Richard Rive

Richard Rive

a partial biography

Shaun Viljoen

WITS UNIVERSITY PRESS

Published in South Africa by:

Wits University Press
1 Jan Smuts Avenue
Johannesburg
2001
www.witspress.co.za

'Mapping' from *The dream in the next body* by Gabeba Baderoon, Cape
Town, Kwela. 2005. Reproduced by permission of Kwela Books.

Bertolt Brecht, 'An die Nachgeborenen' (To Those Born Later)
© Bertolt-Brecht-Erben / Suhrkamp Verlag.

First published 2013

ISBN 978-1-86814-743-4 (print)
ISBN: 978-1-86814-744-1 (digital)

Edited by Alison Lockhart
Proofread by Lisa Compton
Cover artwork © George Hallett
Cover design by Michelle Staples
Book design and layout by Michelle Staples

Wits University Press and the author have made every reasonable effort to
contact and acknowledge copyright owners. Please notify the publishers
should copyright not have been properly identified and acknowledged.
Corrections will be incorporated in subsequent editions of the book.

Printed and bound by Interpak Books

For Ian Viljoen (1929–1991) and Anna Viljoen (1934–)

Hatred, even of meanness
Contorts the features.
Anger, even against injustice
Makes the voice hoarse. Oh, we
Who wanted to prepare the ground for friendliness
Could not ourselves be friendly.

But you, when the time comes at last
And man is helper to man
Think of us
With forbearance.

— **Bertolt Brecht, 'To Those Born Later'**

but our discarded parts,
with their uncertain shifts from
inside to outside,
show that definiteness
is only the edge
of desire

— **Gabeba Baderoon, 'Mapping'**

Contents

Acknowledgements

Michelle Adler, my PhD supervisor, and Tim Couzens, my supervisor in the initial stages of the doctorate, as well as David Attwell, my National Research Foundation-appointed mentor for 2004–2005, helped me do the groundwork for this book. Craig MacKenzie and Stefan Helgesson's examiners' reports were most helpful in rethinking, extending and reformulating ideas, as were the comments of peer reviewers of the final book manuscript, Michael Titlestad and David Johnson.

A number of colleagues at Stellenbosch University generously commented on parts of the book: thanks to Louise Green, Grace Musila, Lynda Spencer, Tina Steiner and Nwabisa Bangeni. Other colleagues, ex-colleagues and friends took time to give me their detailed views on drafts of the book – Sarah Nuttall and Nita Hanmer, my most critical and helpful readers, in particular – as well as Flora Veit-Wild, Milton van Wyk and Dan Yon. Basil Appollis offered continual interest and generous contributions from the start to the conclusion of this project.

Dan Yon, David Medalie and Sandra Swart, dear friends and colleagues, allowed me to share the ups and downs of academic projects and private life and helped to keep this project in perspective. The willing participation and generosity of many of Rive's friends, especially the late Ivan Abrahams and Albert Adams, and also Ursula and Gilbert Reines, made the more personal aspects of this portrait possible. Maeve Heneke and Stephen Yeo shared memories, criticism and a most generous and supportive second home in London. Richard Hauke, in Virginia, very generously gave his wife Kathleen's almost two decades of research on Rive to the National English Literary

Museum (Nelm) and to me, after she passed away in 2004 before completing her own biography on Rive.

Tristan Brikkels, my even-tempered, optimistic partner who bore the brunt of the tantrums and despair, and the rest of my family – Anna Viljoen and Jasper Walters, and Sharon, Dwane, Nicolas and Meghan Harris – were the comedians and cooks who were always interested in my work and helped to keep me going to the very end. Good food indeed played a part in sustaining the writing; thanks to Harald Bresselschmidt and the staff of Aubergine for providing a writing retreat with the best soul food in the world. Constant support and good food came from my Caledon family Elsabe and Dennis Alexander, and Vetesia and Paul Abrahams.

I also wish to thank the following people for their help:

— the numerous interviewees who almost always gave time and shared memories in the most generous ways. They are accredited by name or anonymously in the work. In particular, thanks to George Hallett, who has been very generous in sharing both his photographs and memories;

— Roshan Cader at Wits University Press for her frank questions and comments, Alison Lockhart, the editor who understood what I was trying to do, and Alfred LeMaitre for a most useful initial edit of the book;

— colleagues at Stellenbosch University for their encouragement and support, in particular Meg Samuelson, who gave me her unstinting support on a number of fronts, and also Annie Gagiano, Jeanne Ellis, Mathilda Slabbert, Dawid de Villiers, Daniel Roux, Rita Barnard, Alastair Henderson and Dirk Klopper;

— ex-Hewat College of Education colleagues and friends who were generous with memories and always interested, in particular Marina and Carl Lotter, Jerome and Lilian Van Wyk, Gertrude Fester, Julia Isaacs and Tarnia van Zitters;

— Deborah Britzman at the University of York, Toronto, Canada, and Fernando Rosa Ribeiro at the University of Malaya;

— ex-students and friends Mark Espin and Deela Khan for reading early drafts;

— Berni Searle, Noel Daniels, Dawn Daniels, Rafiq Omar, Sharon Prins, Jerome Thomas, Zubeida Desai, Natasha Distiller, Pamela Nichols and Helen Struthers, who, through fair means or foul, tried to inspire and keep me going;

— Hosea and Ada Jaffe, and Mark Visagie and Daska Grandt-nerova in Britain;

— family members who were interested in my work and supported me in various ways: Pierre Kay and Andy Kay and their families in Cape Town; Jean, Kenny, Marc and Ross Wentzel; Carol Abrahamse and Chris Abrahamse, all in Toronto; and the late Milly and Teddy Roberts, and their daughters Erica, Joanne and Barbara and their families in Brazil;

— student assistants Janine Loedolff, Rico Burnett, Ryan Weaver, Jonathan Maré, François Olivier, Vasti Calitz and Jim Jenkins, and administrative assistants Susan Matdat and Hilary Oostendorp;

— the Fundamentals Training Centre for technical support and help, especially the assistance of Hylton Bergh.

I am grateful to the most helpful staff at the following research institutions where I did much of the archival research: the District Six Museum and Sound Archive, particularly archivist Margaux Bergman; the Police Museum in Pretoria; Nelm, particularly Ann Torlesse; the Magdalen College Archive, particularly Robin Darwall-Smith; Christine Ferdinand at the Magdalen College library; the University of Cape Town administration records and archives; South Peninsula High School principal Brian Isaacs; the Beinecke Rare Book and Manuscript Library, Yale University, in particular Timothy Young; the Schomburg Institute in Harlem, New York; the

JS Gericke Library at the University of Stellenbosch; University of Cape Town Jagger Library and Archive; the St Helena Archive; and the South African National Library, Cape Town.

Financial assistance for this project was received from the National Research Foundation, the research offices of the University of the Witwatersrand and the University of Stellenbosch, the dean of the Arts faculty and the department of English at the University of Stellenbosch, and the Tothill Foundation. The ex-dean and ex-deputy dean of the faculty of Arts and Social Science at the university of Stellenbosch, Hennie Kotzé and Marianna Visser, provided financial and moral support over a long decade.

Photographs

Preface

In a commemorative article on Richard Rive in the *Mail &
Guardian Review* on 7 February 1991, a year and a half after
he was brutally murdered, Nadine Gordimer begins: 'When
someone of marked individuality dies and those who knew him
give their impressions of him, a composite personality appears
that did not exist simultaneously in life.' This biography attempts
to depict Rive as 'a composite personality' but from partial and
selective vantage points. My account of Rive's life assembles a
multitude of voices and perspectives to compose a man who
lived many lives simultaneously and who was a larger-than-life
presence, an exceptional teller of stories who engendered not
merely memories of encounters with him, but memories recast
almost always as exceptional and entertaining stories.

This biography is primarily concerned with the way Rive
embodied a vision of non-racialism in his often angry protest
fiction, his literary scholarship, his interventions in education,
sport and civil society, as well as in an inner life that battled
contradiction between vocal assertiveness and tense silences. It
tries to identify and delve into some of these strange but not
atypical contradictions that pervaded his public and private
personae, especially those related to colour and sexuality that
have marked or masked his sense of self. Even while facets of this
biography will be familiar to many readers, it is a portrait that I
suspect not even the few who knew him well will recognise in all
its aspects. Our experience of others is always only partial. 'His
cultivated urbanity,' Gordimer continues in her tribute, 'glossed
over but couldn't put out a flowing centre of warmth and
kindness within'. Others could find at his centre only arrogance,

self-centredness and abusiveness. Milton van Wyk, an admirer and younger friend of Rive's, highlighted these contraries when he described how many responded to Rive: 'Richard was a generous man if he liked you, scathing and arrogant if he didn't. He enjoyed belittling people and loved attention, but there was a side to Richard very few people saw and that was of a man wallowing in loneliness.'[1]

Rive's main body of work between 1954 and 1989 – twenty-five short stories, three plays, three novels, numerous critical articles on literature, three edited collections of African prose, an edited collection of Olive Schreiner's letters, poems and a memoir – recounts, in a range of tones, the iniquity, brutality and absurdity of life under apartheid. His counter to apartheid backwardness was a strident and articulate egalitarianism that, in his later years, became somewhat muted and refracted through an introspective rather than a declamatory voice. Even his edition of Schreiner's letters reflects his interest in a writer who opposed colonial oppression with an insistent and, in her context, radical liberalism. In some of his earlier short stories, the cry against injustice is too strained and obvious but, even here, his flair for telling a dramatic, clever and crafted story is clearly apparent.

District Six, where Rive was born and raised, was a colourful, cosmopolitan residential area adjacent to the centre of Cape Town. It was declared a 'whites only' area on 11 February 1966 by the Nationalist government, in terms of the 1950 Group Areas Act, and razed to the ground by the early 1970s. Just a decade later, it had become a symbol of all forced removals of people of colour throughout South Africa, an iconic space of contestation and memorialisation. It was symptomatic of a larger resurgence of resistance in South Africa and on the subcontinent after 1976, which resulted in the birth of new, defiant narratives reclaiming space, memory, rites of passage and return. Rive's *'Buckingham*

Palace', *District Six* was one such story and it played a significant role in exposing a new generation of younger readers to his work, ensuring his continued prominence as a South African writer and public intellectual nationally and internationally in the late 1980s and beyond.[2]

The novel *'Buckingham Palace'*, *District Six* has been a popular prescribed text for high school learners at various grades in the Western Cape, as well as elsewhere in South Africa and in other countries. Nine years after his death, in 1998, the District Six Museum in Cape Town hosted a retrospective workshop on Richard Rive and District Six for teachers, writers and academics.[3] These occurrences reflect the continued interest in Rive and his work, particularly as part of a broader national and regional preoccupation with the processes of reconciliation and reclamation. The memorialisation by the District Six Museum of past and present contestations over District Six, as iconic of cityscape, ownership and rights of habitation and access, includes a memorialisation of Rive as one of the writers born in and concerned with the District. The museum and its educational programmes have attracted thousands of young local students and international visitors to its exhibitions, programmes and archives annually. This has played a major role in recreating and sustaining interest in the life and history of the area, and the associated forced removals and current fraught process of return. As a result, wide interest in Rive's life and work has been guaranteed, it seems, for at least the next few generations, not only in Cape Town and the Western Cape, but also nationally and internationally.

A one-man play on Rive's life and work, *A Writer's Last Word*, written by Sylvia Vollenhoven and Basil Appollis, premiered at the Grahamstown Festival in 1998 and was restaged at the One City, Many Cultures festival in Cape Town in 1999. Appollis also directed a stage adaptation of *'Buckingham Palace'*, *District Six* (for which he and I wrote the script) for the Drama department at the University of Cape Town in March 2000, and for Artscape Theatre in Cape Town in 2001. The South African Broadcasting Corporation (SABC) has considered serialising the novel for television and Appollis is working on a film version of the book. Rive insists on continually resurfacing in the decades after his death.

In the period approaching the twentieth anniversary of the 1994 elections, sometimes referred to as the period of post-transition, the field of literary studies is intensely preoccupied with the literature of the present, of the 'now', and with attempts to characterise post-1994 South African literature and culture, particularly with regard to the new forms and subjects of writing that have emerged. This, in part, has resulted in diminished interest in pre-1994 literature, especially in the work of black South African writers. Less attention seems to have been paid to the way the post-1994 period has freed up the act of reading. Just as writing has been freed of the obligatory social and political protest, reading has also been unhinged from old black and white thematics and allowed to proliferate in hugely variegated, exploratory and eccentric ways. New kinds of reading frames will allow us to revisit our literary legacy and find in it new meanings, new pertinence. Certain interpretations of Rive's work in this biography would never have been possible under apartheid. Comrades (and I) would have seen my queer reading of 'The Visits' as defaming Rive, and would have dismissed it as self-indulgent and individualistic, detracting from the priorities of the struggle.

In compiling this biography, particular strands of Rive's life, thought, work and times are continuous refracting lenses in the narrative, skewing the biography into idiosyncratic angles – looking at those parts that interest me. The first of these is a preoccupation with the idea of non-racialism to which Rive not only subscribed, but which I suggest is at (as Yeats puts it in 'The Lake Isle of Innisfree') 'the deep heart's core' of his being, of his private, civic and writing life. This belief in non-racialism co-existed, often in tense fashion, with his angry humanism and, paradoxically, with his own peculiarly racialised self-fashioning. Large swathes of the past from which Rive comes, and which he also helped to form, are fast disappearing.[4] Invaluable and luminous moments of personal memory are thus rapidly fading as his family, associates, colleagues and comrades die or forget. The past of Rive's era is currently being fiercely contested on a multitude of levels.[5]

Rive, in his educational, civic and literary work, entered the conflicts of apartheid South Africa from a consistently non-racial position, to defend people of colour from imposed ignominy and deprivation. This way of envisioning human relations is undervalued and even devalued in post-1994 South Africa because neo-liberal economic and attendant social policies of the South African government, its global partners and corporations, despite the rhetoric of non-racialism, have reinforced old intersecting racial and class barriers which suit their profit-driven agendas.[6] While the term 'non-racial' has been widely adopted currently as nomenclature for the state's position and as a description of the African National Congress (ANC) policy in the days of struggle, what the ANC, now the ruling national party in South Africa, draws on and practises post-1994 should in effect be called 'multiracialism'. Even the liberal 1996 Constitution of South Africa, which insists on the equality of all races, nevertheless continues to use the term 'race' in an unqualified way. Neville Alexander puts this contradiction we live with cogently: 'The fact that the relationship between an unavoidable national South African identity and the possible sub-national identities continues to constitute the stuff of political contestation in post-apartheid South Africa today demonstrates clearly how tenacious the hold of history is on the consciousness of the masses of people.'[7]

The assumed existence of different 'races' or 'sub-national identities' makes reconciliation between groups the most urgent task in contemporary South Africa, rather than, as is implicit in Rive's brand of 'non-racialism', the abolition of the very notion of race. The current terms of the national census and mechanisms of employment equity and redress, particularly the national policy of affirmative action, serve to entrench notions of 'race' and of racialised perceptions and consciousness. These operate on the basis of racial profiling, which serves to advance a minority of black middle-class citizens rather than address much more fundamental questions of poverty, land and employment. This fairly hegemonic 'racialised', 'multicultural' mindset – 'we are different but equal' – common in contemporary South Africa and prevalent elsewhere globally, is identified by Cornel West as perpetuating fraught social relations in the United States in recent years. He instead suggests that, unlike the 'othering' positions of the American conservatives and liberals, we need 'to establish a new framework ... to begin with a frank acknowledgement of the basic humanness ... of each of us'.[8] Rive's notion of non-racialism would completely concur with West's emphasis on a human and national commonality, rather than primarily on racial distinction and ethnic difference.[9]

Does Richard Rive have anything to say to us in the twenty-first century in a markedly changed South Africa, so implicated in a firmly neo-liberal and rapidly fomenting global order and with a persistent, viral residue of the old colonial apartheid past? The prominence of the 'race question' in contemporary South Africa has resulted in renewed debate on questions of race, division, perception and racism in our society. This is not peculiar to South Africa, of course: one finds parallel concerns in other parts of the world, especially in North America, Britain and Europe.

A re-examination of Rive's life and work entails a reflection on his fight against racialism and for a well-defined non-racialism. This book, and the continued interest in Rive's work and life, will, it is hoped, contribute to current debates about what kinds of knowledge we need to generate about ourselves and others to establish a truly 'new' non-exploitative South Africa.

Renewed interest in notions of 'coloured identity', part of an increasing trend in South Africa, which interrogates and/or affirms particular constructions of personal, ethnic and national identity, or what Desiree Lewis eloquently calls ' "new" fictions of freedom and selfhood', has ironically resulted in a resurgence of interest in Rive's life and work.[10] Rive himself resisted the notion that he was coloured and his non-racialism saw this classification as a creation by colonialism and apartheid, as part of the divide-and-rule politics of European domination. In so far as this position was a direct ideological retort by a segment of the oppressed intelligentsia, Crain Soudien's classification of it as 'counter official' is useful, since this stresses the oppositional genesis of this stance to the notion of being coloured.[11] If he were still alive, Rive would probably not only have baulked at being seen as a 'coloured' writer but would in all likelihood have decried attempts to give credence and respectability to this kind of racialised identity.

The subtitle refers to my wanting to go beyond Rive's declarations about his life and struggle. I am interested in the silences in his life and work, and what I find to be encodings of homoerotic desire and alterity, and deeply personal anxiety about the self in his world, in his fiction and some of the other work. Alongside the anger against injustice that sometimes made his authorial voice gratingly obvious, Rive is remarkably silent, in both life and fiction, on questions of homosexual desire and his own homosexuality. The exploration of sexuality and my queer readings of various works are the parts of this biography

that Rive undoubtedly would have deplored. Yet these are dimensions of the man and his work that I found engaging and
which have not yet been explored, except to a limited extent in
a chapter on *'Buckingham Palace', District Six* by Brenna Munro
in her recent work *South Africa and the Dream of Love to Come*.

Exploring issues of homosexuality raises ethical considerations about making public the private, particularly because of the
absence of any direct link between Rive's homosexuality and his
creative output, and also because of his own very evident silence
about his homosexuality throughout his life. Alf Wannenburgh
remarks in his memoir of Rive that 'there were large areas of
his own inner life that he was not prepared to disclose, even to
those who knew him well'.[12] Rive's friends and associates had
widely differing opinions about addressing the topic of his
homosexuality, from 'tell everything', as advocated by Stephen
Gray, to Es'kia Mphahlele, who 'had no idea' about Rive's being
gay, implying, it seems, as many did in interviews, that his
sexual preference was never known to them or, by implication,
of no consequence as far as they were concerned.[13] Yet others
refuse to talk about it and one senses the extent to which for
many, even in our own time, homosexuality remains a taboo
subject or 'irrelevant' – an invasion, it is felt, of the person's right
to privacy. Yet, as William McFeely insists, 'as either the writer
or the reader engages in a biography or autobiography, there is a
conjunction of the private and the public'.[14]

We all draw the line between the private and the public but at
different points. How far do you go? And why go there? A tension
of competing interests marks where the border should be, as
recognised by Gray when he says that 'all literary biography is a
tug-of-wishes between the private being's will to reticence and
the publicist's to disclosure'.[15] As a biographer, I am convinced
by the idea that the personal and historical are inextricably
linked. I nod at Robert M Young when he says that 'one of

the things I most like about biography is that it celebrates ... the history of ideas, narrative, will, character and the validity of the subject's subjectivity'.[16] I am curious about the connection or apparent absence of connection between the private and the public, the subjective and the social, in particular with regard to questions of desire and sexuality. This biography does not 'out' Rive – his being gay was widely suspected, whispered about or guessed at and even known about, especially in his adult years, and his murder and the subsequent widely reported trial of the two young men accused of killing him finally established his homosexuality as public fact. Unlike the dominant notion of 'being homosexual' that pervades Western ideas of identity, Rive's precarious simultaneous state of being and not being gay is far more dynamic, all the more fraught, a space of sexual being that prevails widely, especially in postcolonial contexts where fixed categorisation is often resisted and alien to lived experience.

In writing this book, I have attempted to walk a line between empathy for Rive's own desire for privacy and my own curiosity about silences, queer literary encodings or readings and sexuality. A constant image throughout the project has been an awareness of Rive looking over my shoulder as I write his life; not infrequently I have had to remind him this is *my* version of his story, not his. Rive's sexual life comes into focus to explore possible meanings of these tense, visible or veiled intersections, rather than appearing for their own sake or merely for reader titillation.[17] What level of detail is used and to what end? The exploration of sexuality is carried out, it is hoped, with contextual and ethical considerations constantly in mind. As I explored aspects of Rive's public and private life over the years, I realised how partial I had become to his ideas, his convictions and the way he navigated the trauma, doubt and dilemmas in his work and life. The nature of Rive's strained relationship with his family, his unspoken homosexuality and proclivity for young men and the violent and mysterious circumstances of his death were matters some interviewees found sensitive and chose to avoid, explain away or refuse to talk about altogether. While responses to these questions were formulated and refined and redefined during the process of transcription and writing, I kept falling back on the response that, while attempting to maintain empathy with Rive and his assumed sensibilities, I needed to make the narrative my own, pursuing lines of inquiry I could justify as valid, useful, informed and considered. This work attempts a historically accurate account of Rive's life as far as possible, but combines this with the particular lenses I chose in order to refract his life. I had hoped to unearth some of the fascinating enmeshing of the intensely personal and private on the one hand and the macro socio-economic on the other, but, for the most part, the nature of such entanglements continues to baffle.

Lastly, I read Rive's life and fiction as distorting echo chambers of each other. Reading real authorial life from clues in the fiction – reading the fiction as symptomatic of authorial conscious-ness and life facts – and inversely reading fiction in the light of that life, risks downplaying the mysterious interconnected-ness and often autonomous existence of these two realms. Placing them side by side to compose a fuller portrait of Rive's life is helped by his own insistence that his life and fiction were closely linked; on many occasions he insisted that his stories and novels were 'faction'. Biographer Michael Holroyd believes that the main business of the literary biographer is to 'chart illuminating connections between past and present, life and work', typifying the strong and very productive empiricist tradition of anglophone biography.[18] Such attempts at mapping between life and work are not simple one-to-one matches but are instead intricately threaded conjoining and disjunctures, in constant tension and often contradictory, mediated by the dynamics within and between such diverse domains as individual imagination and macro socio-economic contexts.

This biography proceeds chronologically from shortly before Rive's birth in 1930 to his death in 1989 and slightly into the posthumous period. I give greater prominence to momentary images – large photographs that mark parts of Rive's life on which I reflect closely in an attempt to cohere the narrative around the specific image. I place the photographs in positions where they talk to a segment of the text, rather than, as is more conventional in many biographies, interspersing the photographs, chronologically ordered, in a few compressed folders which form an impressionistic visual narrative illustrative of the story in the text. I do close readings of the images to echo, contribute to or interrogate the main narrative in the text. I use nine images, all but four by George Hallett, a world-renowned photographer who was a pupil and lifelong friend of Rive's, and who believes it was Rive who opened him up to the idea of becoming an artist. These particular photographs also suggest their own mute narrative that Hallett imparts to us about Rive. Only very particular, fleeting moments and gestures become visible, but all other times of Rive's life remain visually unseen.

The cover photograph was taken by George Hallett in 1966 or 1967, when Rive was in his late thirties, just before he left for Oxford to do his doctorate and Hallett himself went into exile. Taken in Rive's flat in Selous Court, Claremont, Cape Town, the image, with the backdrop of books ordered on bookshelves and framed artwork on the walls, features in the foreground the comfortable, confident, even cocky man in a typical gesture of his, arm over the head as if to frame himself as he is framing his words, fingers containing the temple in a gesture associated with thought. He is seated and, with his eyes overlined by those distinctive fulsome eyebrows, he stares directly at the photographer, his protégé, and beyond at us, not smiling but holding forth, claiming a point, loud, yet, as is the way of a photograph, silent and therefore forever ambiguous. He talks to us but he is mute.

Late twentieth century and early twenty-first century work on biography (Paula Backscheider, Michael Holroyd, Hermoine Lee and, in a South African context, Mark Gevisser, John Hyslop and Roger Field, among others) reveals a much greater degree of self-consciousness about its project than earlier work from the late nineteenth century onwards, which reflected more confident, unquestioned assumptions about epistemology and objectivity. What film-maker and photographer Errol Morris says of photography is equally true of biography – photographs (biographies) edit reality; they 'reveal and they conceal' and tell us something of the real but never the whole story; they can document, but they also skew; they can tell us something, a partial truth, but simultaneously remain a mystery.[19]

I have used archival documentation, Rive's own work, writings on Rive, personal interviews and my own memories of the man. Facts of his life *matter* in the biography, and in this regard I have drawn heavily on Rive's memoir, *Writing Black,* as well as other sources, but why specific details have been chosen and how I then make sense of them matters equally. What does one select, why, and then how to connect or resist connecting these chosen facts, and to what end? I have used a combination of conventional third-person narration, with occasional more intrusive first-person narration (particularly in those times when my life overlapped with Rive's in the 1980s and when I worked with him at Hewat College of Education) with interlocking narratives by Rive himself and anecdotes and stories by those who remember him.

I came to know Rive in the mid-1970s through his association with Non-European Unity Movement (NEUM) intellectual Victor Wessels at discussions and parties at Victor's home in Fairways and then in Walmer Estate. I also encountered him in this period at forums like the Cape Flats Educational Fellowship, where he often gave workshops on English and African literature for high school students. I also saw and heard him in meetings on civic and sports issues during the late 1970s and early 1980s, but we were by no means friends. In fact, I thought little of his work and disliked his pompous and affected manner; he in turn thought little of me (or so it seemed), sensing perhaps my reservations about his work (I have not a single signed copy of any of his books), my natural reserve generally and my preference, unlike him, for remaining in the shadows, away from public glare.

It was only during a meeting in London in 1986, when I was a student at London University and he was passing through to secure a visiting professorship at Harvard, that we really spoke to each other over supper in North London at the home of Maeve Heneke, a mutual friend. It was then that he recruited me to take up a teaching post at Hewat College of Education, in fact to take his place while he was on leave teaching at Harvard. He was head of the English department at the college, where I worked closely with him from 1987 to his death in 1989. A friendship of sorts developed, but there always remained a measure of distance between us. Tension increased between us at certain times, such as during my participation in a Hewat College stage production by colleague Colleen Radus of his novel *'Buckingham Palace', District Six* in 1988, when he disliked the way I had rescripted parts of his own script. He nevertheless remained generous and at times very warm towards me, asking me to housesit on occasion, and on his last birthday before he died, we had supper together with two other Hewat colleagues, Marina Lotter and Martin Dyers, both of whom he liked and who in turn really liked him. At the time of his death, my admiration for him as a writer and a man had grown, but I remained sceptical of the literary value of much of his work. The more I thought and uncovered about him and the work over the next twenty years, the larger he has grown in my esteem, tempering an initial ambivalence about him as a writer and a person and learning to understand the limitations of my then narrower notions of what constitutes literature. I began to grasp his immense courage, drive and vision as a writer.

Ten years after his death, I decided to undertake this project while working at the University of the Witwatersrand, Johannesburg. There was no existing biography of Rive. It was also becoming clear that that old racism was persisting in the 'new' South Africa at the turn of the century and taking on new, often insidious forms. A biography of Rive would allow me to share more widely our joint commitment to non-racialism as we had known it and perhaps contribute to local and national debate. It was in the course of this research for more than a decade that I started to rethink some of my harsher and decontextualised judgements about Rive's work and character and came to realise how large he loomed, and still does, as a character with his acerbic wit and humour, how lonely and troubled he was and, above all, what a compelling teller of tales.

There are other overlaps between my own and Rive's life. We were both classified by apartheid as coloured and styled by the times as 'coloured intellectuals' despite our resistance to this; we were the products of the political outlook of the NEUM and felt compelled to assert a (Western) cosmopolitanism that stemmed from resistance to the balkanising tribalism and racism being fostered by the South African ruling classes; like Rive, I have ended up being markedly 'anglophilic' in a certain sense (teaching in English departments, for example) and yet, at the same time, we both found ourselves countering that very impulse and propagating African literature and local writing through our work at secondary and tertiary educational institutions; like Rive, although for different reasons (and a few of the same?), I am uneasy with the label of being 'gay' as definitive of who one is.

Finally, a biography of Rive needs to capture something of the spirit of the man most of those interviewed remember – his wit, sometimes scathing, sometimes entertaining, sometimes self-parodying; his natural ability as a raconteur, making him a memorable teacher, colleague and friend. In the end, I hope the Rive I have refracted is what Virginia Woolf hoped for in her fictional characters: 'I dig out beautiful caves behind my characters … I think that gives exactly what I want: humanity, humour, depth.'[20] Reading Richard Ellmann's biography of Oscar Wilde, one wonders to what extent Rive echoes dimensions of Wilde – the dandy, the raconteur, the Magdalen graduate, the aphorisms, the drive to write, the love that dare not speak its name, the changing of dates of birth to make himself a little younger, the tragic ending – were these a strange case of fate, or perhaps, in part at least, coincidences cultivated by Rive?

In 2011 I found myself in Berlin trying to delve into Rive's connection with the old East Berlin, which was where his first book, *African Songs*, was published in 1963. It was then that I had, for the first and only time, a dream in which Richard appeared.

He visits me in my small townhouse in Wynberg (as he did not long before he was killed) and I am showing him a passage from my biography. He thrusts back the book and sneers, 'That is wrong! You've got it completely wrong.' I am about to say, 'But … I got that part from … Colleen' then choke on my words. We descend the narrow stairs with him behind me. I turn to look over my shoulder and catch Richard about to push me down the stairs. I wake up.

Part 1: *1930 – 1960*

Chapter 1

The great influenza pandemic of 1918 and 1919, 'the Spanish flu' as it was called, is thought to have started in military camps in Kansas, in the United States. From there, it rapidly spread to the rest of the world killing, it is estimated, between 20 and 40 million people, more than had died in the five years of the First World War.[1] The plague reached South Africa within months. In Cape Town, a vital stopover on the route of humans and goods between East and West, a young, married, working-class couple, Nancy and Joseph Rive, 'coloured' in the racialising language of the time,[2] had started a modest home in the area of District Six, abutting the centre of the burgeoning port town at the base of the monumental Table Mountain. The area was created as Cape Town's sixth municipal district in 1867 and by the time Nancy and Joseph moved there, it was less of the edgy area once known for its crime and prostitution and was developing into a vibrant, cosmopolitan and mainly working-class residential area.[3] District Six was, however, like all land in the newly formed Union of South Africa, a contested space where white supremacy and resistance to racial oppression did battle. The ANC had been formed a few years earlier, in 1912, by African intellectuals, 'bitter and betrayed' by their exclusion from the common voters' roll, while the white leadership of the new union divided the country into wealthier white and impoverished black areas with their 1913 Natives Land Act.[4]

It was the District, as it was commonly known to locals, that was to become home to the young Richard Rive in the 1930s and early 1940s, but from which he quickly fled as a teenager to escape the constraints of his family circumstances and to make something of himself. It was the District, however, which would prove to be a perennial preoccupation of his imagination and would be intimately associated with his best work.

In 1918 Nancy Rive gave birth to her seventh child, a little girl she called Georgina, most likely after the British monarch at the time, King George V. Like vast numbers of residents of the District, the Rives were great admirers of British royalty, whose portraits were displayed in their homes. The other six Rive children were Joseph, the eldest boy, and then came David (known also as Davey), Arthur, Harold, Douglas and another girl, Lucy. Soon after Georgina's birth, tragedy struck the family and Joseph Rive (senior) died, a victim of the Spanish flu that, quite strangely for influenza, afflicted mainly younger people in their twenties and thirties.[5] In the wake of her husband's death, in a world ravaged by war and a country ruled by white supremacists, and with seven mouths to feed, the young widow was in for a long and hard time.

Twelve years after Joseph's death, in 1930, when Nancy was thirty-eight-years-old and Georgina almost a teenager, the single mother gave birth to a *laatlammetjie* (Afrikaans, a child born many years after its siblings). Richard Rive's birth, on the first of March that year, was shrouded in controversy and secrecy, and marked him as exceptional from the beginning. Interestingly, in *Writing Black,* Rive gives his date of birth as 1931. However, his birth certificate states clearly 1 March 1930. There is wide discrepancy in published texts – 1930, 1931, 1932 and 1933 are all given as dates of birth. At Hewat College, where Rive worked, it was rumoured that he gave a false (later) date to make himself appear slightly younger. It is strange that, for someone as fastidious about detail as Rive, so many dates of birth prevailed even while he lived. He often got dates wrong, for no apparent reason.[6]

The sizeable age gap between Richard and his siblings was to contribute to the young boy's acute sense of alienation from the family as he grew up. He was very much a part of the family yet also very apart from it. The United States was the source of the tragedy that had robbed Nancy of her husband; it was also the place of origin of the man with whom she had had a fleeting affair, who was to father her eighth and last child. His father was a ship's hand called Richardson Moore, who abandoned him and his mother when Rive was just three months, and was not seen again by either. As an adult, Rive tried on a number of occasions to track down his father in the United States. The only trace of his father was in Richard's name, for his mother had given the name 'Richard Moore Rive' on his birth certificate. In his memoir *Writing Black*, published when he was fifty-one years old, Rive says of his father: 'About my father and his family I know almost nothing. He died soon after I was born and was seldom mentioned in family circles. Perhaps a dark secret lurks somewhere.'[7] Is Rive using 'died' here metaphorically to account for the absent father? For, as is clear from Rive's correspondence with writer Langston Hughes in the late 1950s, the father had not in fact died but rather disappeared leaving no trace whatsoever. Hughes (1902–1967), the iconic black American intellectual, poet, fiction writer and dramatist, and a leading figure of the black American literary explosion of the 1920s, the Harlem Renaissance, was to play a seminal role in Rive's writing life.

In *Writing Black* Rive, for some reason, cannot say directly that his father was a black American but instead suggests this circuitously by recounting an incident at an athletics meeting at which he had performed particularly well, and where a black American woman, an intimate friend of his mother's, commented affectionately to him: ' "They can't beat an American boy, can they?" ... So possibly the Black strain came from my father and came from far over the Atlantic.'[8] Rive was clearly tentative, even reluctant, about revealing this aspect of his life, revealing only certain details to particular audiences. He was restrained not only about his father it seems; in his adult life he rarely spoke about his mother, even to close friends.

By the time the older Rive comes to write this account of his life, he undoubtedly knows more about his father than he lets on, choosing to embed even these spare facts in circumspect and suggestive narrative in his memoir. However, in a letter to Hughes in 1962, almost twenty years before the publication of *Writing Black*, he is much more candid about the silence that attended the question of his paternity in his District Six home, a silence clearly stemming from his mother's deep sense of shame at the affair – a shame compounded by Rive's dark skin:

> *A very interesting feature of my life is that my father is an American Negro, but he left home when I was a mere 3 months old. I never saw him. I believe that he might still be frequenting the New York waterfront. He was apparently a ships [sic] cook. Name Richardson Moore. Interesting if we should ever meet again. My mother is from an upper class family, and the subject of my father is never brought up.*[9]

The question of Rive's paternity, with all its unarticulated proscriptions, shame and even disgust within the family (perhaps even within himself), was the first instance in his life where the equation between shame and silence was a mark on the psyche of the young boy. He is clearly reluctant to reveal the full extent of this 'dark secret' in his memoir. Was it just too shameful? Was it too private? Was it of no import in a memoir that, like his fiction, was primarily concerned with exposing the injustices of racial oppression? In the very first line of *Writing Black*, Rive insists on the selective nature of his autobiography: 'Some [incidents] are locked away in that private part of my world which belongs only to myself and perhaps one or two intimates.'[10] Perhaps the deliberate silence Rive acknowledges, as 'locking away' particular incidents and emotions, is not simply a choice to edit out certain details but a multiple, more complex silence – silence about both the world of his family and, later, the very private and closed world of his sexuality.

The young Richard grew up in a 'huge, dirty-grey, forbidding, double-storied' tenement building in Caledon Street, at number 201. Rive's detailed, filmic description of the place is reminiscent of Dickens's descriptions of inner-city settings:

> [It] housed over twelve family units … with a rickety wooden balcony that ran its entire length. There were three main entrances, numbered 201, 203 and 205. All faced Caledon Street. Behind it and much lower, running alongside, was a concrete enclosed area called The Big Yard into which all occupants of the tenement threw their slops, refuse and dirty water.[11]

The photograph by Clarence Coulson is of this double-storey tenement building in Caledon Street, taken from William Street across the square. Aspects of the photograph were explained to me by Noor Ebrahim and Joe Schaffers in June 2012. Both Ebrahim and Schaffers grew up in the District and knew the young Rive well. Each window represents the living quarters of a separate family and the Rives rented the first dwelling on the left on the top floor, with only a bedroom and a small kitchen, according to Ebrahim and Schaffers who visited the Rive house. The square served as a playground for the pupils from the nearby St Mark's Primary School during the week. On the left is the community hall, which was also used by the school. The image here is of a Sunday morning, in the early or mid-1960s according to Ebrahim, with the uniformed lads from the St Mark's Church brigade preparing for their march, which would begin with the tolling of the church bell. An intensely curious audience of dozens of children and adults can't wait for the show

Caledon Street, District Six (photographer: Clarence Coulson)

to begin. The evident physical density and dilapidation of the space is overwhelmed by the sense of bustle and expectation, of adults and children living the rituals of a special time and day, a Sunday morning in the District.

This row of dwellings was, fifty years later, transformed by Rive's memory and imagination into the row of five conjoined, bustling homes called 'Buckingham Place', the locus of communal life portrayed in his novel *'Buckingham Palace', District Six*. A more realistic and possibly more accurate picture of the domestic life of the family in their home is suggested by Andrew Dreyer, the protagonist in Rive's first novel *Emergency* (first published in 1964). The description of Andrew's home reflects the cramped, overcrowded, Victorian conditions in which Rive's own working-class family lived in the District:

They occupied three dingy rooms on the first floor of a double-

storied tenement flat at 302 ... One first entered a landing which
smelt damp and musty and echoed eerily when the wind blew
through it ... Then up a pitch-dark staircase till one fumbled
at the knob at No. 3 and entered a shabby bed-sitting room
grandiloquently called the dining-room. This was dominated
by a huge four-poster bed with brass railings, an old-fashioned
couch with chairs to match, and a side-board cluttered with
Victorian bric-à-brac. A cheap but highly polished table was
squeezed between the bed and the sideboard. A bedroom led
off this, occupied by James and Peter-boy. Here another four-
poster bed was situated in the centre, with an ancient tallboy
leaning against the wall, adorned with a pink and white basin
and picture. Two broken French doors led to an unsafe, wooden
balcony. One had to go back to the upstairs landing to reach
the Boys' Room which Andrew, Danny and Philip occupied. It
contained two beds and a chest of drawers and had the musty
smell of stale air and perspiration.[12]

Growing up in such conditions, confining and dilapidated yet
with a sense of respectability and even grandeur, with Nancy's
ambiguous love and care, and an intimacy with only some of
his siblings, Rive undoubtedly, like many other youngsters with
talent entrapped by circumstance, often retreated into the world
of the mind – to books. He also found refuge in the friendship of
neighbourhood boys who accepted, admired and were intrigued
by his way with words and his wit.

Rive's brother-in-law Freddie Josias, husband to Georgina,
the sibling to whom Rive felt the closest (possibly because they
were the two youngest), describes Rive's family as existing in
circumstances that forced them 'to live from hand to mouth'.[13]
A schoolmate of Rive's, Gilbert Reines, says Rive did not have
shoes at one time (like many of the children in the Coulson
photograph) and that he came from 'a really poor family'.[14]
Rive himself talks of their living 'in an atmosphere of shabby

respectability', playing down somewhat the level of poverty but putting his finger on the quest for middle-class respectability and a 'decent' life.[15] As a single mother, Nancy struggled to make ends meet, but the cost of keeping the household going by the time Richard was growing up and going to school was supplemented from the wages of older siblings like Georgina, who worked at a city printing firm, Herzberg and Mulne, and the second-eldest brother, Davey, who worked at Flack's furniture store in the city.

As a respectable churchgoing Anglican, Nancy Rive had her baby boy baptised and later, in his early teens, confirmed at St Mark's Church on Clifton Hill in the District, just a short walk from their Caledon Street home. One of the few fleeting references to his mother comes in Rive's memoir and is prompted by his visit, in 1963 while on an extended tour of Africa and Europe, to the Piazza San Marco in Venice. There, he recalls accompanying his mother to present the family Bible to the church and remembers St Mark's in terms that suggest the church was a refuge from the hostilities of the outside world for the young boy: 'And the cosily lit warm interior on a Sunday evening when the south-easter howled outside … I was a boy in St Mark's on the Hill, comfortably dozing through the warm monotony of Evensong.'[16]

While St Mark's Church was to feature prominently as a site of communal ritual and resistance in Rive's work, as it did in the history of resistance to forced removals in the District, he turned his back on religion in his adult life, becoming an atheist – as were many of his left-wing mentors and friends who defended their atheism by, for example, quoting Karl Marx's dictum about religion being the opium of the people and circulating Bertrand Russell's polemical essay 'Why I Am Not a Christian', which attacked Christian hypocrisy and mystification. The fact that the policies of segregation pre-1948 and those of apartheid after that were rationalised using Christian doctrine increased the alienation of many intellectuals of the time from Christianity (in particular) and religion in general. Many others, though, were drawn to religion and the church as part of their lives; some of Rive's close friends in his youth – Albert Adams and John Ramsdale – were active churchgoers. One of Rive's early short stories, 'No Room at Solitaire' (1963), exposes the hypocrisy of the Afrikaner characters who profess to be Christian but rudely turn away a sick and pregnant black woman and her husband from their inn. Although a jarringly obvious allegory on the plight of Mary and Joseph on Christmas Eve, the story ends with the racist Afrikaner men having an epiphany of the import of their inhumane act – an ending that reflects Rive's persistent belief in the possibility for good in everyone, a quality present in all his creative work. Unlike his contemporaries Alex La Guma and Dennis Brutus, Rive was impelled not by a strong sense of anti-imperialist or anti-capitalist ideology, but rather by more liberal convictions about individual and human rights. In this sense, Rive shared more common ground as a writer with his friends and fellow writers Es'kia Mphahlele and James Matthews.

Surrounded by 'dirty, narrow streets in a beaten-up neigh-bourhood', his family, Rive claims, was marked by an obsessive hankering after respectability: 'We always felt we were intended for better things.'[17] The gently parodic tone in which this is said in his memoir, written forty years after this period of childhood, indicates a measure of distancing from these familial aspirations. As a young man in his twenties, though, Rive still identified with them, needing to be 'respectable' and 'civilised', able to transcend the 'decrepit' place he inhabited. He would, in his second letter to Langston Hughes in 1954, excitedly and assertively introduce himself: 'Age 23 years. I was born in District Six (one of the most terrible slums in Cape Town, although I come from a cultured family).'[18] The early letters to Hughes are clearly trying to impress the older, internationally acclaimed figure with the young writer's knowledge of place and his sense of being 'cultured'. In this description of himself and his origins, Rive interestingly distances himself from District Six, calling his birthplace a 'terrible slum', unlike the affirmative and often nostalgic portrayal in the later novel *'Buckingham Palace', District Six*. In this description to Hughes of the District and of himself, it is interesting that the qualifier 'although' is used to separate the District from the notion of being 'cultured'. 'Culture' was elsewhere and, like his sister Lucy and his brother Joseph, Rive 'fled the District as soon as possible'.[19] Thirty years later, however, when the resistance to forced removals had reached a pitch in the struggles of the oppressed, District Six, like numerous other residential areas (for example, Sophiatown in Johannesburg and South End in Port Elizabeth), became, for him, the country and the world, an iconic space of unjust displacement and of justified reclamation; a place of reinvented and celebrated pasts textured as both real and imagined.

The young Richard sensed himself on the margins of the family – not only was he much younger than his siblings, but he was much darker in complexion and had a different father. This sense of estrangement from family is only fleetingly dealt with in his autobiography where he says that 'in [his] loneliness', he cultivated friendships with down-and-out, working-class boys whom his family derogatorily called his 'skollie friends' (gangster friends).[20] *Writing Black* is particularly silent on family; Rive's main focus is to fashion his young self as a reader, budding writer and metonymic voice against racism, an individual who simultaneously represents and transcends the oppressed condition. Above all, Rive's memoir is protest, an indictment of racial tyranny and its attempts to categorise, to confine and silence him, and to erase the spaces that define him. But of his inner life as a child in a family, the work is remarkably silent. There is no mention, for example, of the death of his mother or what it meant to him. There is more descriptive detail in the portrayal of the character of Mary, 'proprietor' of the local brothel that the four-year-old Rive stumbles upon in his neighbourhood. As is the case in the later fictional work, the memoir is marked by the invocation of alternative forms of family and intimacy constituted by fellow writers, work colleagues, sportsmen, a few friends and the young men he befriends. The twenty-four photographs that open *Writing Black* carry not a single image of the family – there is one of the District and the rest are images of Rive himself in the company of or, through the mechanism of photographic collage, associated with prominent South African and African writers.

Writing Black recounts Rive's childhood primarily through eyes that see the racial conflicts and dilemmas in South Africa as pervasive. His father's side provided 'the Black strain', the 'strain' Rive insisted in his adult life on proclaiming and defending in contrast to the marked silence about it within his family.[21] Nancy Rive, who was born into the Ward family from Klapmuts, a small settlement in the Boland area on the outskirts of Cape Town, proudly displayed her father in a mounted photograph (showing him in a cheese-cutter hat with a droopy moustache next to his champion racehorse) which had a special place on the dining-room wall. He is described by Rive as 'unmistakably white'. Stephen Gray, a fellow writer and long-standing friend of Rive's, describes Rive's hair as 'Saint Helenan kinky', suggesting that some of Rive's forebears were from the South Atlantic island.[22] One wonders if Gray heard this bit of family genealogy from Rive himself. Nancy's father was, it seems, a descendant of the Ward family on the island of St Helena. The St Helenan diaspora in the Cape and in other coastal areas of South Africa – Port Elizabeth, Durban, Port Nolloth – often asserted their connection to Britain and were generally resistant to being pigeonholed into racial categories, particularly under apartheid, as 'Cape Coloureds'. While this attitude marked a progressive resistance to apartheid's grand plan, there was also among some an attitude that having St Helenan ancestry made you 'a better coloured'. Nowhere is there any textual reference by Rive to these island origins. If Nancy's father's side was fair-skinned, his maternal grandmother, however, Rive guessed, was dark-skinned, as Nancy turned out to be 'beautifully bronze' and 'little was ever mentioned ... other than that she [his maternal grandmother] came from the Klapmuts district'.[23] There was no proudly displayed photograph of Nancy's mother. As was the case with vast numbers of South African families living with the intensely colour-conscious and hierarchical legacy of a colonial and segregationist history, darker-skinned relatives were often regarded as shameful and *personae non gratae*, and were marginalised or completely excised from memory, or relegated to the realm of taboo and silence.

In his first novel, *Emergency*, Rive bestows on his main character, Andrew Dreyer, elements from his own life. Andrew has a tense and ambivalent relationship with his mother, feeling both intimacy and alienation at the same time. The novel accounts for the estrangement from the mother because of colour:

> She had always been strange in her attitude towards him. Sometimes gay and maternal and then suddenly cold and impulsive. He wondered whether it had anything to do with colour. She was fair, like James and Annette, whereas he was dark, the darkest in the family. Sometimes when they walked together in the street, he had a feeling that she was ashamed of him, even in District Six.[24]

Added to this, the young boy in *Emergency* gets blamed for his mother's death from a stroke after she had to brave the wind and cold as Andrew refused to run an errand for her. His elder brother accuses him of being a lying 'black bastard' and a murderer, violently beating up the younger Andrew, who then runs away from home, never to return.[25]

Rive's brother-in-law Freddie Josias remembers him as a clever, even brilliant boy at school. One of the teachers at St Mark's Primary School, Ursula Reines (née Strydom), who later became a close friend, remembers that 'in those days there was the famous old composition that you had to write. Give you a title and sit down and write a composition. And Richard just excelled. I think he had a gift for words.'[26] It was Georgina and Davey's wages that helped keep Richard at St Mark's until Standard 4 and then at Trafalgar Junior School until Standard 6.[27] In *Emergency* Daniel, an echo of Davey it seems, is the only brother with whom Andrew feels some kinship in the home:

> *Andrew got on well with Daniel. He was quiet and an introvert, something like himself, without the bitterness and resentment. Daniel was good-looking, soft-spoken and understanding. A regular church-goer, he had very little in common with the rest of the family other than his mother and Andrew. They often spoke, Danny and he, in the quiet hours of the morning while they lay next to each other. His brother was appreciative and honest in his opinions. He liked Danny best of all.*[28]

Josias remembers the young Richard as a very independent boy, even at this early age, who did exceptionally well at primary school. Alf Wannenburgh, another fellow writer and a friend until their relationship soured after decades, believes that St Mark's, which was Anglican, 'instilled Anglo-Saxon virtues' in the mind of the young boy.[29] These, however, were already present in Rive's home and the connection to St Mark's Church and in the royalist sympathies both at home and in the community, so perhaps it is more true to say that the school cemented the values of his home environment. Rive's own experiences at the primary school are transmuted into fiction in *Emergency*, as were other aspects of his outer and inner life. Andrew Dreyer fondly reflects on his origins in District Six in an early flashback:

> *The boys played games during the first lunch-break, but he was too self-conscious to join in. He stared with wide, black eyes at the teachers and the classrooms and the Biblical pictures on the wall and the miniature tables and chairs and the neat pile of worn readers in the cupboard. See me, Mother, can you see me? And life was beautiful and golden-brown on those apricot days when he was seven.*[30]

What he describes here as the boy's 'wide, black eyes' reflects quite literally Rive's striking dark eyes but also prefigures the title of his memoir *Writing Black*. Rive's alluring eyes are described by his old friend Ursula Reines as 'doleful'.[31] In this passage from the novel, the young boy is sensitive, self-conscious, very observant, immersed in texts and on the outside of the throng, often distanced from family yet immersed in neighbourhood, and with a deep subliminal longing to recreate an ideal mother-child bond. His childhood was not only a dreary and often trying time, but equally 'beautiful and golden-brown'. The image of the time as 'apricot days', the sweet and sour of growing up in the District, is more fully and successfully portrayed in *'Buckingham Palace', District Six*.

While there are echoes in his fiction of his strong sense of alienation from his family, especially after the death of his mother, while he was still at high school, Rive did not write about this in his non-fiction or in reflections on his childhood or his adult years. He shared the more private aspects of his life with only a very few close colleagues and friends. Interestingly, in *Emergency*, after Andrew has just left his home following the traumatic death of his mother, his fraught relationship with his siblings is described: 'He had a kind of revulsion about hearing the news of his family, yet his curiosity got the better of him.

He would have preferred to wipe out their existence from his mind.' Earlier in *Emergency*, we hear that Andrew 'was afraid of his elder brother; James had beaten him for breaking one of the dining-room chairs. James was very fair-skinned, a play-white, always cold and aloof' and '[James] … despised Andrew, whose dark skin he found an embarrassment.'[32] Rive, like his creation Andrew, felt the internalised racism that was prevalent in his family and caused untold strife and disruption, apparently leading to lifelong animosity between him and many in his family. Josias, however, denies that family members who were only 'a shade lighter' than Rive were prejudiced against him because of his dark skin. Long-standing friends of Rive's, Ariefi and Hazel Manuel, recall Rive's sisters who lived in Woodstock and that Richard was the darkest of the siblings and that this *was* patently an issue in the family. Much of the time Rive was raised by his maternal grandmother rather than by his mother and, by his teens, he had left home to board elsewhere. He maintained some contact with Georgina, who kept in touch with him throughout his life.[33]

In Rive's short story 'Resurrection', first published in 1963, there is a similarly fraught family scenario. Mavis, the main character with whom we empathise, has fair-skinned, play-white brothers and sisters who refuse to acknowledge the existence of their dark-skinned sibling. This story dramatically recounts the terrible pain and humiliation felt by Mavis, spurned and ignored as if she did not exist by those supposed to be closest to her – intense emotions that peppered Rive's relations with his mother and his siblings. And while these emotions undoubtedly affected him in deeply personal ways, he seemed able to confront them only from the distance provided by fiction, rather than in the closer-to-home autobiographical accounts of his childhood and adult life. In this regard, Rive embodies what Virginia Woolf suggests about the almost impossible act of capturing the momentous social and personal forces that constitute one, the 'invisible presences' that elude self-memorialisation: 'How futile life-writing becomes. I see myself as a fish in a stream; deflected; held in place; but cannot describe the stream.'[34]

Another factor that kept Rive at a distance from his family, particularly beyond his teenage years and throughout his adult life, was his sexuality. He attempted to conceal his homosexuality from family members and most of his friends for as long as he lived. Many, especially those of his generation or older, only realised he was gay because of the circumstances of his murder which, especially after the trial of the two accused, pointed to the murder of a gay man by young boys with whom he had or intended to have sex. Some of his friends, colleagues and fellow writers suspected that he was gay, while a few knew that he had had relations with younger men. As if out of respect to Rive the influential public figure and educationist, the son of the community who had made a name for himself locally as well as internationally and did them proud, and also perhaps respecting his own obvious wish to remain closeted, combined with the conservative ethos of the times in South Africa, there was, during Rive's lifetime, a public silence about his homosexuality. Josias claims that Georgina would have been horrified had she known he was gay. She never did realise he was gay or, like many of her generation, possibly refused to recognise something that was beyond her comprehension or moral universe. Josias also says that Rive became especially estranged from his sister Lucy because her husband was hostile to him – perhaps, Josias speculates, because they were jealous of his achievements or perhaps his homosexuality became evident at a later stage and so the hostility increased. Rive must have sensed even at a very early age this fairly widespread socially encrypted disgust for homosexual men and this increased the distance between him and his family. At what age he realised he was gay, or what the terms he used to think about his own sexuality were, remain unknown.

One of Rive's enduring friends was the artist Albert Adams. They met as fellow students at Hewat College, where Adams was a year ahead of Rive. Adams was much more comfortable with being a gay man at that stage than Rive was and accounted for the difference in the following terms:

I think even in '53 I knew Richard was gay ... Dennis Bullough was a gay chap who lived in Bree Street and he had a partner, John Dronsfield, who was an artist, and Bullough and Dronsfield kept a kind of open house for artists and the like. And Bill Currie was a close friend of Dennis Bullough, and if you knew Bill [as Richard did] you were invited to Bree Street ... it was a group of gay people and, you know, if you were ... there, you were gay ... Already then I knew that Richard was gay; we all knew that he was gay. Although our gayness, I think, was a little bit more open than Richard's. Richard had this macho-image of course, he was also a sportsman ... So he was involved with sports and young people, and I suppose ... I don't know to what degree that also [kept] a halter on him to keep his gayness under cover ... It would really not have, not have been accepted had he worked with young men, you know, on the sports field ... it was also simply part of Richard's insecurity. I'm thinking ... underneath all this kind of bravado, and this really extrovert, public image that he gave, I think there was a, a real sense of ... insecurity on Richard's part. I'm ... almost sure about that.[35]

Adams was one of the very few friends with whom Richard was open about his gayness, but even with Adams he was reticent about revealing any details of his private sexual affairs.

Rive decided, it seems, not only to keep his sexuality an intensely private matter, but to deflect it by recreating heterosexual stances that could be perceived as indicating his 'normality'. Writer Es'kia Mphahlele, who first met Rive in 1955 and became a lifelong friend and mentor, was bothered by Rive's lack of family attachments and also wondered whether his father was from Madagascar because the name 'Rive' is so close to 'Rivo' or 'Rivero'. Mphahlele also remembers that Rive did not relate to his brothers because they were not from *his* father. There was clearly a distance between him and his family, Mphahlele says, and Rive seemed to have cut all family ties, claiming he would leave his house to his nephew instead.[36] Rive left his house to Ian Rutgers, who was not a relative but the man to whom Rive was extremely close for a long, long time. Ian lived in a room in Rive's flat and then house for many years. He was the brother of Andrew Rutgers, whom Rive had befriended when Andrew was a young student of his. Rive became very friendly with the Rutgers family. Ian regarded Rive as a mentor and even father figure and did not or could not reciprocate the physical attraction Rive felt for him. 'Nephew', unbeknown to Mphahlele, was not indicative of a blood relative but was, instead, often a code word used by Rive for a young man he felt close to, and to whom he might have been sexually attracted or involved with, and whose presence he had to explain away, ironically by invoking conventional familial relations.

Those of us who worked with Rive during his years as a lecturer at Hewat College remember being introduced, during suppers at his home in Windsor Park or on the sports field, to a number of his 'nephews' and many of us knew what that meant. In a short story that partially fictionalises my attempts to create a biography of Rive, I focus on the attempts of the character called Richard to disguise the boys he surrounds himself with, and to whom he is attracted, as 'nephews'.[37] The story questions Rive's silence and secrecy about his sexual life and his need to disguise real relations with fictitious familial ones.[38]

While Rive did on occasion consciously enact what Judith Butler calls 'parodic replays' of heterosexual convention, at other times he used these conventions to disguise his secret life as a

homosexual man.[39] These heteronormative peformances can be
read as symptomatic of his deep yearning to be 'normal' – part
of conventional, mainstream social existence and, as a sporty
man, to assert what Adams calls the 'macho image'. Yet at the
same time these performances by Rive can be read as poking
fun at these very conventions and their language.

Rive had numerous friendships with young men, often
stemming from his keen desire to help the youth, especially those
who came from poor backgrounds like he did, to realise their
academic or sporting talent. A number of these friendships must
have been sexually charged but remained clandestine and silent; perhaps these unspoken relationships were unintentionally
encoded in *Writing Black* where he fleetingly describes these
moments of taboo friendship with 'the local guttersnipes' in the
poetic line which is also prophetic of the despair that marked his
love life: 'We used to sit in darkened doorways, and our silence
was full of the hopelessness of our lives.'[40] While Rive here also
notes that 'discovery by my socially insecure family was fraught
with danger', he does not acknowledge, even in the most subtle
or euphemistic way, that there might have been taboos other
than crossing class lines that were implicated in his attraction to
boys marginalised by conventional society.

Despite the dominant thread of deep disaffection with family,
Rive certainly had moments of intimacy with certain members
of his family, which he hardly mentioned and rarely wrote about
in his autobiographical writings. He seemed particularly close at
times to his mother, as can be gauged from the rare references
to her in his work and from the accounts of close friends.
Georgina was the sister with whom Richard had most contact;
the character of Miriam in his novel *Emergency* has shades of
Georgina – the sympathetic, supportive and, significantly, 'dark'
sister who never quite gives up on Andrew, in contrast to the
hostile, fair-skinned sister, Annette: 'Miriam was easier to get on

with than Annette. She was almost as dark as himself, quiet and detached. He had never really known her. She had married a bus driver when Andrew was eight and had gone to stay in Walmer Estate, seldom visiting District Six.'[41] In later years, Rive visited Georgina and her husband at least once a year, and they in turn visited his Selous Court flat in Claremont where he lived for a long time. Rive wrote to Georgina on a regular basis when he travelled and Josias remembers her receiving letters from Rive when he was visiting Japan in the mid-1980s.

One of the nieces whom Rive had time for was Georgina Retief, the daughter of the eldest of the Rive children, Joseph Rive. Retief says she was named after one of Richard's sisters – 'his favourite, Georgina Rive.'[42] She has fond memories of her Uncle Richard, who brought her to St Mark's Primary School in District Six and insisted she went into an English-medium class even though she was Afrikaans-speaking. He was also a student-teacher at her school, a fact she was very proud of as a young pupil. Retief also mentions that Rive stayed with Georgina and Freddie for a short while. She confirms that most of the family distanced themselves from Rive because of his homosexuality and he in turn had very little to do with them. Retief does not make any reference to colour prejudice within the family, but it is probably easier for families, in post-1994 South Africa, to admit to homophobia than to internalised racism in order to account for intra-familial hostility. The opposite seems true of Rive's early years – it was 'easier' to blame the distance in his family on his 'darkness', rather than on his mother's shaming affair or his homosexual 'difference' – both things that were much more taboo in those days than race.

As a top-performing pupil at Trafalgar Junior School, Rive was awarded a municipal scholarship at the age of twelve to fund his studies at the prestigious Trafalgar High School in the District, where he studied 'subjects with a ring about them' – Latin,

Mathematics and Physical Science.[43] Richard Dudley, a leading intellectual, educationist and member of the Teachers' League of South Africa, remembers encountering the teenager at Trafalgar. Dudley was doing research at the school in 1944 when Rive was fourteen and in Standard 7: '[The young Rive was] an earnest, bustling, bright young lad, as yet unsure of himself … Among a group of really gifted pupils, he was one who drew attention to himself.'[44] Dudley here shows glimpses of the larger-than-life character that Rive was to become – articulate, sharp-tongued, with an impish sense of humour.

There are disappointingly few details about Rive's school days at Trafalgar High, where he matriculated in 1947. The only mention of the school that played a seminal role in developing his thought and politics is in a chapter of *Writing Black* called 'Growing Up':

> *Much of what I wanted to know about myself I later found out in books written by people who were able to articulate their experiences better than I ever could. From my primary school days at St Marks and Trafalgar Junior I read avidly and indiscriminately anything I could lay my eyes on. By the time I was at Trafalgar High my reading was partially to escape from the realities of the deprivation surrounding me.*[45]

In the photograph from his high school days, Rive appears reticent, reserved, almost shy, hands just touching the shoulders of his classmate kneeling in front of him. Kneeling just to the left of Rive, in the centre, is my father, Ian Viljoen. This was the most uncanny moment of my research into Rive's life. It was only sometime after I came across this photograph that I recognised my father. I had no idea he had been in the same class as Rive and he had died long before I embarked on this research. Julia Williams, the young woman kneeling on the far left, married Ivan Abrahams, who was a fellow student with Rive at Hewat College and later a colleague at the college (it was

Richard Rive (back row, fifth from the right) with some of his Standard 10 classmates at Trafalgar High in 1947 (photographer: unknown) Reprinted by permission of UCT Libraries (BC1309: Richard Rive Papers. A3. Photograph of the matric class of Trafalgar High, 1947)

she who helped to compile information about this photograph in June 2012). Abu Desai, standing on the far right, became vice-rector at Hewat College while Rive lectured there. (How segregation and apartheid created these intimately connected colour-coded villages within the city!) The mathematics teacher, Mr Roux, stands at the centre.

Rive's high school years coincided with the reign and fall of Nazism and the renewed vigour of worldwide debate about freedom, equality, democracy and national independence. His years at Trafalgar High were to be formative intellectually and ideologically. Dudley captures the decisive intellectual influence the school had on Rive's outlook on life:

> At Trafalgar a climate and ethos had been created which was unequalled in any institution for the oppressed at that time. For

among the teachers were distinguished scholars like Ben Kies, Jack Meltzer, Suleiman (Solly) Idros, George Meisenheimer, Cynthia Fischer and the equally distinguished science teacher, H.N. Pienaar. This generation of teachers ... were the articulate bearers of a new outlook in education, a team dedicated to excellence and selfless in their service to their pupils ... It is here where the teachers brought into the classroom, from all corners of the world ... writers and their works to [nurture] the minds of their pupils ... Through these teachers ... these scholars learnt that oppression was created by mankind, could be ended by mankind, and that a new society could be created too by mankind.[46]

Many of the teachers Dudley refers to were part of an intellectual tradition coming out of the left-wing reading and discussion circles and broad social movements in South Africa at the time.

Ben Kies was the most influential of these scholars and teachers at Trafalgar High. He was regarded as the leader among the Non-European Unity Movement (NEUM) leadership. His tall and sturdy bearing complemented his incisive intelligence, encyclopedic knowledge and frank, forthright manner. Kies was part of the leadership that propagated the notion of a principled, programmatic struggle propounded by the All African Convention (AAC) and its constituent organisations, formed in 1936, and later by the NEUM, formed in 1943. Both these organisations propagated a struggle against racial oppression and economic domination on the basis of a minimum programme of demands, aimed at breaking with the dependence on ruling-class concessions that was the premise of the nationalist politics of negotiation adopted by the ANC at the time. These more radical intellectuals saw the limitations of narrow nationalism and were inspired by the ideals of the French and Russian revolutions, by the works of Marx, Lenin and Trotsky and by the ideas stemming from the internationalist, anti-colonial movement emerging from the period after the Bolshevik revolution. The NEUM, a broad front of civic and political organisations, reached the peak of its popularity in the late forties and early fifties but then fragmented and was eclipsed by the more popular ANC and later Pan-Africanist Congress (PAC). The ideology of the NEUM, however, remained influential in the 1950s and beyond and was marked by subscription to a radical anti-imperialist internationalism and to a policy of 'non-racialism'. Non-racialism challenged the existence of the category of 'race' and insisted on a common humanity of all people and on a definition of national identity that stressed common interests rather than differences among South Africans. This particular conceptualisation of non-racialism was to be at the heart of Rive's work as a teacher, sports activist and writer. Ironically, while Rive revered him as a teacher and an intellectual, Kies was later disparaging of Rive's character and dismissive of his creative work. In the mid-1970s, Kies told me that he felt that Rive tended to be an opportunist and a poseur and that his work was trite and reinforced stereotypes.

The far-reaching ideas seeded during his high school years were further developed when Rive went to study at Hewat Teacher Training College on the Cape Flats after high school and then again during his years as a teacher at South Peninsula High School in the southern suburbs of Cape Town, where a number of his colleagues were NEUM intellectuals. Later in his career, as lecturer and eventually senior lecturer and head of the English department at Hewat College, he was also among colleagues who were leading and active members of the Teachers' League of South Africa. At South Peninsula, Rive made his mark as an English and Latin teacher. Through his friendship with fellow Latin and Mathematics teacher Daphne Wessels, Rive became a very close friend to Daphne's husband, Victor Wessels. It was largely through Wessels, but later also under the influence of prominent NEUM members such as Ivan Abrahams, a colleague at Hewat College during the 1970s and 1980s, and Harry Hendricks, with whom Rive worked in the Western Province Senior School Sports Union and in the South African Council on Sport, that Rive consolidated and refined the intellectual leitmotifs of his life – commitment to the underdog, non-racialism, progressive nationalism, principled struggle, universal equality. While 'Rive never publicly belonged to any national liberation organisation in South Africa',[47] he was a product of, and consciously aligned himself to, the ideological positions of his political teachers and mentors in the NEUM. For most of his adult life, Rive was at one time or another a founding or leading member of civic organisations such as school-level and national sports bodies.

In a letter of 30 July 1954, Rive, a highly articulate and well-read twenty-four-year-old teacher at South Peninsula High, committed to the struggle and to the ambition of becoming a writer, describes to Langston Hughes, in the understandably overblown terms of a wide-eyed and overawed young writer in the making, himself and his political ideas:

> … *[I] am avidly fond of reading and fanatical about politics.*
>
> *I belong to a school of thought, Trotskyite and Leftist in its outlook (shades of Senator McCarthy) who believe in non-collaboration as a political weapon. After becoming a gold-chorded [sic] King Scout in the Boy Scout Movement I was almost forced out because of speeches and reports attacking Imperialistic indoctrination and the division of the movement on racial lines. I'm out of it now.*[48]

While at school, Rive joined the Scouts movement rather than the church brigade, as the family thought the former more respectable than membership of the church lads' brigade, which entailed 'marching through the streets behind a blaring, tinny band'.[49] It was while he was in the Second Cape Town Boys'

Scout Troop that Rive first met artist Peter Clarke, who was to become a good friend and fellow writer. Rive's already developed sense of the iniquities of racialism and his courage to speak out against injustice, which he relates to Hughes, were hallmarks of his outlook and character even in these early years. In slightly later correspondence with Hughes, Rive gives more revealing detail about the incident in the Scouts:

> *Concerning the Boy Scouts, in South Africa it is divided into racialistic groups. When Lord Rowallen, chief scout of the world, visited South Africa, a preliminary meeting of Scouts was called to 'decide on the questions he was to be asked'. People started asking silly questions like official length of garter-tabs and colours of scarves. Everyone shirked the political issue till I asked 'whether the division of Scouts into racialistic groups as practised in South Africa was in accordance with true Scouting principle and tradition'! Complete chaos. When we met Rowallen I asked the same questions and of course things were made so hot for me that I resigned. My troop threatened to resign in protest. But I objected.*[50]

We glimpse in this letter, in both the actual event recalled as well as in the rhetorical representation of himself in the narrative, with its evident sense of rhythm, drama and climax, the fearless, outspoken leader of the troop, the irrepressible and just voice of a leader of the silent, oppressed masses. The young Rive is keenly, even boastingly aware of the transgressive nature of his ideas, of his talent for words and courage to speak out, and of his ability to play leader.

His fearless breaking of the silence on racial issues must have been spurred on by his own experiences of racist attitudes because of his dark skin. While the progressive teachers at Trafalgar High were to help him formulate his non-racialism, there were others whose bigotry must have wounded him deeply. Gilbert Reines, who was a fellow pupil at Trafalgar and later the husband of Rive's primary school teacher Ursula Reines, remembers one such Standard 6 teacher they had at the school:

> *You know, in those days, you had to bring your mug to school to receive milk, and if you've forgotten it, [this teacher] used to put a saucer on the floor with milk in it, and make you lick it, you know, lap it up like, like a cat … And … he always tried to catch Richard out, I think, for something or other. But one day … he said to Richard very seriously, 'Oh d'jys 'n slim kaffir' ['Oh, you're a clever kaffir'].*[51]

In the classroom, on the sports field, inside the home – wherever he turned, it must have seemed to the young Richard Rive, he was being assaulted by soul-destroying hatred based on the colour of his skin.

Besides highlighting the racial situation of the time of his childhood, the early chapters in *Writing Black* focus on two other areas of his youth so fundamental to Rive's whole life – sport and his ambition to be a writer. Even at an early age, Rive was a superb athlete (as he revelled in recounting when he was an older, rotund and quite out-of-shape man), winning prizes at amateur competitions organised by the well-meaning social workers in District Six. Peter Meyer, a long-standing colleague in the sporting world and fellow educationist, traces Rive's development as a sportsman:

> *His interest in athletics started at primary school and developed under the guidance of physical education teacher 'Lightning' Smith at Trafalgar High School … He excelled particularly in the four-hundred-yards hurdles … and the high jump. During the late 1940s he became the South African champion in these events, participating in the colours of the Western Province Amateur Athletics Union and in competitions of the South African Amateur Athletics and Cycling Board of Control.*[52]

According to Joe Schaffers, Smith was a well-known wrestler and a member of the 'exclusive, upper-class "Coloured"' Aerial

Athletics Club, which Rive also joined. Even his earliest aspirations of developing his talent as a sportsman were frustrated by the politics of racism and prejudice: 'At first the members, all fair-skinned, were worried about my dark complexion, but relented because not only was I a mere junior but I attended Trafalgar High School.'[53] This attitude, which tempers overt racism with overlays of class considerations, encountered by Rive early on in life, surely increased his determination to get the best education he could and, in addition, to flaunt it as a retort to people judging him by the colour of his skin.

Besides his participation in organised sport, Rive was also keen on mountain hiking, often walking up the numerous tracks on Table Mountain with friends and students. The walks through the mountains above Kalk Bay and the paths up Table Mountain from the Pipe Track were favourite routes. He loved swimming and the sea, and occasionally went spear-fishing. One of his spear-fishing friends was Jim Bailey, owner of *Drum* magazine. Rive knew Bailey even before he made a long trip in 1955 to Johannesburg to meet the staff of *Drum* and Es'kia Mphahlele in particular.

Every other aspect of life selected for display by Rive in *Writing Black* – childhood, sport, teaching, studying, travelling – is consciously and demonstratively linked to the colour question and oppression in South Africa. The autobiography is as much protest literature, or 'anti-Jim Crow' as he calls it, as it is memoir. In fact *Writing Black* grew out of a keynote paper Rive delivered at the conference of the African Literature Association of America held at the University of Indiana in Bloomington in 1979. His paper was called 'The Ethics of an Anti-Jim Crow' and used the story of his childhood in District Six and young adult life to emphasise the complete exclusion of people who were not white from civil society in South Africa.

In both the paper and the memoir, Rive links his drive to

be a writer to his being a keen reader as a child, a connection commonly made by many other writers when recounting memories of childhood, as documented in Antonia Fraser's edited volume *The Pleasure of Reading*. Rive read voraciously and indiscriminately everything he could get his hands on 'to escape from the realities of the deprivation surrounding me'.[54] He also insists on capturing the racialised assumptions about the world of books embedded in the perceptions of his young self: 'I never questioned the fact that all the good characters, the hero figures, were White and that all the situations were White … Books were not written about people like me. Books were not written by people like me.'

The initial chapter, which covers the period between 1937 and 1955, is in fact primarily about Rive becoming a writer. It is noteworthy that a number of aspects of his childhood reading are foregrounded and conflated in his recreation of these early years. He establishes that he was a keen reader as a high school student and states that he was drawn to the classics of English literature. He names Shakespeare, Wordsworth, Scott and Haggard in particular. Rive was not only genuinely inspired by these writers, but was also consciously establishing and asserting his credentials as a cosmopolitan intellectual and writer. In addition, he has an acute awareness of how the received literary tradition was constructed and functioned as a Eurocentric way of seeing the world. The United States was not only the place of origin of Rive's enigmatic father but also, ironically, the source of the inspiration to be an 'African' writer; to feel that his life, his place and his times were worthy subjects for serious literature.

Chapter 2

It was the discovery of the writers of the American Harlem Renaissance – Rive mentions in particular Richard Wright, Langston Hughes, Countee Cullen, Jean Toomer and Cedric Dover – that allowed the young Rive to find representations in literature that spoke more directly to his own dilemmas and contexts, and to break the illusion that books were for and about 'White Folks'.[55] In 'On Being a Black Writer in South Africa: A Personal Essay', Rive claims to have first encountered the work of Langston Hughes when he read *The Ways of White Folks* at the age of twelve, a book he found on the shelves of the Hyman Liberman Institute Library in Muir Street, District Six: 'A new world opened up. This was about me and depicted my frustrations and resentments in a world obsessed with colour.'[56] One senses here Rive's epiphanic moment, a moment of self-discovery that changed his life as a writer and his very sense of self. It is also fascinating that Rive captures this turning point in an image that echoes the isolated Miranda's excitement at glimpsing a 'brave new world' in Shakespeare's *The Tempest*. Unlike a writer such as Ngũgĩ wa Thiong'o, who tried to effect a radical break from the English canon and its prevailing humanist assumptions in order to establish an independent African aesthetic, even attempting to move away from using the English language in creative work, Rive comfortably and consciously asserted his identity as an African writer, as he simultaneously claimed the great English literary tradition and the English language as his own.

The influence of the black American writers of the Harlem Renaissance was also refracted through the work of the writer who most directly influenced the whole *Drum* school of writers,

Peter Abrahams. Mphahlele makes the point that the previous writing tradition by black authors located itself in folklore, in the oral past, in the (often Christian) allegory, the didactic and in the epic; it was with Thomas Mofolo, Herbert Dhlomo, RRR Dhlomo and AC Jordan that elements of realism were being favoured in work by black writers. Mphahlele continues:

> *Realism, however, really burst into full blossom for us when Peter Abrahams published* Dark Testament *(1940) … Abrahams acknowledged the influence of Afro-American writing on his own … Abrahams' novels were to provide an inspiration for later fiction – that of the next decade.*[57]

Realism, a particular style of writing that represents place, time, people and things as they appear in everyday life, was attractive to black South African writers in the 1950s as the post-war, anti-colonial movements gained momentum around the world and defiance marked the anti-apartheid mood at home. Abrahams's gritty realism, detailed depiction of local settings and autobiographically inspired content are narrative elements in the work of American Harlem Renaissance writers. In South Africa, Abrahams became a model for both black journalists and fiction writers of the 1950s. Rive, who always spoke of himself as a member of 'the Protest School of writers', acknowledges his debt to both Abrahams and Mphahlele: 'There were many factors which gave momentum to [the Protest School] which had started hesitantly in the forties with Peter Abrahams and Ezekiel Mphahlele.' He also talks about Abrahams in the following terms: 'Abrahams was intent on showing social conflict in the broad, political sense of the word.' Rive claims that Abrahams's realism also derives from the social realist traditions fostered in the prose emanating from the Soviet Union. Rive found the stylistic conventions of realism – the insistence on authentic and detailed description of place and time – a mode of expression that enabled him to articulate an anti-racist, humanist position and, like Richard Wright, say, 'Listen, White man'.[58] Apartheid impelled Rive to be a writer; even at a young age, he dedicated his talent and directed his anger to writing against apartheid – in the conventional sense of the word as socio-economic relations that dehumanised and destroyed lives but also, less commented on then and now, apartheid that infiltrated and scarred the innermost life.

Rive dates his first 'raw, angry prose' from about the time he gained his school-leaving Senior Certificate and, after the death of his mother, moved out of District Six to the abutting neighbourhood of Walmer Estate – to Flat 3, 17 Perth Road – a relatively middle-class area with larger, more modern housing often owned by the occupants rather than rented.[59] Walmer Estate was literally and in terms of social hierarchy higher up than the District. Rive was extremely glad to be out of the slum existence in which he had grown up. In *Emergency*, the narrator recounts Andrew's feelings towards his home neighbourhood as a teenager in his final year at high school:

> *Andrew was determined to blot out the memory of the slums, the dirt, the poverty. He remembered the feeling of shame and humiliation he had experienced when Miriam had told him that Justin and Abe had come to pay their respects in Caledon Street after his mother had died. He was glad he had not been home. He wondered how they had reacted. Had they realised before that he lived in a slum?*[60]

Rive had made the first of many moves towards middle-class comfort and respectability, but later he noted that 'paradoxically I also became more aware of my own position as an unenfranchised, Black non-citizen'.[61] As his experience for the rest of his life was to prove, no matter what his financial, literary or educational achievements were, he remained an inferior being in the eyes of the authorities and of those who had internalised racist assumptions.

After Rive completed high school in 1947, he worked as a clerk at a furniture retail business, Phil Morkel, 'but after two years', Harry Hendricks suspects, 'he must have felt that business talk was too limited a field for him'.[62] Perhaps he had already decided to bide his time, earning the money he needed to pay his way through college. In 1950 he registered at Hewat Training College, then in Roeland Street in District Six at the site of the present Harold Cressy High School, where he trained to become a high school English teacher. At Hewat, Rive met fellow students Ivan Abrahams and Albert Adams. Abrahams remembers first meeting Rive when he arrived as a first-year student at Hewat and Rive was in his second year. Rive was a keen athlete and became a champion 440-yard hurdler. Abrahams, also an avid athlete and runner at his old high school, Athlone High, helped to encourage Rive's sporting career, even carrying his tog bag!ized[63] How Rive must have relished having a first-year student at his heels.

Abrahams also remembers Rive having a very impressive style of sprinting, using shorter rather than longer strides, which, he claims, Rive picked up from the Americans. The connection to the United States loomed large in his parentage, his sense of himself as a black writer and even as a sportsman. The connection to Britain was to the home of Englishness, to English literature and London as a nerve centre of African literature, and to the apotheosis of his educational achievements – his doctorate from no less than the great Oxford University. And, enmeshed with these transatlantic locations of belonging was the connection from the Cape to the north, to Johannesburg, to East and West Africa, from where he drew inspiration for his sense of being an African writer.

In 1951 Rive became a second-year representative on the editorial board of *The Hewat Training College Magazine*. The board was headed by Adams and the pieces of dialogue that Rive wrote for the magazine under the name 'R.M. Rive' are called

'Variations on a Theme', 'With Apologies to William Shake-speare', 'With Apologies to Alan Paton' and 'With Apologies to H.W. Longfellow' and are a far cry from the 'angry prose' of the short stories associated with *Drum*, which were to launch his name as a writer a few years later. But like parts of some of the *Drum* stories, these student pieces are marked by an obvious and sometimes grating derivativeness. The first piece, 'Variations on a Theme', imitates an absurdist exchange between Stranger and Tweedledee; the second imitates, in overblown Shakespearian diction, an exchange between Stranger and Tweedledadio; the third is a paternalistic exchange between Alan Paton and a black man ('Umfundisi' and 'my child'); and the final one imitates the style of Longfellow, with dialogue between Stranger and Hiawatha. The young writer clearly wants to show, even show off, his knowledge of great writers. At the same time, there is an element of parody present, in that the pieces are so obviously flaunting the characteristic diction of each of the writers. This makes them somewhat funny but in a self-consciously learned, yet at the same time satirical fashion. Lastly, the piece on Paton includes a local, South African reference. From even this early stage as a writer, Rive was intent on engaging with his own conditions, with the work of South African writers, even though he was enchanted by the giants of the canon. This coterminous assertion of the local and the Euro-American persisted throughout his life. He was, he insisted, a citizen of the world.

According to Hendricks, Rive completed his two-year teacher training course at Hewat College by the end of 1951 and then 'taught at Vasco High School for a year and during that year was one of the teachers instrumental in the formation [and] the founding of the Western Province Senior Schools Sports Union'.[64] After Vasco High, Rive joined the staff of South Peninsula High School, where he eventually became the head of the English department. At this stage he still lived in Walmer

Estate, but he later moved to take up a room in Second Avenue, Grassy Park, 'with an aggressively respectable family, who insisted on ignoring their even darker neighbours', in order to be closer to South Peninsula, which was in the nearby suburb of Diep River.[65] At the start of his career at South Peninsula, he taught Latin and English, and his principal was Attie de Villiers – one of his former teachers at Trafalgar High.[66] This was a moment of great pride for Rive – acquiring a post at a highly respected school and having the honour of working with one of his own teacher-heroes. He taught at South Peninsula for almost two decades, until 1974, spending just a few of those years travelling, studying and working abroad. Towards the end of his time at South Peninsula, he did a short stint at Athlone High School, in 1973, while he was on leave from South Peninsula to complete his doctoral degree.

Together with fellow South Peninsula High colleagues such as Wilfred King, Rive helped to establish a reputation for the school as a top-performing contender in inter-school athletics championships. After a hard day of teaching English and Latin, he would spend time in the after-school hours, weekends and school holidays as an athletics coach and sports administrator. In addition, he remained an active member of the Western Province Senior Schools Sports Union and served on the executive committee of the body until his appointment at Hewat College in 1975. As if this was not enough to prove his sense of commitment to education and sport, he helped to form the South Peninsula Athletics Club in 1958 in order to consolidate and extend the work being done in sport at school level. With the formation in 1961 of the national umbrella body, the South African Senior School Sports Association (SASSSA), Rive became a national player in the field of athletics administration. Peter Meyer remembers:

Richard became a Western Province delegate to the South

African Senior School Sports Association and served on the
executive for many years. His wit, his irony, his sarcasm and
eloquence in debate made him a fierce and feared opponent ...
He could analyse a situation to the point of being clinical and
could formulate resolutions and motions very concisely and
accurately. But he was sometimes very impatient and arrogant.
He came across as somewhat of a braggart.[67]

At the start of his career as a teacher, in 1952, while teaching
full-time, Rive decided to register as a part-time student for his
Bachelor of Arts degree at the University of Cape Town, majoring
in English. He continued to write creatively in his spare time.
Teaching, writing, organising sport and studying made their
demands on his time and he eventually graduated with his BA
more than ten years later, in 1962. His degree courses included
Political Philosophy (II), History (II), Economics and Economic
Geography. It was in one of the registration queues, in 1959, that
Rive and writer Alf Wannenburgh first met.[68]

The twenty-four-year-old Rive paints for Langston Hughes a
detailed, fascinating picture of his typical day at this time when
he begins to make a name for himself:

I awake at six in the morning at my home in Walmer Estate
(a select Coloured area where Africans are seldom seen, but
don't blame me), and catch a bus to Cape Town Station. I am
allowed to sit anywhere in the bus, but in Johannesburg I can
only sit upstairs, three seats from the back and in Durban I
will be allowed to sit where I like (because I'm Coloured) but
Africans and Indians must sit upstairs.

At the station I board a section of the train where anyone
may sit, but under no condition may I sit in the compartments
labelled 'Blankes Alleen' as those are reserved for Whites. I have
regular friends I meet on the train, Hepburn who is a Master
of Arts and has a keen sense of humour, Bill Currie who is
an outstanding actor but will never be able to act in National

Companies because of his Colour and Arthur whom I suspect seeks solace in Roman Catholicism. Our conversation reaches a high standard, most probably far higher than most of our counterparts.

At Diep River I alight and walk 200 yards to pleasant South Peninsula High (a school for Coloured pre-University students) where the students are well-dressed and fed and come from better-class homes. Here I meet fellow lecturers who mostly belong to the Teachers' League of South Africa (a militant teachers' body now outlawed by the Department of Education). I lecture in Latin and English Literature and in addition take students for track athletics and swimming. After finishing here I attend lectures of the University of Cape Town (one of the two Universities in South Africa where no colour-bar is in operation) and am allowed in the same lecture room as white students. I should have mentioned that there is no academic segregation but a rigorous social segregation is observed, and I am not allowed to represent my University at Sports or functions attended by Apartheid Universities. After my lectures I usually go home and then to the Athletics Track which we are allowed to use on two nights a week when the whites do not use it. After this I either go to a political lecture, N.E.F. (New Era Fellowship, a militant Non-European Unity Movement (NEUM) organisation) or M.Y.S. (Modern Youth Society, a group of radical youths with Leninist tendencies) or listen to the Cape Town Municipal Orchestra (no colour bar) or have the option of attending a Coloured cinema where a notice is usually displayed bearing the legend 'Not for Natives (Africans) and children under 12!!!' Or I watch the University Ballet in which Coloured Artists are allowed to perform or drama at the Little Theatre. I belong to the University Library, Public Library and Educational Library (in any other Provinces there would be no library facilities for Non-Europeans whatsoever).

> *Were I an African, life would by no means be quite as*
> *pleasant. I would have to live in a location about 30 miles*
> *from Cape Town (Langa) earn a mere pittance and find a*
> *social if not economic bar to most cultural matters. I would*
> *also be open to abuse from both Whites and Coloureds. An*
> *African friend of mine, Mchigi, was almost knocked over by a*
> *Coloured skolly (hooligan) and told 'Voetsek Kaffer!' while in*
> *my company. Mchigi holds an M.A. degree in philosophy but is*
> *spurned as a Kaffer. The favourite term of abuse for Coloured*
> *people is 'Hotnot' or Hottentot. I have been called 'Kafferboetie'*
> *(friend of Kaffers), a frustrated intellectual, a perniculous [sic]*
> *influence, geleerde Hotnot (educated Hottentot), cynic, etc etc*
> *etc. During vacation I usually travel extensively through South*
> *Africa, and that is when the fun starts. It is then that I am*
> *made to feel my colour and see the system in operation.*[69]

This letter is remarkable for the manner in which it conveys a
finely observed sense of how racial politics infiltrated and de-
meaned every aspect of the young man's daily life; for what it
reveals of the writer's eye for class distinctions present within
the more obvious divisions along lines of race; for his empathy
with those like Mchigi who were even worse off than he was;
for his strong sense of himself and his circle as cultured, urbane
intellectuals and members of a radical resistance to racial
oppression; for his ability to portray character in concise and
vivid ways; and for his irrepressible wit and the humour that
cannot help but mark his writing. Despite all the trials of being
a black man in a white man's country, this letter exudes a lust for
life that persisted through most of his life.

It was about this time that Rive met Barney Desai, who was
Cape Town editor of the *Golden City Post*, a national newspaper
aimed at black readers. Desai commissioned Rive to do a short
story, launching the long association Rive was to have with the
popular press throughout his life. Rive's memoir suggests this

story was written in his 'early twenties', which implies a date prior to 1955, but the *Golden City Post* started only in 1955. The story appeared in its companion paper, *Africa*, in July 1955. Is this another indication of Rive's penchant for making himself a little younger than he actually was? Or is it his unreliable memory for dates? Rive called his piece 'My Sister Was a Playwhite', a piece of journalism in the style of an agony/confessional column. It is narrated by a young, dark-skinned, coloured girl who tells the story of her fair-skinned sister, Lucille, who is encouraged by their also fair-skinned mother to live 'as white'. It depicts the painful and humiliating divisions arising within the District Six family, where dark-skinned members are disowned, shamed and displaced, as a result of the aspirations of the mother and elder sister to exist as 'white' in a racially ordered society. The final paragraph reflects the didactic tone and mock confessional style: 'I am writing this confession, distasteful as it is, because Lucille has asked me to do it to sound a word of warning to all Coloured persons who entertain a desire to "cross the line" and pass for White.'[70]

There are obviously strong autobiographical elements to the story – the home in District Six, the divisive family attitudes to racial identity, the fair mother and dark father, the narrator being a top performer at St Mark's School but getting no acknowledgement for her academic achievements from father or mother – and perhaps even the name Lucille hints at Rive's own sister Lucy. These thinly disguised aspects from his own life would clearly embarrass his family if ever they read the story, which is probably why Rive chose to use a pseudonym as well as to change the gender of the narrator. The piece pre-dates any of the stories Rive composed for *Drum* shortly hereafter and is intriguing for the insights into what were fictionalised aspects of Rive's childhood and the terrible strain that existed within the family. A dominant strand of Rive's second novel,

'*Buckingham Palace*', *District Six*, is already very evident in this, the earliest of his work set in District Six – the lyrical and deliberately celebratory recreation of the fabric of past life in a place constantly under threat of erasure. It begins a lifelong use of fictionalised autobiography in his creative work and a preoccupation with District Six as a setting for the exploration of the antithetical interconnectedness of the personal and the political, of nostalgia and despair, and of loss and hope. 'My Sister Was a Playwhite' is one of only two fictional works in which Rive uses a female narrator, the other being the short story 'Mrs Janet September and the Siege of Sinton' (published in 1987 in *Contrast*, two years before his death). Unlike the earnest confessional of 'My Sister Was a Playwhite', this last short story Rive wrote is told by a sixty-seven-year-old coloured woman, Janet September, who insists on being arrested along with protesting scholars from Sinton High School. The tale of this 'oldest lady terrorist in Athlone' is a hilarious, over-the-top and camp parody of the idiom of an older generation of coloured folk (like Rive himself).[71] At the same time, the story celebrates fearless resistance to the police brutality of the dying apartheid state.

It was in Desai's office, in 1955, that Rive again met artist Peter Clarke, and for the first time got to know photographer Lionel Oostendorp and writer James Matthews, all of whom were to become his very good friends. Clarke, writing to Langston Hughes in 1955, recalls a gathering of these friends, capturing the cultural earnestness and hunger for ideas of the young men at the time, as well as their love of a good party:

> *I saw Richard on Saturday, in fact I spent the afternoon at his home. He was having a party for a small group of us which included another writer friend James Matthews and photographer Lionel Oostendorp and one other friend (DRUM was responsible for our getting to know each other). It was quite*

a happy little affair and we spent the time eating and drinking and being merry while talking books and stories, art, poetry, music and that great old one and only subject, W-O-M-E-N … We listened to Beethoven as rendered by Malcuzynski, we listened to Borodin's 'Prince Igor', Prokofiev, Smetana, excerpts from 'Hamlet' and 'Macbeth' and John Gielgud reading T.S. Eliot's 'Preludes'… There was Chopin and Delibes. Richard has a fine collection of records which make truly enjoyable listening.[72]

Despite both growing up in a slum, Rive and Matthews had very different dispositions and asserted very different social class allegiances, and also had very different ideas about writing and intended audiences. Rive describes the bond and the differences that marked their friendship from the very start and all the way through their long and often affectionately acrimonious association. The differences between them were already apparent in their first encounter in the office of the *Golden City Post* in Corporation Street, District Six:

So here was James Matthews, whose stories I had read in the Weekend Argus; *the telephone operator who wrote fiction in his spare time. I knew … that he came from a slum area above Bree Street, as beaten up as District Six, and that he had the merest rudiments of a secondary education. I had also heard he was a member of a powerful gang. I realised immediately that he saw in me everything he despised. I was not only Coloured middle class, but I spoke Coloured middle class and behaved Coloured middle class.*[73]

Matthews, in a tribute to Rive in 1989, makes a similar remark about the differences that marked the two men as writers and friends: 'At times we were the opposite sides of a coin. My habitat the shebeens. Yours the drawing room of academia, our writing the strong bond.'[74]

Rive embodied a not atypical paradox that was characteristic of the divided subjectivity of black intellectuals in the colonised world during the anti-colonial struggles for independence – being a part of, yet apart from; being black and engaged in struggle, iconic of and giving voice to the oppressed mass, yet being an educated, well-travelled writer and academic, living in fairly comfortable, middle-class conditions. Throughout his life Rive experienced the tension of such straddling of worlds; Matthews was far less wracked by the division, always living in a working-class area, spurning the comforts of suburbia.

It was not only writing that was the strong bond between Matthews and Rive, but also a shared conviction and the courage to speak out against ever-encroaching dictates of white minority rule. A fomenting spirit of defiance and cultural assertiveness marked the early to mid-1950s in South Africa. Through short stories, reportage and photography, Rive, Matthews and the writers associated with *Drum* asserted their humanity and cosmopolitanism in a fusion of African and American themes and styles as a retort to ruling-class attempts to dehumanise and tribalise. *Drum*, Michael Chapman says, 'was part of the socialising process of the fifties: it helped to record and create the voices, images and values of a black urban culture at the precise moment that the Minister of Native Affairs, [Hendrik] Verwoerd, was setting out to render untenable any permanent African presence in the so-called "white" cities'.[75]

One of Rive's first short stories, 'The Return', written in 1953 or possibly even before, was entered for a *Drum* short story competition which was judged by, amongst others, Langston Hughes. He was asked to be a judge by the assistant editor of *Drum*, Henry Nxumalo. Hughes not only agreed but also offered to do a column about *Drum* in the *Chicago Defender*. Nxumalo sent Hughes the eight stories entered into the competition in December 1953. Rive's story got second prize.[76] Hughes was very impressed with the stories and his exposure to young writers in South Africa gave birth to his idea for the publication of an anthology of African short stories. He began writing to various African writers about his idea, first testing it on Peter Abrahams in London, who promised to contribute stories. He also wrote to the young Rive very soon thereafter:

As one of the judges of Drum's *recent Short Story Contest it was my privilege to read your very beautiful short story, 'The Return'. I am wondering if you have any more such stories or sketches that you could send me?*

There is great interest at the moment in America in Africa, particularly South Africa, it being so much in the news these days. And the books of Alan Patton [sic] and Nadine Gordimer, among others, have been well received here. So, I have talked recently with one of the best American publishers about the possibility of an anthology of short stories by African writers, and he was most favorable to the idea, asking me to assemble such a collection, and promising to give it very careful consideration when gotten together. If accepted for publication, there would be the usual pro rata payment to each writer for his work used therein.

Should you have a half dozen or so more stories concerning the problems, inter-group relations, or folk life of the people, I would be most happy to see them as soon as you can conveniently send them to me for consideration in such an anthology. I liked the story of yours which I have very much and would want to include your work in the book. Peter Abrahams has promised to send me some of his stories from London, and we both feel that a very interesting volume can be assembled. I hope to hear from you soon.

With all good wishes to you for continued good writing,
Sincerely yours,
Langston Hughes[77]

This letter from the great American poet and storyteller must have made a huge impact on the young South African writer.

It marks the start of Rive's writing career and reputation nationally and internationally. The letter is remarkably similar in formulation to one sent to Peter Clarke (who was using the pseudonym Peter Kumalo at the time for his short stories) as well as to several other African writers, such as Can Themba and Amos Tutuola. Clearly Hughes was not only spurring on African writers but was also driven by his vision for a pan-African anthology of writings. It was the start of an often very detailed and fascinating correspondence between Hughes and Rive that lasted thirteen years, until Hughes's death on 22 May 1967. Hughes wrote to Peter Clarke, 'Richard Rive ... writes wonderful letters'.[78] The correspondence is particularly intense until around mid-1955, after which there is an unexplained gap until it is resumed in 1960. Interestingly, there is a similar gap of about three or four years in the correspondence between Hughes and Mphahlele and between Hughes and Clarke. Timothy Young, curator of the Hughes collection, cannot account for this gap.

Rive, replying to Hughes, is clearly inspired to respond to the hugely encouraging words but does so in a rather polite and formal tone:

> I have received your very interesting and encouraging letter. I am afraid I do not conform to the pattern of starving-in-the-attic writer. I merely felt like it so I wrote. I have only three or four other short stories, but at the moment it is University vacation (I am at University of Cape Town) and mean to write, I assure you that within six weeks I will be able to send you at least half-a-dozen short stories following the theme of 'The Return'.[79]

'The Return' is the story of a nameless stranger whose 'sallow complexion betrayed that he was not European'. The stranger returns to a small town in the Karoo where he is greeted with crude and foul racist insults by white youngsters and older folk in the main street. He finds refuge in the coloured location, where he seems vaguely familiar to the people, but where he also finds intense mistrust of 'the kaffers'. Both white and coloured folk justify their bigotry in terms of Christian doctrine and when the stranger attempts to enter a whites-only church, he is bundled out by the church warden. The concluding paragraphs reveal that the stranger is in fact Christ returning, only to discover that in this racialised society 'there was no understanding in their hearts'.[80]

As in the stories Rive was to write a year or two later, 'The Return' highlights the hatred amongst people bred by racist attitudes, which were shockingly evident even in boys as young as eleven-years-old in the story. Especially in its use of dialogue and Afrikaans, the story depicts the crude racist labelling and entrenched master-servant attitudes that prevailed in both rural and urban South Africa. As in some of his other stories ('No Room at Solitaire' and 'Resurrection'), Rive uses the contradiction between the professed Christianity of the characters and their very unchristian prejudice in order to expose the hypocrisy inherent in racist behaviour. Rive reworks Christian mythology in order to expose the oppressive nature of racist attitudes, as Ngũgĩ wa Thiong'o would later do in his early novels. In this way, Rive reasserts as moral and just his egalitarianism vision.

The realism of parts of 'The Return', particularly the hard attitudes and an inhospitable setting, invokes similar descriptions of brutal encounters in Peter Abrahams's autobiography, *Tell Freedom*, especially when the young narrator, Lee, and his friend Andries encounter three white boys. The dialogue and narration that ensue in Abrahams's story, in which the black boys are called 'Hottentot', 'bloody kaffir' and 'ugly black baboon' before a violent fight breaks out between the two groups of boys, find an echo in Rive's story in the racist and violent encounter at the start between a white boy and a black boy. Abrahams's gritty detail and his depiction of the harsh realities of a divided society were, as Mphahlele has argued, models for Rive and other writers of the *Drum* school faced with similar social conditions.[81]

Another telling element in Rive's story, which can also be found in many of his other short stories, is the overt or muted identification of author with protagonist. The stranger is described in terms that have been used by Rive to describe himself elsewhere: 'The nose was sharp and aquiline and the hair burnt in [*sic*] rich brown through exposure. His eyes attracted most attention. Their light-brown, almost hazel colour contrasted oddly with his dark complexion.'[82] Character and author, the realms of fiction and of fact, interplay and repeatedly echo the trauma of the racialised outsider, the skin as singular marker of who we are and our place in the order of things.

'Times were giddy,' Rive remarked about 1955, a turning point in his own life as a writer.[83] Events seemed to have catapulted him into the world of South African and international writing and writers. In May 1955, at the age of twenty-five, Rive saw his short story 'Black and Brown Song' appear in *Drum*, becoming one of his first stories to be published.[84] 'Black and Brown Song' was billed by *Drum* as 'Richard Rive's grim prize-winning story of the brutish ignorance of Cape Town's slum hooligans, who fear the white man, despise and victimise the African – or "Kaffer"'. A story called 'Dagga Smoker's Dream', written under the pen name 'Richard Moore' – a practice the young Rive regarded as 'adventurous and way out' – won a short story competition run by *New Age* and was published in September 1955. Rive labels some of his very first stories and those of his contemporaries published in left-wing magazines and newspapers such as *Fighting Talk*, *Drum*, *Africa* and *New Age* as 'protest fiction'.[85] The elements of protest – the declamatory tone, the insistent politicisation of content, characters oppressed by social and political circumstance, the belief in human reason as antithetical to the dominant racist logic – were to recur in his fiction, marking even work of his last decade, such as the posthumous novel *Emergency Continued*, albeit in more muted tones than in the earlier writings. These traits were particularly prevalent in the early short stories.

'Black and Brown Song' and 'African Song' both use songs and their lyrics as counterpoints to the harsh realities of racial oppression experienced by the protagonists. In 'Black and Brown Song', Johnny-boy, Amaai and Braim, rough, ruthless and violent gangsters, hang around outside the movie house in District Six waiting to pick off unsuspecting victims when they confront a black man and, in attempting to rob him, Johnny-boy slits open his face with a knife. This story depicts the way racist stereotypes constructed by the social system have been internalised by the coloured gangsters who treat the 'Kaffer' as subhuman, and regard the 'White man' as a superior being. The refrain, in the form of lyrics/poetry that frame and interrupt the narrative, gives an authorial perspective deploring the divisions between 'Black' and 'Brown' songs and the consequent debasement of relationships in a highly racialised society.

Even more horrific than the racial abuse and the stabbing in the story, though, is the fact that 'the watching crowd was as passive as ever. No one thought of interfering while the three boys were beating up the African.'[86] The cruellest irony comes with the ending, when the black man who was beaten up is treated as the criminal by the police when they arrive, leaving the reader feeling indignant and helpless. 'Black and Brown Song' starkly portrays the vicious and inherently violent hierarchical pyramid of apartheid society; this kind of impassioned indictment of the apartheid system was particularly revelatory for readers outside of South Africa.

'Dagga Smoker's Dream' uses as its protagonist a down-and-out, working-class, coloured man from District Six, Karel. He has just violently beaten up his girlfriend Honey and he is clearly high on marijuana (dagga). He boards a train from Cape Town to the southern suburbs and begins to harass the other commuters in the third-class, 'non-white' compartment he is forced to occupy:

> *A crowded train going God knows where. But then he was going God knows where. And why should he sit even if there were seats? Standing against the door people could see him, and laugh with him, or maybe at him. Maybe see Honey's bleeding face through him. They were his friends at the back of the carriage, that was why they laughed at him. Laughed at Honey. He was popular at the back of the carriage, and everyone getting up and grinning.*[87]

Through a mix of third-person narration and Karel's internal speech and dialogue marked by a dialect that hints at Cape gangster slang, Rive is intent on depicting a desperate man who is trapped by circumstance and who has been turned violent, aggressive and anti-social. Yet, by the end of the story, we see Karel as pathetic and deluded because of the gap between his bravado and false sense of self and the failure he really is.

In both these stories, we are given a slice of raw Cape Town life of the time but Rive also insists in the fiction on distancing and contextualising the 'bubbling life'[88] for the reader to help make sense of the social conditions and their dire consequences. These stories caught readers' attention locally and abroad because of the colour and realism in describing setting, confrontation and character and, above all, for the plea implicit in such stories at the time: *look, dear reader, see what we have become under these harrowing conditions.*

Jayarani Raju and Catherine Dubbeld list first publication dates of Rive's other short stories from the mid to late fifties – 'My Sister Was a Playwhite' (1955), 'Rich Black Hair' (1955), 'The Bench' (1956), 'Willie Boy' (1956), 'African Song' (1956), 'Moon over District Six' (1956) and 'Rain' (1960) (oddly, they do not mention 'The Return'). The stories combine a sense of angry or sometimes more muted and pained protest at the unjust and dehumanising nature of racial oppression. In *Writing Black*, Rive identifies this range of tone in protest writing: 'Sometimes our protest is quiet and subdued but bubbling and frothing below. And sometimes it is turbulent and spouts out, and the ashes scatter widely and burn.'[89] The protest is often combined with a vision of a single, egalitarian, non-racial nation, best expressed in the epigraph poem to the story 'Black and Brown Song':

Where the rainbow ends,
There's going to be a place, brother,
Where the world can sing all sorts of songs,
And we're going to sing together, brother,
You and I,
Though you're white and I'm not.
It's going to be a sad song, brother,
'Cause we don't know the tune,
And it's a difficult tune to learn,
But we can learn it, brother,
You and I,
There's no such tune as a black tune,
There's no such tune as a white tune,
There's only music, brother,
And it's the music we're going to sing,
Where the rainbow ends.[90]

Rive's poetic expression of a non-racial vision for South Africa goes far beyond the limited 'separate but together' vision implied in the concept of the Rainbow Nation popularised forty years later. These words became widely anthologised, in South Africa and the United States, as a poem called 'Where the Rainbow Ends'.[91]

The focus of Rive's early stories is clearly a condemnation of racial oppression and he speaks, as Chapman puts it, 'eloquently

for racial justice.'[92] The short story was the dominant form chosen
by the *Drum* generation because, according to Mphahlele, 'the
situation was not conducive to the novel. In the short story one
could get the message across in a few broad strokes. We also
used the short sentence from Afro-American prose. La Guma
produced longer short stories but longer prose pieces were
often written outside the country.'[93] Rive, in his critical essays
on South African literature, would often echo these reasons for
the dominance of the short story genre during the 1950s. These
man-in-the-street stories in *Drum* were, according to literary
scholar Ursula Barnett, illustrative of what many other short
story writers – Peter Clarke and Can Themba for example –
were publishing in the magazine during the mid-1950s:

> *In* Drum *the black man could give expression to what one of
> its contributors, Peter Clarke, called a very virile, passionate,
> conscious entanglement with living our lives. Can Themba's
> reply to people who queried the cheeky abuse of English in*
> Drum *was: 'Confound the cultural ideas of these men! All we
> seek is the fullest expression of the bubbling life around us and
> the restless spirit within us.'*[94]

These early stories by Rive, like all of his fiction, even at its
most overtly autobiographical, focus on those stigmatised and
marginalised individuals who are caught in the tensions that
define the hostile spaces they inhabit.

The publications in *Drum* gave Rive wider exposure than
he had ever had before and drew him into the national writing
scene. Es'kia Mphahlele became fiction editor of *Drum* in
January 1955 during the last months of Anthony Sampson's
editorship of the magazine.[95] This marked the birth of what
Rive calls the 'Protest Movement' in South African literature,
which, according to him, was 'faintly reminiscent of the Harlem
Renaissance'. In 1955, Rive took the long train trip from the
Cape to Johannesburg to visit Desai, who was then manager of

a cinema in Martindale in Johannesburg, and to make contact with the writers at *Drum*. At the time of his visit to the office of *Drum* in the city, he met Bloke Modisane, Casey Motsitsi, Todd Matshikiza and Lewis Nkosi – all well-known South African writers who wrote for *Drum*. But it was clearly Mphahlele whom he seemed to admire above all the others, describing him as 'the Grand Old Man' of South African letters.[96]

While in Johannesburg, Mphahlele and his wife Rebecca took Rive to a party at Nadine Gordimer's house in Parktown, enabling him proudly to proclaim in *Writing Black*, 'I had dined with Nadine Gordimer'. At times like these in his memoir, one can almost *hear* him make this claim in his inimitable, puffed-up, cocksure, Oxbridge voice, though not without the edge of self-parody that was sometimes present. Gordimer was, at the time, helping to support and encourage the new generation of black writers. Rive admired Gordimer's work and courage and was, for example, full of praise for the solitary stand Gordimer took during the dark period of the mid-1960s when, in 'How Not to Know the African', she spoke out against the Suppression of Communism Act of 1966, under which writers critical of the regime were named and banned. Despite his admiration for Gordimer, Rive was openly more ambivalent towards her than Mphahlele was. He always disliked what he saw as the paternalism of many English-speaking white South Africans and yet, at other times, he resisted such sweeping categorisation and would echo Mphahlele's way of thinking about Gordimer – 'Nadine is not White nor Black. She is just a good South African.'[97] They admired each other's work, but it is clear that at the time, even in avant-garde circles where there were conscious, deliberate transgressions of legislated lines of social separation and strong assertions of the common interests of forward-looking writers, the divisions between white and non-white lives ran deep.

Barney Desai introduced Rive to two of the judges of the *Drum* competition, writers Jack Cope and Uys Krige. Rive struck up what were to be important and lasting friendships with these two men. The friendships gave Rive access to the world of writers, particularly Afrikaans writers, as well as helping him to establish international connections. Krige's intervention resulted in German translations of four of Rive's stories for publication in Peter Sulzer's *Christ Erscheint am Congo*.[98] In fact, the dedication in Rive's *Selected Writings* is to 'Jack Cope – who taught me how to write'. In *Writing Black* Rive makes it clear, in a remarkably objective and accurate summation of his work in the mid-fifties, that Cope was the most important writing teacher at the start of his career:

> *Jack was tall, good-looking, gentle and understanding ... I was receiving recognition out of all proportion to the quality and quantity of my work. There was far too much international recognition and praise based on a handful of unpolished short stories and Cope ... painstakingly made me account for every word I wrote.*[99]

A close friendship developed between the two men and Cope attended all of Rive's graduation ceremonies – at the University of Cape Town, at Columbia where he gained his master's and at his doctoral graduation at Oxford.[100] Cope's role in nurturing black writing talent stemmed from a deeply held conviction that he could assist 'these young men and beginners ... to master the full range of techniques. They are moving away from the folk-tale and religious influences and looking at life with clear, merciless eyes.' Cope made this claim in a letter to Hughes in 1954. The letter was a response to a prior letter from Hughes, it seems, outlining the latter's attempt to compile the anthology of African writing. Interestingly, Hughes, a polite and prolific letter writer with secretarial aid, does not continue the correspondence (at least there is no archival evidence to that effect), perhaps dismissing Cope as white and irrelevant to his project, which focused on black writing. Anticipating Hughes's interest in black African writers, Cope describes himself in this letter of 27 October, saying 'the best I can claim is the old African compliment: Your skin is white but your heart is black'.

Through his association with Afrikaans writer Krige, Rive met Krige's fellow Afrikaans writer intellectuals Jan Rabie and Marjorie Wallace at a gathering of writers at the couple's home in Green Point, Cape Town. Included in this circle of writers and friends was Breyten Breytenbach, a fellow student at the University of Cape Town. In his biography of Krige, JC Kannemeyer describes the home of Jan Rabie and Marjorie Wallace in the late 1950s as a refuge and a meeting place for artists at a time when apartheid was increasingly constraining social and cultural life:

> *Jan-hulle se huis was gou 'n bymekaarkomplek vir kunstenaars, skrywers, politieke dissidente en boheme, soos Jobst Grapow, Kenny Parker, Richard Rive en die jong Breyten Breytenbach [Jan and Marjorie's home quickly became a rendezvous for artists, writers, political dissidents and bohemians, like Jobst Grapow, Kenny Parker, Richard Rive and the young Breyten Breytenbach].*[101]

Rabie in turn visited Rive at his Grassy Park home. On one such visit in 1957, Rabie brought with him Ingrid Jonker, whom Rive found 'a beautiful, withdrawn young woman with wide, haunted eyes and a penetrating stare. [I] was fascinated by Ingrid.'[102] The two became very close friends. Rive recalled that 'sometimes I would drive her around central Cape Town and Sea Point on a motor scooter and we would pretend to be brother and sister because Marjorie said we looked alike'. In fact, they seemed so close that Mphahlele thought they were lovers.[103]

During this period, while Rive spent a lot of time on his writing and with fellow writers, he continued to earn a living as a teacher at South Peninsula High School, where he proved to be, to many of his more talented pupils, a source of inspiration to read widely and make something of their lives. As a teacher, Rive made a lasting impression on many and became a loyal comrade and friend; to others, he was pompous, arrogant and affected. Carol Abrahamse, who was a student in his class for four years (from 1959 to her matriculation in 1962), remembers him as the most inspiring and thought-provoking teacher she ever encountered. What I found interesting about the comments of Abrahamse, who has lived in Canada for over forty years (emigrating just a few years after leaving school), is that she sees Rive as being *the* formative influence during her time at South Peninsula but she is not uncritical:

> He was a very enthusiastic and dedicated teacher and was very hurt when his family shunned him in the street when they saw him coming because as you know he had a very dark skin. As far as the English class was concerned, the way we read and discussed in depth Shakespeare and other plays – this gave me a lifelong love for the theatre. He could be pretty cruel; he used to hit me on my hands for my handwriting and the pen I used, so being a rebellious teen I used a thicker and thicker nib every time and my hand writing got worse … I was not one of his groupies who would sit at his feet and adoringly listen to everything he said. I have never liked this in most of the gurus I have encountered. As a result of seeing his ego so inflated – it gave me a lifelong dislike of joining any group led by a strong male ego.
>
> The good stuff was the political awareness and all the political discussions we had in class instead of English. It gave me a lifelong interest in world politics, political systems and local politics. I remember one very important moment when he asked the class to vote on whether we thought people should have a certain amount of education in South Africa to be able to vote, or if everyone eighteen and over should vote. I voted for everyone to have a vote. Our class had the top five

*students who were brilliant and I was in the next five close
to the top ... All the top students voted that only the more
educated people should be eligible to vote. We discussed it and
he argued that everyone should vote regardless of education.
I was proud of myself for choosing everyone. That moment I
realised a lot about myself. I took care of a woman from Cortes
Island [Vancouver] a few months ago who had both her knees
replaced and had to have it done in Vancouver. She paid me the
biggest compliment, because next to her I am pretty wealthy
and she told me I was one of the few wealthy people who doesn't
think I am better than anyone else. I think that discussion with
Richard Rive and our class helped me with that.*[104]

A good friend of Rive's, Ariefi Manuel, was also a student in his
class of matriculants in 1957. Manuel remembers Rive taking
students to the University of Cape Town's Little Theatre in the
city, one of the few theatres that had not been segregated, and
they were also taken to the open-air theatre at Maynardville,
where annual performances of Shakespeare plays were staged
in late summer. He introduced his students to classical music
and Manuel remembers Rive loving Beethoven but disliking
Tchaikovsky. He used to have a portable record player to
play the LPs to the class. Rive loved to quote from Chaucer's
Canterbury Tales and Dylan Thomas's *A Child's Christmas
in Wales*.[105] Manuel's memories bring to mind these very
qualities in Andrew in *Emergency*, which Rive was to begin to
write three to four years after Manuel had him as a teacher. It
is strikingly clear, however, that in his classroom Rive opened
up worlds to young minds which the ruling National Party's
Christian national educational and segregated social order was
determined to confine and indoctrinate.

In his leisure time, when he took respite from teaching and
sport, Rive would often visit the homes of friends to chat, smoke
and have a drink. On a visit to the home of Dennis Bullough and

his partner John Dronsfield, where he went with Albert Adams sometime in the early 1950s, he met Gilbert Reines, who would later share his Selous Court flat in Claremont for a year.

It was about 1958, Reines recalls, that Rive approached him to share a flat as he needed to move out of his lodgings in Grassy Park but could not afford to rent a place on his own. Reines agreed, as his girlfriend (Ursula Strydom) lived nearby, and the two men then moved into Selous Court in Rosmead Avenue, Claremont, a double-storey block of four flats. Living in close quarters with Rive means that Reines remembers quite vividly some of Rive's personal habits and peccadilloes, such as his constant loud sniffing, picking his nose and scratching his groin as he sat with legs spread apart. He tells of Rive's preoccupation with being raided by the security police at the time, a fear that might have been real, but from Reines's account during our interview, it is made to seem more like paranoia on Rive's part:

> *There was this whole thing about the police going around doing dawn raids and looking at people's books, looking for subversive material, and I know Richard used to come in and ... I [would] find him sometimes burying things in my room under the bed, and I'd say, 'What are you doing?' [laughing] And that was just Richard, and I said, 'Stop being a drama queen' ... I said, 'They're not coming'. 'Oh no, they're coming at any time and they've been peering through the curtains' [laughing]. 'They might come any time,' he said, 'and raid the flats' and at the end of the day, I said, 'Richard, they are not coming today, Richard'. I think how quite disappointed he was.*[106]

Reines also remembers that Richard 'had no respect for boundaries because he [had] a kind of communal attitude – "what is yours is mine"'. He continues: 'I used to come home and he and his friends [were] invading *my* bedroom, sitting on *my* bed, you know, sitting around smoking, you know, and the last thing you want to do is come in at night into a warm bedroom which you had nothing to do with warming!'

He also paints a picture of a fairly untidy and scatterbrained flatmate, who in the morning rush would let the porridge boil over and cake on the stove and, on more than one occasion, locked himself out of the flat with the keys inside:

One evening he came and said, 'You know what happened to me today? I was getting dressed in such a hurry, this morning, semi-darkness … and I got to school and they were all standing on the stage for assembly. The kids were standing in the front, and they were putting their hands together to say prayers … and so one kid's eyes were wide open looking at my feet and I looked down – I had one brown shoe and one black shoe.' And of course it whipped around the school like mad: 'onpaar skoene, onpaar skoene!' [odd shoes, odd shoes] … and you know, that was Richard.

Like many others who knew Rive at this time, Reines remembers him rushing around on his silver-blue Vespa scooter. Often friends would ride with him and Reines recalls the story, often repeated by Rive, about the incident where the very quiet-natured Peter Clarke was riding pillion with Rive to the small settlement of Tesselaarsdal more than one hundred kilometres away in the Overberg, sometime in mid-1959:

All I know is that they were talking and Richard was driving of course and talking away and Peter was very monosyllabic in his responses, he was a very hard person to talk to … And of course after some time Richard was getting no response to his questions and when he turned around Peter wasn't there! He'd fallen off the Vespa. So he turned round and drove back about ten or fifteen miles and there was Peter Clarke sitting there like … the thinker on one of those milestones, you know, sitting there!

Clarke had first gone to Tesselaarsdal in 1956 for extended stays to get out of the city and draw inspiration from the rustic community and landscape, and went there from early September to just before Christmas every year until 1960.[107] His entry in his diary for the trip when Rive took him on the scooter recalls a small part of their extended and daring trip:

> *We had gone through the Solitaire Valley to Hermanus. The road was terrible in places, at times as rough as a mountain track. Richard wanted to see Hawston & the road as far as Bot Rivier, along which he had once hiked … Afterwards we went via Onrustrivier to Bot Rivier, then to Caledon, then home via Dunghye Park.[108]*

Rive made it patently clear that, unlike Clarke, he was not keen on the pastoral.[107] Good friends such as Clarke and also James Matthews understood him and knew his views, so were not put off by his strident opinions. Others were, and Gilbert Reines tried to explain when he remarked in our interview that Rive was 'a very angry young man'. Reines claims that Rive never spoke about his family except for one of his sisters and that 'there was something that was driving him to make a name for himself as a writer'. Little did Reines or even Rive himself know that within the next five years or so, Rive would be catapulted into the international arena, in no small part due to the friendship he had already established with Langston Hughes.

Arnold Rampersad, in his definitive two-part biography of Hughes, confirms that the idea of the publication mentioned by Hughes in his letter to Rive was in fact born from his exposure to the works submitted to him as a judge in the *Drum* short story competition.[110] Rampersad elaborates on this project, aimed at showcasing African voices in the United States, saying that it failed to find favour with American publishers for a number of years:

> *Just as he had done with Mexican writers some twenty years before, he began to assemble an anthology of short stories by Africans (probably the first such venture in the history of*

American publishing), and he was undeterred when Simon &
Schuster rejected the first six stories he submitted as a sample.
Carefully he wrote to virtually every young writer whose name
had come to him, including Amos Tutuola, Efua Sutherland,
John Mbiti, Gabriel Okara, Davidson Nicol, Cyprian Ekwensi,
Peter Clarke, Richard Rive, and Ezekiel Mphahlele ... Few
American publishers were then interested in foreign literature,
and almost none in that of Africa.

Hughes's persistence, assisted by an increasing awareness of
and interest in the tide of nationalism sweeping through Africa
towards the end of the decade, triumphed in the end. In 1960,
An African Treasury: Articles, Essays, Stories, Poems by Black
Africans was published by Crown Publishers. In a letter to Peter
Abrahams, Hughes makes an interesting observation about
the collection of African prose pieces: 'The South Africans
will be best represented – along with the Nigerians. And their
differences are interesting: the Nigerians have a lot of humor
in their writing, and the South Africans a lot of sadness and
poetry.'[111]

The anthology received good reviews in the United States
and was published in 1961 by Victor Gollancz in London.
Mphahlele, already in exile for two years, was excited about
the publication and exclaimed in a letter to Hughes: 'You have
done an excellent job of this anthology of African writing:
congratulations! It simply bristles with life & newness, unlike
Peggy Rutherford's ... *Darkness and Light* ... which is cluttered
with statuesque pieces' (Rutherford's anthology was published
in the United States under the title *African Voices* and appeared
simultaneously with Hughes's collection).[112] In South Africa,
Hughes's book was quickly banned and anyone in possession of
it could be fined or jailed.

Stephen Gray recalls one of the young-writer anecdotes
Rive liked to repeat. Like many of the anecdotes for which Rive

became notorious (be these true or apocryphal), it casts him in the light of articulate, well-versed and witty storyteller, making light of what touched him to the quick all his life – the colour question. Gray makes a crucial point about the question of authenticity, memory and self-fashioning. He says that, in the end, it does not matter whether or not such anecdotes are true because the *thought* that the story evokes 'freshens one's sense that literary history is a sequence of such mythical moments'.[113] The incident was about Rive's meeting with Sarah Gertrude Millin, author of *God's Stepchildren*, in which she relegates the 'coloured' to the inferior status of the stepchild. Gray recalls what was told to him by Rive:

> *So up stepped Richard Rive in his brilliant twenties, with a sheaf of short stories about 'his people' … When the colour-bar dowager encountered this upstart, she was evidently struck with genealogical confusion. All she could blurt was: 'What are you – Indian?' To which Richard suavely replied: 'No, ma'am, I am your stepchild.'*[114]

But it would be a while yet before Rive developed the self-confidence that would allow this kind of witty, parodic play with the question of colour, which had, since his earliest memories it seems, dominated his life, causing pain, anger and acute dislocation of body and spirit. The question of colour would, in fact, never go away.

Part 11: *1960 – 1970*

Chapter 3

'1961 and 1962 were prolific years for me,' recalls Rive in his memoir.[1] The 1960 Sharpeville and Langa uprisings had shaken the apartheid regime and once again exposed the brutal nature of the South African state to its people and to the world. The events gave Rive the setting for his first novel, *Emergency*, which he wrote in 1961 and 1962, and which was published by Faber and Faber in 1964. It was the first novel to be set against the backdrop of the Sharpeville crisis,[2] and the first to be banned in South Africa. Rive overtly states that the life of the main character, Andrew Dreyer, 'in some ways ran parallel to mine'.[3] This autobiographically inflected protagonist finds himself in Cape Town in the maelstrom of the uprisings against the pass laws, organised by the Pan-Africanist Congress (PAC), from 28 to 30 March 1960. While these events provided creative impetus for Rive's first novel, they were also the start of a state of emergency in South Africa that lasted until the early 1970s and were a severe setback, not only for organised political resistance, but also for writers and artists in the country, who feared reprisals for freely expressing themselves. The fifteen-year period from the mid-1960s to about 1980 also marked the leanest period in Rive's creative writing life.

In *Emergency*, Andrew Dreyer grows up in District Six and becomes a high school teacher. Dreyer's main dilemma in the novel – choosing greater political involvement in the struggle or escaping to safety – was in fact Rive's own dilemma at certain points in his life when the option of living abroad was open to him. In the novel, Dreyer decides to stay. His increasingly middle-class material circumstances, compared to those of his old friends who remained in the slums of his youth, and his ambivalent relationship to the struggle of working people can also be read to exemplify the uncertain relationship that Rive and many other members of the urban intelligentsia had towards mass struggle.

Rive was elated at the publication of his first novel and there were many accolades from friends and fellow writers. Overall, newspaper reviews in London and Ireland lauded the work as a successful novel of political protest.[4] The banning of the novel in South Africa soon after publication meant that there were few published reviews in the country. The fact that more was being written about the novel outside South Africa was clearly symptomatic of the repressive nature of the times.

Among those who were most encouraging about the novel was Es'kia Mphahlele, as always the gentle and broad-minded doyen of younger South African black writers. It was Mphahlele to whom Rive had turned for an opinion on the draft manuscript of the novel in 1963, before it was accepted by Faber and Faber later that year, an indication of how deeply he valued Mphahlele's views. In his introduction to the 1970 Collier edition of the novel, Mphahlele gives his very generous and context-sensitive assessment of Rive's achievement:

The novelist in the South African setting has to handle material that has become by now a huge cliché: violence, its aftermath, and the responses it elicits. In this, he travels a path that has many pitfalls. He can depict a situation so immense and characters so tiny that we fail to extract a meaning out of the work; he can create symbols and 'poetic' characters so that reality eludes us; he can be melodramatic; he can be too documentary. Richard Rive has avoided these pitfalls …

> *His prose maintains its tension and its pressurised drive*
> *throughout. And the reader is pleasantly struck by the novelist's*
> *economy of diction and structure.*[5]

Certain other scholarly reviews that were much more critical
also started emerging. Rive must have been deflated by the
critical reception of his novel in some quarters. The most hostile
was a review in 1965 by Lewis Nkosi, who slated the novel in
extremely harsh terms:

> *To read a novel like Richard Rive's* Emergency *is to gain a glimpse*
> *into a literary situation which seems to me quite desperate. It*
> *may even be wondered whether it might not be more prudent*
> *to 'renounce literature temporarily,' as some have advised, and*
> *solve the political problem first rather than grind out hackneyed*
> *third-rate novels of which* Emergency *is a leading contender.*[6]

Two years earlier, in 1963, Nkosi had been most critical of Rive's
African Songs in a review published in the Johannesburg-based
magazine *The Classic*. The terms of Nkosi's harsh criticism of
stories such as 'Moon over District Six', 'Resurrection', 'The
Return' and 'No Room at Solitaire' reveal features that he regarded
as 'irritating beyond endurance' and 'slipshod calamities of style'
in Rive's prose – his penchant for archaic diction and literary
cliché, his obvious reliance on pathetic fallacy and his creation
of caricature (especially for black and white figures) rather than
well-rounded characters.[7] While Nkosi's criticism reveals his
own bias towards nineteenth-century European realist prose
and the grand posing of a South African in exile freed from the
immediate context of home, he does put his finger on certain
formal weaknesses evident in the stories he dislikes. In response
to what must have been the most damning criticism of his
literary work ever, Rive wrote an equally vitriolic retort in the
next issue of *The Classic*:

> *There are two types of criticism the non-white writer in South*
> *Africa must guard against. Firstly, the over-sympathetic pa-*

tronising type which is merely a manifestation of inverted racialism; secondly, the destructively nihilistic, done for motives personal or otherwise, of which Mr Nkosi's review is symptomatic ... By all means, let us have criticism, it is necessary for the writer, strong, healthy criticism, but spare us the smart-alec [sic] vituperations of the Nkosis which are primarily intended as a display of pyrotechnics.[8]

Rive could clearly give as good as he got, demonstrating in this response his own mastery of combative rhetoric. While Rive does not convincingly deal with Nkosi's at times trenchant but spiteful criticism, he manages to control the damage done by Nkosi's views on *African Songs* by contrasting the clearly lopsided review with one by Mphahlele, who offers a more measured, critical condonation of Rive's talent.

The second bout of criticism from Nkosi's pen, in the form of his review of *Emergency*, must have piqued Rive severely, and this continuing fracas no doubt led to the subsequent ongoing enmity between the two writers. Rive recalls his reaction to Nkosi's review, calling Nkosi his '*bête noire* ever since he had reviewed a book of mine not only scathingly but inaccurately that I had been forced to reply in order to point out gross errors of fact'.[9] Most obviously, an additional point to make in response to Nkosi would be that the cessation of creativity he was proposing was patently deterministic and exactly what repressive apartheid legislation was attempting to impose, and that to wait for a new and favourable political turn could have meant capitulation for writers and artists. Daryl Lee aptly criticises Nkosi's view of *Emergency*, identifying some of the assumptions that underpinned Nkosi's view of the work of protest writers at the time:

[Nkosi] relies upon a droll and cruel humour to denigrate black fiction by South Africans in the sixties, en masse, as politically trite and monotonous. Nkosi bases much of his

negative argument on the perceived failure of protest fiction to conform to conventional left-Leavisite criteria of universal moral relevance and modernist 'freshness'.[10]

By the time Rive wrote his memoir, some good faith had been restored in the relationship between the two writers, Nkosi having been one of three judges who voted Rive's *Make Like Slaves* the top play in a BBC competition in 1971. Rive still, however, gets a dig in when he describes his first meeting with Nkosi at the offices of *Drum*, using a backhanded and euphemistic compliment: 'Sylvester introduced me to ... a bright young reporter, Lewis Nkosi, who I felt later developed into an over-enthusiastic critic.'[11]

While Rive could easily dismiss in terse and disparaging terms criticisms of *Emergency* coming from what he called a 'pseudo-politician', he seemed to listen more carefully to certain academic reservations about his work.[12] One of the most considered assessments of the novel was made by Bernth Lindfors in 'Form and Technique in the Novels of Richard Rive and Alex la Guma', published in the American *Journal of the New African Literature and the Arts* in 1966. Lindfors's assessment, unlike that of Nkosi, takes into account the social context of production that so radically affected writers such as Rive and La Guma, who remained in South Africa despite the fascist conditions:

The writers remaining in South Africa have had three alter-natives: to stop writing, to write innocuous short stories for South African publications, or to send their manuscripts abroad. The best writers have had great success in getting their work published outside South Africa. Short stories have been easiest to export, but in recent years ... three novels – one by Richard Rive (Emergency, London, 1964) *and two by Alex la Guma (A Walk in the Night, Ibadan, 1962; And a Threefold Cord, Berlin, 1964) have appeared. This too has been a literature of protest.*[13]

Lindfors goes on to account for the very evident tone of protest and lack of experience on the part of South African writers in this period with the more protracted and demanding form of the novel:

> *Such literature is difficult to write well. The author must be able to view his subject with sufficient detachment and emotional balance to write objectively. He must be able to control the passionate intensity of his own feelings and to coolly translate these feelings into a work of art which will move other people. If his tone is too shrill or his message too obtrusive, his writing will deteriorate into sheer propaganda. In South Africa it has been hard for non-white writers to achieve discipline, detachment and emotional balance in their writing. It has been hard for them to avoid writing propaganda.*[14]

With these comments as preface, Lindfors goes on to highlight the strengths and more evident weaknesses he finds in *Emergency,* the work of a 'promising' novelist.[15] He finds that 'Rive very adroitly manipulates prose rhythms and leit motifs [*sic*] to achieve a stream of consciousness effect' and also that many scenes 'display Rive's sensitive control of space' by controlling and varying sentence length.[16] These strengths Lindfors sees as the hallmarks of the good short story, but he adds that Rive is not able to make these techniques 'serve a larger purpose' as is demanded in a novel. In short, he summarises his critique of the novel by resorting – quite playfully, considering Rive's own pride at his youthful athletic prowess as a hurdler – to a running metaphor: he accuses Rive of 'shortwindedness', of being 'a good performer in short dashes but he can't run long distances very well'. The other weakness he identifies is the use of flashbacks to give detailed biographical sketches of Andrew's past. It 'is unnecessary for it does not help us to understand Dreyer's thoughts, impulses or actions on the three critical days in his life'. 'Dreyer,' Lindfors continues, 'remains a sketch, a figure without depth or dimension who would be more at home as the hero of a short story.'

Lindfors's contextualised criticism was echoed in the 1980s by Ursula Barnett, who perhaps sums up what many other critical commentators of the decade 'Piniel Shava', for example, think of the novel:

> *All the ingredients for a deep study of the options of a man under pressure in crisis have been assembled in* Emergency, *but Rive's novel is disappointing in that he fails to dramatise these ideas credibly. The events and characters remain flat on paper. The reader never really becomes involved in Andrew's dilemma.*[17]

Barnett also makes a valid criticism of the character of Dreyer when she notices that 'Andrew seems to have little regard for those close to him', pointing to the way *he* decides what is best for his girlfriend Ruth at the end of the novel, as well as his not being empathetic to the plight of other characters, such as his brother-in-law and his landlady.[18] Like Lindfors, Barnett finds that La Guma's characters display more fullness, more humanity and more understanding towards others. The assessments of South African literature at this time by critics such as Lindfors and Barnett, outsiders who saw themselves as champions of the literary cause in the far South, seemed intent on balancing formal and contextual considerations compared to the no-holds-barred criticism by Nkosi who, at that stage, seemed impatient and fed up with the fiction of writers in South Africa who seemed to rely too much on strident tone and obvious content and less on modernist reflectiveness and interiority.

It is Lee, though, who comes closest to recognising the political vision that underpins the novel and Rive's stated concern with 'the social and political emergence of the main character'.[19] While Lee agrees that the work has its weaknesses as a novel, he nevertheless identifies its political thrust:

The novel, Emergency, *is unsubtle in its representation of prominent political tendencies within the national liberation movement in the late fifties and early sixties in Cape Town. Abe Hanslo and Justin Bailey, two central characters who grow up with the main character, Andrew Dreyer, are used in the novel to dramatise the ideological tension and dialogue between the Non-European Unity Movement (NEUM) and the Congress movement, respectively.*[20]

Abe and Justin can be read to represent the tensions between the different ideological and pragmatic approaches of the NEUM and the PAC movement, at the time of the 1960 Sharpeville crisis. In addition, these two characters represent polar opposites in the mind of Rive himself as he was testing the strengths and limitations of his NEUM-based ideas of struggle and non-racialism at a time of an acute social crisis. I suspect that Rive was compelled by the crisis to rethink the very foundation of his political being – that is, his belief in non-racialism and the need to conduct day-to-day struggles on the basis of principles as articulated by Abe in the novel. The scene where Abe and Justin pit their views against each other about whether or not to intervene in the mass struggle unleashed by the PAC is perhaps the most sustained exchange between these two contesting positions:

[Abe] continued addressing Justin.

'The people must at the very start be made to recognize the indivisibility of oppression. They must look upon themselves not as African, Coloureds, Indians or whites, but as a people seeking to abolish national oppression. Racialism cannot be fought with racialism, or with localised stunts.'

'Hear! Hear!' said Braam contemptuously.

'That's all very well,' Justin replied impatiently, 'but where does it get us? Where do we go from there? Do we sit on our backsides discussing the finer points of political theories?'[21]

It is significant that the views expressed by Abe use left-wing political catchphrases that marked the NEUM's hesitancy about getting involved in mass struggle. Justin's viewpoint is, however, far less coherent and persuasive, relying on sentiment and activist notions, but shows a commitment to the struggling people that is lacking in Abe's intellectual position. One reason Rive wrote the novel, I speculate, was to think through these contending ideas and connected practices. While Andrew continually questions Abe's thinking by playing it off against the outlook of Justin (which must have held allure for Rive, who wanted to *do* something), he concedes, by the end of the novel, the validity of Abe's views but demonstrates a completely independent line of action by refusing to go into exile with Abe:

'You know, Abe, all my life I've been running away. I ran away from District Six. I ran away the night my mother died. I ran away from Miriam's place. I've been running away from the Special Branch. Now I am hiding in Lotus River, like any common criminal. Maybe I've been running away from myself. But that's all over now. I am determined to stay. And I don't know why you had to deliver a sermon on non-racialism to me. I agree and always have with most of the things you say. But I still retain my right not to give up the fight against every form of racialism and therefore I shall remain here, not run away to Basutoland or Europe. I shall fight with all the others whenever and wherever I can identify myself with them. If there is another march in Cape Town I shall be in it. I want to live my own life.'[22]

Andrew remains in Cape Town, finally returning with his white lover, Ruth, to her flat. Perhaps Rive, like Andrew, was asserting that the best contribution he could make was to remain and not run. By doing so, he chose to engage and challenge racial oppression head-on and he would do this not according to the dictates of any organisation or ideology, but as his own conscience and will dictated. Rive's text confirms for himself and others that he would remain in South Africa and that he would be committed to the struggle against apartheid – as a teacher, a writer and a sportsman, but never as a member of a political party.

Two other aspects of *Emergency* are noteworthy. In the novel classical music represents the creative world that provides a refuge for Andrew and is an antidote to the ugliness and pain in his life. Andrew continually listens to recordings of Smetana, Beethoven, Rachmaninov, Mendelssohn and other well-known composers. These iconic names of European culture occur together with numerous instances where Andrew lists book titles by and quotations from the greats of the Western canon, such as Chaucer, Shakespeare, Spenser, Tolstoy, Hardy, Hobbes and Locke. These claims, in Andrew's eyes – and clearly in Rive's, too – intimate a familiarity with Western culture that demonstrates Andrew's/Rive's cosmopolitanism. This alignment with the West is in direct contrast to the barbarism of the white *Herrenvolk* and their attempts to ghettoise, tribalise and isolate the non-whites spatially and culturally. These references, though, repeated on numerous occasions throughout the book, begin to rankle and frustrate the reader, making one think of Andrew at times as a pompous and pretentious Europhile and pedant – in short, a prig – a view some people had of Rive. This blinkered view ignores the commitment of both the fictional character and the author himself to the local and the African, to the struggles, the literature and future of country and continent.

Another interesting aspect of the novel is the relationship between Andrew and Ruth. Their transgressive 'inter-racial' love exposes the ludicrous anti-human philosophy of the apartheid state that forbade love between white and black people. The partnership also embodies Andrew's non-racialism. The odds were clearly stacked against the relationship between Andrew and Ruth. The Immorality Act criminalised sexual relations between white and non-white, and the hostility to such affairs displayed by Andrew's landlady, Mrs Carollissen, shows that she has adopted such racialised assumptions about human relations. By the end of the novel, even though Andrew chooses not to run off with Abe into exile but instead to return with Ruth to her flat, we know their relationship has no hope of surviving under the circumstances. The sequel to this novel, *Emergency Continued* (published in 1990), confirms that the relationship soon succumbs to the pressures of its context, and Andrew and Ruth never see each other again. Andrew is a frustratingly egocentric character who seems to dictate the terms of the relationship and relate to Ruth in rather unfeeling ways. Ruth, in turn, remains a one-dimensional woman defined by her selfless love for Andrew. The relationship between Justin and his wife Florence is also dysfunctional because of his total commitment to the struggle, which leaves her feeling abandoned and betrayed. Andrew's sister, Miriam, is extremely unhappy in her marriage to Kenneth, who in his drunken state beats her and brings home prostitutes to their bedroom. Mrs Carollissen dominates her very passive husband; and Andrew's principal and his wife, with whom he briefly takes refuge, are a conventional, religious and wooden couple. Andrew's mother raises her children without a father. As with almost all heterosexual and conventional familial relationships in Rive's fiction, the ones in *Emergency* are tenuous, fraught, lifeless, violent or doomed to failure.

Even when they are together, the love, even physical love, between Andrew and Ruth seems awkward and forced, with Rive using far too obvious cinematic-type metonymy, cuts and music to symbolise their passion and repetitively describing them as engaging 'hungrily' with each other in the one love scene between them:

> *The Concerto moved into its beautiful second movement. He could hear her breath coming in short, quick pants.*
>
>   *'Ruth?'*

'Yes, Andy?'
They kissed hungrily.
'Please, Ruth.'
'I know.'
Passion overcame him, as he felt her hanging on to him.
Hungrily he sought her. Days with Miriam and little boys with
hymn-books. And Rachmaninov. Vltava? No, Rachmaninov.
Rhapsody on a theme. A nocturne movement. A long coda.
Beautiful. Hysterically beautiful.[23]

Interestingly, the only successfully captured scene depicting
sensuousness and sex in any of Rive's fiction is the one in this
novel between Braam and a prostitute he has brought home to
his flat. Both are drunk. Rive conveys the desperation of their
lust with a remarkably convincing build-up and frank and
disturbing realism uncluttered by obvious technical artifice:

They drank for a long time. She was becoming more drunk and
Braam found the longing raging inside him. There were two
open sores on her leg, but that didn't matter.
'Too much light?'
'Yes, too much light.'
He switched off and then blew out the lantern. He lay back
on the sleeping-bag, pulling her next to him. She felt warm and
sweaty.
'You want me?'
'Yes,' he said hoarsely, feeling for her clothes. The room
became uncomfortably hot and he perspired profusely. After-
wards, when he lay back exhausted and dissipated, a feeling of
revulsion came over him. Now that it was all over he wanted
to get rid of her but she was snoring gently next to him. Braam
turned away from her in disgust.[24]

The relationship with Mrs Carollissen's young son, Eldred,
who is also a student in Andrew's class, carries very muted,
homoerotic encoding in the way the narrator describes the

boy and the way he relates to Andrew's 'physical presence' in the novel. Their initial meeting is described as follows: 'There was a boy in one of his Junior Certificate classes he had always noticed. Good-looking with greenish-grey eyes. Intelligent as well.' Through Eldred, Andrew later comes to board with the Carollissen family and then he further describes Eldred as 'a healthy, bronzed, solidly built Matriculation student at Steenberg High – in Andrew's class in fact … At sixteen he worshipped his teacher, and Andrew in turn found him the only approachable member of the Carollissen household.'[25]

When the police raid Andrew's room at the Carollissens' house, Eldred, to his mother's horror, loyally and courageously defends his teacher, refusing to tell the policemen where Andrew is. Andrew is forced to leave because of pressure from Mrs Carollissen, who is being pressured by the police. On leaving, he describes Eldred again: 'He had never really been aware of the extent of the youngster's attachment to him. True, Eldred had always been around … Now that Andrew was leaving it was different. He would miss the boy's inane questions, over-enthusiasm, his physical presence.'[26]

The manner in which Rive encodes a homoerotic meaning to the phrase 'physical presence' becomes more overt in a later story, 'The Visits' (1977), where an older teacher is much taken with the 'physical presence' of a young student.

In an interview in 1980 with Chris van Wyk in the magazine *Wietie 2*, Rive reflected in a frank and self-critical fashion about *Emergency*, with the benefit of hindsight:

> *I'm not very happy speaking about 'Emergency' because I think it's dated and I'm hoping to have more stuff that will be far more relevant. Look, I think it was very relevant for its time and it might very well be relevant now, but there are other things to write about now. But I think a careful reading of 'Emergency' (and some critics have been able to spot this) is*

that it is basically a series of short stories with a particular
character in common. And the reason for that is that I am
essentially a short story writer, not a novelist.[27]

Why Rive succumbs to Lindfors's formalist criticism of his
first novel, more than fifteen years after its publication, is puz-
zling. While too self-conscious a work overall, *Emergency* does
read like a novel and not a series of short stories. With the
publication of his next novel, the hugely successful *'Buckingham*
Palace', District Six, just six years later, Rive was to prove himself
wrong: his legacy would become that of both short story writer
and novelist.

During this artistically productive yet politically and emotionally testing period of the early 1960s, Ariefi and Hazel
Manuel, a young couple who needed a place to stay, were
generously given refuge at Rive's flat, 2 Selous Court, Rosmead
Avenue, Claremont, where he had recently moved. Ariefi had
been a student of Rive's at South Peninsula High School during
the late 1950s and they later became friends. As a teacher, Rive
had made a lasting impression on the young Ariefi, who tells
of how Rive brought his portable record player to class to play
them classical music LPs, and how he took them to the open-air
theatre at Maynardville and to the Little Theatre in the city. The
Manuels remember Rive listening to a lot of music, particularly
classical works, and that he had done so while writing part of
Emergency. At the time he wrote mainly in the mornings or at
night, with a grey Parker Pen with a silver cap and fine nib, using
his distinctive diminutive cursive script in 'foolscap manuscript books with red taped spines and stiff black covers'.[28] The
Manuels remark that they often sensed anger in Richard and
that he could at times be a lonely person. People reacted sharply
to him, they say, either loving him or hating him, but always
fearing his tongue: 'When he was a younger man, he did not
hesitate to tear someone apart, but when he liked you he was

gentle and endearing.' In one of his letters to Langston Hughes in 1954, Rive describes himself thus: 'I am also extremely emotional, love arguments especially on political themes, verge on cynicism and [am] violently anti-social in certain respects.'[29]

In recalling Rive, Wannenburgh captures in astutely observed detail another dimension of Rive's social life at the time – his cultivation of and cultivation by liberal white circles:

> As a consequence of winning a few local short story contests in the late fifties, Richard had been 'discovered' by a host of well-meaning people on the fringes of the arts, and invitations were plentiful. Although he suspected that, no matter how pure the motives of those who invited him seemed to themselves, he was being paraded as a drawing-room curiosity, he generally accepted and took me along for moral support. I would hold my breath when someone in the company entered a danger zone in conversation and finally uttered the trigger words 'coloured intellectual' or 'coloured writer', waiting for him to snort, 'What's that; can you eat it?' and leave them wondering what they had done wrong. And afterwards he would remark wryly that I, as a white, would have to wait longer to be 'discovered'.[30]

Rive continually crossed the white-coloured and also, but less frequently perhaps, the coloured-black 'race barrier', despite the indignity or embarrassment the former sometimes entailed. Unlike many of his 'coloured' friends, fellow writers, comrades or colleagues who did not cross these lines because they were such entrenched barriers (or because it was too dangerous, or illegal, or just too awkward and seemingly pointless), Rive persisted, meeting some of his dearest friends and fellow writers in the process, forming a writing camaraderie in the Cape, which Nadine Gordimer called 'a sort of colony along the coast'.[31] He always made the effort to look up or invite home writers from elsewhere in the country as well – colour was no consideration, of course. Why was the crossing to the black side far less frequent? Perhaps the contact was more difficult, as the control of entry to black townships, more geographically isolated from other areas especially in the Cape, was strictly policed and in fact illegal without a permit. Perhaps his drive to be a writer meant that for him to succeed, the most important contacts were obviously white. Perhaps Rive's middle-class and Western cosmopolitan aspirations made him look to those in South Africa who seemed to represent that particular world.

In 1963 Seven Seas (based in East Germany) published Rive's *African Songs*. The collection included several of the stories written in the late 1950s and early 1960s, such as 'The Bench', 'Moon over District Six', 'Rain', 'Willie Boy', 'African Song', 'No Room at Solitaire', 'Resurrection' and 'Strike'. Rive's account of how *African Songs* came to be published is testimony to his tenacity and dogged belief in himself as a writer of national and international import. He says of *African Songs*:

> *I then prepared five manuscript copies and sent these unsolicited by surface mail to five different overseas publishers. I did not even consider that any local publishers would display the slightest interest since the contents were politically outspoken. By airmail I sent advance warnings to the five publishers that the manuscripts were on their way. Four ... [sent letters to say they] regretted they were unable to risk publishing relatively unknown writers. The last publisher to reply was Seven Seas, based in East Berlin, which brought out works in English ... I then started a drawn-out correspondence with their editor, Gertrude Gelbin.*[32]

Rive recalls in his memoir how, soon after the publication of *African Songs*, he accepted an invitation from the East German Writers' Union to visit East Berlin and East Germany and in late 1963 met up with the American-born Gelbin. He also met her husband, German writer Stefan Heym. Literary scholar Peter McDonald says: 'Seven Seas (1958–1978), an English language paperback series published out of East Berlin, was a product of the cultural cold war.'[33] Gelbin and Heym were its founders, 'exiles from McCarthyite America – and, given the inexpensive price of the books, it was most probably heavily subsidized by the Ministry of Culture in the GDR. As its name indicated, it was internationalist in outlook and ambition.' Rive was impressed neither by what he witnessed in East Germany, nor by Gelbin and her circle, and was scathing about her and other American expatriates in East Berlin:

> *The parties to which I was invited were crowded with American expatriates, White and Black, trying hard to justify their defection. I felt it all so unnecessary. It was like trying to justify South African exile. Gertrude's attitude was typical … She tended to overenthuse about all things communist, whether the buildings in East Berlin, its works of art, or the waiter serving at our table. My natural reaction was to sink into an aggressive cynicism.*[34]

Rive, free to travel beyond the confines of apartheid South Africa by American CIA (Central Intelligence Agency) funding (more on this later) and at the same time published for the first time in book form by the communist-inspired Seven Seas, was caught up in the Cold War battle for the hearts and minds of intellectuals and writers. The West clearly wins in Rive's mind. His experiences in East Germany and his encounters with Gelbin in East Berlin confirmed his fear that communism was 'a deliberate emasculation of individuality and an over-emphasis on conformity.'[35]

Also published in 1963 was *Quartet: New Voices from South Africa: Alex La Guma, James Matthews, Richard Rive, Alf Wannenburgh*, edited by Rive. This collection of sixteen short stories was dedicated to Mphahlele: 'For Zeke Mphahlele, in admiration and regard for his work for literature on the African continent in general, and … our country, South Africa, in particular.' The foreword was by Alan Paton and it was published by Crown in New York, a result of Rive's contact with Langston Hughes. Crown had published Hughes's *African Treasury*.[36] Heinemann Educational Books, London, republished *Quartet* in 1965 though unfortunately without Paton's introduction.[37] The four writers in *Quartet* had been members of a literary discussion group based in Rondebosch, Cape Town, which Rive had started.[38] Each writer had four stories in the collection, a playful symmetry evoked in the title with its resonance with classical music composition. Alf Wannenburgh recounts the meetings of the group of *Quartet* writers and Rive's role in particular:

> *Back in the early sixties, during a brief period when Alex La Guma wasn't restricted by banning orders, Richard, Alex, James Matthews and I met occasionally over a gallon of Lieberstein to read and discuss the stories we later published in our* Quartet *collection. Richard ... was then the most widely published of the group, and, as he was five years older than I and 'established', I considered him my mentor. I had known Alex longer, but he was little disposed to literary discourse, preferring to play his guitar and set up shot glasses and tumblers for proletarian friends, whereas Richard was, as he often joked, 'grossly over-educated', and enjoyed nothing more than talking about books and writing.*[39]

The four stories by Rive in *Quartet* appeared in *African Songs* as well – 'Strike', 'Resurrection', 'No Room at Solitaire' and 'Rain'. This insistent creative output and unflagging drive to be a writer, especially given the circumstances under which Rive had to work, led JM Coetzee to remark that 'as early as the 1960s Rive was regarded – everywhere but in South Africa – as among a vanguard of engaged writers'.[40]

In 'Strike', the very first story in *Quartet*, the narrator describes the protagonist, Boston, who happens to be a writer, in terms that are patently autobiographical. Boston is said to be in his late twenties in the story. If we assume that the story was written in the year before publication, it means Rive was about thirty-one at the time of composing this description. The setting of the story, on 27 May 1961, was just four days before the declaration of South Africa as a republic on 31 May 1961. The story fictionalises a local response to a predominantly ANC (African National Congress) call for a three-day strike, the last day of which was to coincide with 31 May. The strike was a consequence of heightened political activity post-Sharpeville and in part called for a national convention.[41] Boston is an image of Rive as he perhaps saw himself at the time:

> Boston spoke with a slightly affected accent that made people look at him twice in conversation, and wonder where he came from; it offended at first until one became used to it. His face was dark brown, with heavy, bushy eyebrows and a firm jaw. His hair was black and wavy. In Durban he could pass as an Indian, only his accent gave him away. He was soberly dressed except for a brown suede jacket that he hoped gave him a Bohemian touch. Just sufficient to indicate that he wrote short stories. He was in his late twenties, and just starting to put on weight.[42]

This self-portrait is remarkable for the manner in which it depicts, with photographic accuracy, physical features of Rive himself at about thirty. Yet there is also present in the description of Boston a fascinating idiosyncratic reflection on race and skin colour. The character defies standard racial categorisation – he is labelled 'dark brown', he looks 'Indian', has an unsettling accent and in dress is somewhat Bohemian. If there were a category Boston fitted, it was, it is suggested through slightly humorous self-parody, that of the short story writer. But not only is the description a conscious defiance of the apartheid mindset, with its obsession for racial profiling, but also perhaps a less conscious, internal grappling by Rive with who he was, how others saw him and how he saw himself.

Concurrent with Rive's highly conscious and ideologically well-developed opposition to racism was, it seems, a fraught subjectivity with regard to his own dark complexion. Rive was widely known to students at South Peninsula High School, and at Hewat College of Education where he lectured, as 'Chokka', an affectionate but nevertheless bigoted reference to Rive's very dark skin colour (the word *tjokka* is Afrikaans for 'squid' or 'cuttlefish' and alludes to the creature's intense black secretion).[43] Milton van Wyk, who came to know Rive and his work in the mid-1970s and 1980s, says about this nickname:

> [Rive] was also treated with contempt by some of his students, who resorted to calling him 'Chokka', a corruption of 'chocolate', because of his dark skin. This was a label which he totally abhorred. On the other hand he also enjoyed making fun of himself by saying: 'I'm so black, I'm navy blue.'[44]

It was, however, not a nickname anyone dared use to his face, as there was an intuitive awareness of his sensitivity, and also, possibly, users understood that the name, despite its affectionate or playfully deflationary connotations, carried derogatory and racist overtones – whether intended or not.

Rive refers to his complexion on a few occasions in his lengthy correspondence with Langston Hughes during their eleven-year friendship. He gives, in the initial letter in 1954, detailed portraits of himself. In this letter he describes his childhood and his experiences of racial prejudice, yet his only reference to his colouring is in the following ambiguous and euphemistic terms:

> Some of the students I teach are very fair and can easily cross the Colour line. So they all trundled along and went to see a 'White Only' performance of 'Julius Caesar' while the lecturer (myself) who is a graduate in English Literature was unable to enter, because of his deep tan.[45]

He is 'deep tan' and could not, it seems, directly refer to himself as black or dark-skinned. While said in jest, the Van Wyk quotation above belies a truth – it turns his blackness into another colour, navy blue. Elsewhere in the correspondence with Hughes, Rive describes himself as having 'Aryan features' (a term he undoubtedly knew was fraught with racist overtones of whiteness and Nazism), but the self-fashioning in these terms seems to reflect a resistance on the part of the young man to being black. Perhaps there are some subconscious internalisation of the very bigotry that was so consciously, so stridently and continually fought at all levels his whole life.

Almost twenty years later, Rive entitled his memoir *Writing Black*. This memorable title, asserting writing as an action which was at the core of who Rive was and simultaneously asserting a racialised identity as the very object of that act, stands in strong contrast to the title of JM Coetzee's *White Writing* (1988), where writing is the object examined and whiteness a category controversially already in existence. This deep fracture between white and black writing has long marked the literary sphere in South Africa and, despite our many attempts to bridge it both pre- and post-1994, its shadow still lingers even in a social order not legally racialised.

The title of Rive's memoir is also an accurate polemical statement of Rive's political allegiances and possibly also an astute marketing strategy for the book, for Black Consciousness had become a popular philosophy and its rhetoric provided a persuasive new, defiant and in some ways unifying vocabulary by the time the book was published. The title also reflects assertiveness about being 'black', not merely as literal skin colour, but primarily as proclamation of a positive and resistant identity for all those classified as non-white. In fact 'black' replaced 'nonwhite' as the widely acceptable term for describing all disenfranchised racial groups – black, coloured and Indian. 'Black' had become a positive, political signifier inspired by Fanonism and the confidence that came to the oppressed with the rise of the Civil Rights Movement in America and its refraction in South Africa, the Black Consciousness Movement of the late 1960s and 1970s. It was perhaps for Rive what Lee calls 'a strategic blackness'.[46]

Concurrent with this Africanist rhetoric, one continued to hear Rive's very pronounced Oxbridge (to the South African ear, at least) accent, deliberately cultivated even before he spent time at Oxford in the early 1970s completing his PhD on Olive Schreiner. He asserts this marker of educated Englishness as a very conscious antidote to racialised and ghettoised 'coloured' identity imposed by apartheid when he proclaims in *Writing Black*:

> *I, personally, am able to empathise with no world other than that of Western European sophistication and unsophistication. I have never had the opportunity to identify, like Langston Hughes in 'The Weary Blues', with*
>
> > *The low beating of the tom-toms,*
> > *The slow beating of the tom-toms ...*
>
> *I cannot be what the propounders of negritude or the African Personality cult would have me be. I am Johannesburg, Durban and Cape Town. I am Langa, Chatsworth and Bonteheuwel. I am discussion, argument and debate. I cannot recognise palm-fronds and nights filled with the throb of the primitive. I am buses, trains and taxis. I am prejudice, bigotry and discrimination. I am urban South Africa.*[47]

Here, it is as if Rive is defiantly saying, 'You see me and place me as a black man, inferior, primitive, but I defy you – I am not your "black"; I am cultured, cosmopolitan, and, as the accent would testify, have the best education in the world.' Rive's manner of speaking is another reflection of his paradoxical self-construction. Lee very perceptively describes this contradiction, asserting that while, on one level, 'the literary and cultural lineage of the dandy appealed to Rive's elitism and intellectual background', on another,

Rive's country gentleman image was also a self-indulgence
which amused him, and manifested his sense of self-irony.
Rive's sartorial and verbal style recalled the indolence, languor
and sophistication of the Victorian dandy and the clubbiness
and snobbery of his cricket-loving, cravat-wearing colonial
counterpart. As such, Rive's implication in this identity
subverted apartheid notions of black South Africans as willing
manual labourers and undermined the central apartheid tenet
that black South Africans were culturally incommensurable
with Western (white) civilisation.[48]

Recent critical works by Grant Farred and Desiree Lewis explore
the articulation of identity in Rive's work, focusing especially
on the contradictions between Rive's more consciously held
notions on race and nation, and meanings discernible in the
fabric of both his fictional and non-fictional work. Lewis, in a
most insightful analysis of how Rive constructs a set of identities
in his memoir *Writing Black*, asserts that the tension in the
memoir 'is between a univocal political persona and facets
of self that are intricately entangled in racial discourse.'[49] She
elaborates as follows:

Rive's autobiography, fiction and non-fictional writings
frequently condemn 'Coloured' as an official category and any
expression of coloured self-consciousness as evidence of false
and imposed identity. It will be argued here that despite this
Rive directly and obliquely engages with the entrenched myth-
making surrounding an official label in ways that indicate an
insistent absorption with areas that his conscious disavowals
appear to resolve.[50]

While by the late 1970s Rive been persuaded by certain arguments propounded by Black Consciousness about the need to be
more assertive about black identity, he continued to be absorbed
with how to reconcile these new ideas with his cherished non-
racialism as articulated by the NEUM, which criticised the

ideas and jargon of the Black Consciousness Movement as racialising and as imported from the United States.[51] While the title of the memoir was *Writing Black*, between the covers the condemnation of what apartheid had done to writers was fired by Rive's foundational belief in non-racialism rather than black identity. The book bore testimony to his conviction that non-racialism was the most powerful retort to what he called 'the single most important theme in my life: constitutionalised racism.'[52]

But this tension between non-racialism and the pull of Black Consciousness was yet a long way off. In 1962, in the aftermath of the Sharpeville crisis, Rive was writing as if possessed. The publication of *African Songs*, *Quartet* and *Emergency* would serendipitously happen while he was on an extended trip overseas. Without his knowledge initially, his dear friend Mphahlele had secured for him a substantial grant as a promising young African writer that would entail extensive travel in countries of his choice: 'I reached for my school atlas and compiled a long list starting with Afghanistan and ending with Zanzibar.'[53] He finally decided on Africa and Europe. In December of 1962, he departed from Cape Town harbour for Durban, accompanied by Alf Wannenburgh, who would be travelling with him as far as Durban. He was seen off at the quay by a number of his admiring pupils and his ever-supportive friends Jan Rabie, Marjorie Wallace and Jack Cope.

Chapter 4

The year 1963 was a watershed for Rive in terms of making a name for himself as a writer and this coincided with months of intensive travel and adventure. At thirty-three he was travelling outside of South Africa for the first time. From December 1962 to September 1963, he travelled up the coast of southern Africa by boat and then through Africa, on to southern Europe and finally to London. The trip was funded by a Farfield Foundation Fellowship secured for him by Es'kia Mphahlele. Mphahlele had decided to leave South Africa in 1957, and in 1963 was director of the Congress for Cultural Freedom in Paris.[54] Rive mentions that this Congress was 'an American-based organisation … [whose] purpose was to combat the cultural inroads of communism, but no-one in the organisation seemed to take that aspect seriously'. Here Rive skims over a controversy of which he was aware, as later in his memoir he admits to the Congress being 'reputed to have accepted funding from the Central Intelligence Agency'; the Congress was in fact funded by the CIA as a way of soliciting pro-Western sympathy from writers in anglophone Africa, who were perceived to be more radically critical of the West than their assimilated francophone counterparts.[55] The Farfield Foundation had also helped to fund the establishment of the literary journal *The Classic* in Johannesburg, at the start of the 1960s. Rive took his cue for a strategic involvement with the Congress from Mphahlele, rather than from his political associates in the NEUM, who would have suggested he refuse such collaboration. He would continue to find himself in such 'compromising' positions and his decisions seemed to be guided by his belief that a writer should be independent of any party political line even as he aligned himself ideologically with particular NEUM positions. In deciding to accept the funding, he risked being seen as a CIA spy and being ostracised by more radical friends at home. This perhaps accounts for the silent treatment he got from some of the writers in exile, such as Todd Matshikiza, whom he met up with on the London leg of his trip.

Writing Black gives detailed descriptions of his encounters with people and places on this trip. The first experience of ocean-liner travel is marked for Rive notably by the manner in which white South African passengers recreated segregationist boundaries that humiliated and ostracised the non-white passengers. Rive's first port of call on his ten-month trip was Durban, from where he travelled inland to meet Alan Paton at his Kloof home. His main purpose was to secure Paton's agreement to write an introduction to the manuscript of *Quartet*. Alf Wannenburgh, who travelled with Rive as far as Durban, captures the intense jousting in the first encounter between Rive and Paton:

> We were duly ushered into the presence of the great man in the rondavel he used as his study. There we spoke for a while before Mrs Paton appeared with the typescript of the introduction – 'Four Splendid Voices' – which Mr P perused, signed and handed to us. In parting he suggested we go to a performance of Sponono, a stage version of one of his short stories ... On the way back to our lodgings Richard, mindful of the Liberal school of writing that Paton represented and the nascent Protest school of which he was the founder, said something unflattering about Sponono that unintentionally, but perhaps revealingly, gave the impression that he had been purely opportunistic in asking Paton to write the introduction ... some years later, when Richard asked [Paton] to contribute a short story to an anthology he was compiling, Paton replied through an intermediary that he didn't think that Mr Rive would be interested in anything he had written.[56]

What Rive thought of Paton is also clear from correspondence with Langston Hughes in which Paton is discussed. When Hughes first wrote to Rive in 1954, he mentioned Paton and his work in very appreciative and sympathetic terms: 'The books of Alan Patton [*sic*] and Nadine Gordimer, among others, have been well received here.' In a letter to Peter Abrahams, Hughes described how he had just met Paton, who was on a trip to the United States in May 1954, 'at a big colored party … [and he] spoke most effectively'.[57] In his next letter to Hughes, Rive expressed his ardent view of Paton as 'extremely unpopular with the non-Europeans. He represents a school of thought accepting white trusteeship where all men are equal (but some more equal than others).'[58] His memoir also depicts the meeting as iconic of two different schools of thought in South African literature:

> *He represented the high point of Liberal Writing in South Africa. I was representative of the nascent Protest School. Liberal Writing may be loosely defined as writing mostly by Whites about Blacks to move Whites out of their socio-political complacency … Protest Writing on the other hand is written mostly by Blacks articulating their position to a White readership they feel can effect change. Sol Plaatje and Peter Abrahams were amongst its progenitors.*[59]

Ironically, from a post-apartheid vantage point, Rive's formulation reveals that the two schools he identified had very similar audiences and intentions in mind! Yet, at the time, black and white writers must have lived in worlds that were poles apart. That Rive and the other *Quartet* writers had agreed to have Paton write the introduction to their publication was in fact probably a mix of qualified admiration for the man's work as well as a strategic choice – Paton carried weight on the national and international literary scene.

The African leg of Rive's journey took him through East Africa, visiting Mozambique, Tanzania, Kenya, Uganda, Sudan,

Ethiopia and Egypt. That Rive chose to visit this array of eastern and northern African countries at a time when travel to and through them could be arduous might have been a condition of the funding, but it is also testimony to his view of himself as an African writer and to his commitment to African literature. The mission through Africa, along with his plan to connect with African writers and publish a collection of African prose, is clearly also inspired by and modelled on Hughes's earlier attempt to make contact with and publish African writers. In Mozambique, then firmly under the rule of the Portuguese colonial administration, Rive was visited by Luis Bernardo Honwana, who showed him the manuscript of his short story in Portuguese, 'We Killed Mangy Dog'. Honwana eventually became the minister of culture in post-independence Mozambique but never published any other creative work beside this and a few other short stories.[60] Dorothy Guedes, with whom Rive was staying in Lourenço Marques (now Maputo), along with her architect husband Pancho Guedes, was part of a small set of artists and intellectuals working in the city. Dorothy was an English teacher at the English Primary School and had edited the third issue of *The Classic*, which focused on writing in Mozambique.[61] She translated 'We Killed Mangy Dog' for Rive and Pancho was to design the cover for the first edition of Honwana's story collection. Rive liked the short story a lot and arranged for a translation to be included in his *Modern African Prose*, soon to be published by Heinemann.

In Uganda at Makerere University he met Gerald Moore, a leading African Literature scholar who had just published his critical work *Seven African Writers*, as well as Ngũgĩ wa Thiong'o, then still known as James Ngugi. Ngũgĩ was a second-year student at Makerere at the time and had written a play and two short stories. Rive remembers Ngũgĩ for 'the intensity with which he approached his work' and does so interestingly in terms that style himself as the mentor figure:

He was slightly built, long-faced and had large, dreamy eyes. He was untidily dressed, giving the appearance of a genuine lack of interest about matters such as clothes. But he was bright and alert and drank in all I had to say ... Ngugi and I sat down at his desk to work our way through his short story, 'The Martyr'. The bell rang for lunch but he insisted that we continue.[62]

Rive had been invited by Mphahlele, writing from Paris on 25 January 1962, to attend the important Makerere conference of African Writers of English Expression:

We are having a writers' conference at Makerere, Uganda ... Is it possible, in any case, for you to attend this conference? You will be the guest of Mbari Writers' and Artists' Club in Ibadan who are calling the conference under our [Congress for Cultural Freedom] sponsorship ... We plan to have 22 writers at this conference from different parts of Africa, for the main purpose of giving them an opportunity to meet and know one another ... It would be very good to have someone from South Africa direct as well as exiles. I am also inviting Alex la Guma.[63]

Rive regretted not being able to go to Makerere for the conference in June 1962 because of the obvious difficulty in getting 'official approval' to attend such a gathering but also probably because of teaching commitments. He clearly grasped the significance of the gathering in debating future directions of African literature:

The conference had been an historic occasion, the first assembly of African writers to be held on the African continent itself. There had been forty-five participants, including twenty-nine writers and five editors of political and critical reviews. I had been invited but, like most other South Africans, had been unable to attend, as official approval was out of the question. The South African delegation had been reduced to a handful of exiles and two Whites from Cape Town who had no problems getting out.[64]

After leaving Uganda, Rive travelled to Ethiopia, Egypt, Greece, Italy and Switzerland, finally reaching Paris, where he stayed with Mphahlele and his family at their home on the Boulevard Saint-Michel. Mphahlele read Rive's manuscript of *Emergency*. Rive must have been proud to share this work with his mentor and no doubt took seriously what criticisms Mphahlele had. In Paris, he met up again with his writer/artist friends from Cape Town, Peter Clarke and Breyten Breytenbach. The latter took him to meet the famous South African painter Gerard Sekoto, who was living in exile in Paris. Rive's critical comments on Sekoto and his work reflect Rive's own fear of breaking with his homeland and going into exile, excising the very source of his creativity:

> *His eyes seemed vague and lost but would suddenly brighten intensely when a chord of recognition was struck. He painted Africa from memory, but it was a romanticised, coffee-table memory. He had been away far too long. He had become far more French than African … To me he epitomised the effects of prolonged divorcement from one's subject matter.*[65]

In Paris he also celebrated the publication of *African Songs*. A party was held and the gathering of exiles and locals celebrated in a fashion typical of South African writers' circles then – with laughter, smoking, wine, song and dance. The achievement of an individual talent was a milestone for the group as well, and of course a victory against the barbarians who ruled back home. He then travelled to London with Peter Clarke and spent a few days at the Regent's Park home of Sylvester Stein, one-time editor of *Drum*, and later moved into a hired room further down Regent's Park Road to a house in which Todd Matshikiza was also living with his family. Matshikiza gave both him and Clarke the cold shoulder, which led Rive to think about the perceptions of differences that his non-racial beliefs had been resisting so firmly – differences between 'coloured' and black, between those forced into exile and those allowed to travel on valid passports. There are a number of such sincere and awkward moments of self-questioning in the memoir that reveal Rive's capacity to empathise at times with views quite contrary to his own; these moments offset the preponderance of self-assured assertions about politics and people he was prone to make. It is as if he momentarily forgets that he has constantly to perform and position himself, and lets doubt surface fleetingly.

At the African Transcription Centre in Dover Street, London, a meeting place for African writers and artists, he met Nigerian writers John Pepper Clark, Christopher Okigbo, Wole Soyinka and Chinua Achebe. Achebe, he remarked, was 'gentle, quiet, unassuming … one of the greatest writers of the twentieth century'.[66] Rive was approached by Keith Sambrook of the recently established Heinemann African Writers Series and asked to compile an anthology of African prose, probably with prompting from Rive, leading to *Modern African Prose* coming out in 1964. Stephen Gray sums up the importance of this compilation in its day and for many decades thereafter:

> *Modern African Prose [was] the first anthology to assemble a continent-wide English selection including Chinua Achebe, Ezekiel Mphahlele, Cyprian Ekwenzi, Amos Tutuola and Ngugi wa Thiong'o. In parts of independent Africa this title became the educational setwork to insert after* Julius Caesar *and the 'Immortality Ode'. Richard later refused to update and revise it, for it did have its historic position in the rise of African Literature and is still used as is … Heady and optimistic, assertively forward-looking, as were Richard's own stories – impressionist slivers of the poor life, singing of dignity and scenting freedom.*[67]

In London Rive also met two South African writers whom he admired very much – Dan Jacobson and William Plomer. Jacobson interviewed Rive for *New Comment*, a BBC Third

Programme radio feature. Plomer, who was about to turn sixty, had in his novel *Turbott Wolfe* initiated the theme of inter-racial love in South African fiction that Rive drew on in *Emergency*. Rive admired his compatriot's 'strong reaction to racialism, prejudice and bigotry [that] could hardly make his works popular with the authorities in the country about which he wrote so vigorously'.[68] He admired the fiction of both these writers:

> Both were iconoclasts impatient of shibboleths. Both put their society under a searching microscope … Whereas Jacobson relied on nuances and innuendo, Plomer used rapier thrusts which went straight to their target. Both in no uncertain terms exposed the sham that is still often passed off as the traditional South African way of life.[69]

Plomer and Rive dined together in Charlotte Street where Plomer intrigued him with stories of Roy Campbell, Laurens van der Post, Pauline Smith, Sarah Gertrude Millin and the *Voorslag* movement.[70] Seventeen years later, in 1979, Rive would spend much time in the Humanities Research Center at Texas University examining the letters of Plomer, who had died in 1973. Did Rive have any idea that Plomer was homosexual? As was the case in Rive's own work, homosexuality did not feature overtly in any of Plomer's fiction.

While in London, Rive received the news that Faber and Faber had agreed to publish *Emergency* and Alf Wannenburgh wrote to him from home that Crown Publishers in New York would publish *Quartet*. This plenitude of success led him to declare in the somewhat quaint idiom he was fond of: 'There was a spring in my step and birds whistled happily over the way in Regent's Park.'[71]

The long trip was filled with numerous encounters with writers, artists, publishers, friends and strangers, demonstrating Rive's zest for engaging with people and his compulsion to immerse himself in the world of writing and African writers in particular. The proliferation of names mentioned while on this trip, and on three subsequent trips over the next seventeen years recounted in *Writing Black*, seems initially to irritate JM Coetzee in his review of the memoir, but on reflection he accounts for it in an interesting and illuminating way:

> One wonders what all these chance brief acquaintances are doing in the story of Rive's life till one gets the point: that the sections of Writing Black *set outside of South Africa are intended to provide testimony of how it is possible for a South African to interact on perfectly ordinary terms with perfectly ordinary and even dull people in societies not based on racial divisions.*[72]

There is, however, an additional way of reading the panoply of names in the book –as name-dropping. Rive, the memoir signals to the reader encountering this litany of names, is by association clearly a member of the community of well-known writers. This mode of self-construction, while not untrue (Rive had by then established himself as a major South African writer), nevertheless reflects the strong self-inflation that was characteristic. The narrative is a performance of his stature as writer. Athol Fugard, jokingly but not without a note of seriousness, remarked to Rive when he first met him in the late 1950s, 'With your arrogance and self-assurance I'll make an actor out of you.'[73]

Another, less self-absorbed side emerges in the memoir as well. There are incidents that reveal a selfless and genuinely caring man. In Kenya he attended a party with all social classes of people and ended up holding forth in his pompous way in his Oxbridge accent to three working-class British soldiers. They told him that they did not understand the 'fancy words' he was using, and that he sounded like 'a bleeding BBC announcer'.[74] He realised he had been engaging in a monologue rather than making conversation, and then began to ask real questions and listen to the men talk about their lives. In the memoir he clearly empathises with their marginalisation in Kenya, with their loneliness, and even understands their dislike of the 'wogs'. In another incident, when he entered Sudan, Rive assisted a young South African political refugee who was penniless and, despite finding him a shady character, puts him up and helps him. It was often young, marginalised men, much like himself in his family circle as a teenager in District Six, whom he sought out and engaged with in this way. It also happened to be the profile of the kind of man to whom he was sometimes sexually attracted.

On other occasions in the memoir, when Rive is less conscious of himself as the subject, he becomes enthralled by particular characters he describes. His meeting in London with the Nigerian writer Christopher Okigbo is one such incident. Rive's descriptions of Okigbo are vivid and touching; he was clearly moved at Okigbo's untimely death in 1967 while fighting on the side of the Biafran separatists. But perhaps it was his flattering claims to Rive that they were the two younger African writers 'destined to rescue African literature', as well as his evident affection for Rive, that endeared him to Rive. Interestingly enough, he also labelled Okigbo 'a sartorial dandy' – clearly the two were kindred spirits.[75]

When in London, Rive visited and stayed at the homes of various friends who had immigrated to Britain from South Africa – Albert Adams, Cosmo Pieterse and Gilbert and Ursula Reines. The Reines were struggling to adapt to a new life and at times found Rive demanding and overbearing. According to Ursula Reines, he told, rather than asked, her to type out the whole manuscript of *Modern African Prose*, which he was preparing for publication. Rive did, on the other hand, recognise their contribution in his acknowledgements in the book. Gilbert Reines remembers Rive's boundless energy at the time and that 'he couldn't sit still for five minutes … his company was always quite stressful in a way, and you were always sort of saying "when is he going?" … He had his catchphrases [and] he used to quote the same things at me often!'[76]

The highlight for Rive of his stay in London, though, was undoubtedly his first meeting with Langston Hughes. It represented the most important meeting of the ten-month trip. Rive called Hughes 'the man who had created Simple, the Shakespeare of Harlem, the greatest living Black writer in the world'.[77] He revealed his awe and excitement, tinged with his wry humour, at the prospect of the meeting: 'I … dressed in my only suit, put on my best necktie and made my way down to the Dover Street Hotel.' He was appalled at the casual way the receptionist at Brown's Hotel in Mayfair responded to his request to see if 'Mister Hughes' was in: 'She made it sound so matter of fact, as if they regularly had one of the greatest writers in the world staying over. I felt her attitude was almost irreligious.' Hughes was having a shower but asked Rive to come up to the room. Rive's description of what follows is a fascinating mixture of 1950s movie script, farce, bathos and humour:

I knocked. I could hear a shower running somewhere inside. I knocked louder, then heard a voice shouting something. I opened the door and entered. The shower was switched off for a moment.

'That you, Dick?' said a voice in an unmistakably broad American accent.

'I am Richard Rive.'

'Glad to meet you, Dick. Make yourself comfortable and have a scotch. Be with you in a second.'

I made myself as comfortable as possible under the circumstances, poured a stiff whiskey, downed it in one gulp, poured another and sat nervously on the edge of my chair. What a dreadful anticlimax if I were to see this great writer coming out from under a shower. He would be wet and drying his paunch with a towel. He might even have ingrown toenails. I speculated that he would look like any 'Coloured' uncle from District Six. When he did appear in dressing-gown and slippers, I found him pleasantly roundfaced and with close-cropped curly hair, and he goggled owl-eyed through heavy-rimmed spectacles. He chainsmoked and talked all the time with a cigarette dangling from his lips.[78]

The two went off to a performance of *Black Nativity*, a musical written by Hughes, at the Strand Theatre in the Aldwych. The manner in which the famous writer courted attention at the theatre – to the extent of blowing kisses at the actress as she was about to sing, causing her to stop the show and shout 'Lang' – fascinated Rive and is reminiscent of his own self-indulgent behaviour twenty-six years later at the time that *'Buckingham Palace', District Six* was being rehearsed at the Baxter Theatre in Cape Town. He would continually refer to '*my* play' and to himself as 'a true thespian'.[79] Hughes, as a black writer at ease with himself and at home in the world, was clearly the strongest role model for the younger South African. Rive dedicated *African Songs* to Hughes, taking the cue for his title from Hughes's poem 'The Weary Blues':

Ah, we should have a land of joy,
Of love and joy and wine and song,
And not this land where joy is wrong.

On his return to the Cape, in September 1963, Rive had arrived as a writer, but in a country still controlled with an iron fist by a white supremacist regime that had banned both his books – *African Songs* while he was travelling abroad and *Emergency* soon after he arrived back. In 1965 *Quartet* was also banned. With his wry humour, he claims in the memoir, 'I was now part of a small élite of South African writers not allowed to read their own works in case they became influenced by them.' Just before returning home from this trip, he had, he says, 'serious doubts about the wisdom of returning'.[80] It is clear that he grappled with the dilemma – to stay in London would mean freedom from all he had fought against; to return meant facing a harrowing, uncertain and unsafe future, and given the onslaught on writers, even the death of his creativity. He finally chose not to stay in London, where he felt he could 'avoid all this', but to return to what was after all his home. He does not say what swung the balance, but does speak of an intense longing for home that took hold of him towards the end of his long and frenetic trip:

> *I longed once again to hear the traffic faintly roaring past my flat on Rosmead Avenue. I longed to dive into the cold water outside Gif Kommetjie and prickle the fleshy lace-edge of abalone between the rocks. I longed to climb along Waterfall Buttress under dark caves wet with dripping ferns. I wanted to share the hilarity of interschool athletics with rosettes, caps and warcries. I wanted to sit at the quiet of my desk in the very early morning, working away at my writing.*[81]

The yearning for the landscape and rituals of home, for the sea and the mountains of the Cape peninsula, and the strong sense of obligation and self-fulfilment, even exhilaration, that attended his work in education and sport, were what drew him back. But perhaps also, as his reflections on Sekoto's work implied, he felt that the pain of home, of the intensely local, was simultaneously the source of his creative life. In addition perhaps, it was his sense of commitment to a writing life and struggle back in South Africa that compelled him to return. Or perhaps, as possibly the least articulated reason, he wanted to return to the place where he had left behind a young man, a student of his, to whom he had grown furtively and closely attached – Ian Rutgers.

Rive returned to a country in which the repressive force of the post-Sharpeville regime was pervasive. He described the two years that followed his arrival back home as a time when 'not much happened, but some of the things which did occur were scarring and bitter'.[82] There were many acquaintances, for example, who cut ties with Rive on his return as he was perceived to be a marked and dangerous man whose books had been banned by officialdom. The 1960s were the darkest times for the disenfranchised majority and for all artists and writers who overtly or even subtly opposed the status quo. Most of these writers had gone into forced or self-exile by the middle of the decade. Mphahlele was amongst the first to leave. Can Themba sought refuge as a schoolteacher in Swaziland. Alex La Guma, one of the last, was forced into exile, along with his wife Blanche and two young sons, in 1965. Rive and James Matthews were amongst the few remaining *Drum* writers left in South Africa.

In July 1965, two traumatic events occurred that were deeply unsettling to Rive. They were also symptomatic of the dark times in South Africa. Ingrid Jonker drowned herself in the sea at Green Point and Nat Nakasa threw himself off a New York skyscraper. Ariefi and Hazel Manuel remember Rive being extremely upset, especially at the death of Jonker. On his return to South Africa, Rive had resumed his close friendship with Jonker. The intensity of feeling that he had found in her from the start of their friendship continued to strike him: 'She was always strange, sometimes withdrawn, often impulsive, and always unpredictable'.[83] Like other writers who describe Jonker in Jan Rabie's *In Memoriam Ingrid Jonker* (1966), Rive sensed that she was a prescient, almost childlike medium embodying the intense, irreconcilable and tragic conflicts that wracked the country. Rive claims he was 'one of the few people to see her off on the Union Castle liner' when she left on a short trip to England after winning a major literary award in 1963. At her funeral, he thought back to when she gave him a copy of her collection of poems, *Ontvlugting*, inscribed with the words, '*Vir Richard – sonder die liefde is die lewe nutteloos.* [Without love life is worthless]'. Perhaps Jonker was one of the

An impish, delighted, camp Richard Rive, performing with Marjorie Wallace what seems to be a mock award ceremony, with George Hallett playing the audience (photographer: Jan Rabie, using Hallett's camera; courtesy George Hallett)

very few who impelled Rive to reflect on the nature of love and abjection in his own life.

Her death brought the circle of friends together. Rive frequently visited Jan Rabie and Marjorie Wallace at their home at 6 Cheviot Place, Green Point, and regularly spent part of his December vacation with them at their holiday home in Onrus outside the town of Hermanus. One story goes that Rive, Uys Kriger and Jan Rabie were in Hermanus and Jan quietly asked a restaurateur he knew well if they could bring Rive into the whites-only establishment. The owner hesitated and asked, 'How many of them are there?' and Rive, hearing this, piped up, 'All 18 million!'[84]

The week before Rive departed for his 1962–63 trip, he received an unexpected visit from Nat Nakasa at his Selous Court flat. He had heard of the writer but had never met him before: 'There stood Nat, case in hand, a trifle dumpy and stuttering with shyness at what he felt was an intrusion … He had come from Johannesburg for a week and hoped to find accommodation with me.'[85] Nakasa had also come to see if Rive was interested in *The Classic*, a magazine he was about to launch. Rive and Nakasa kept up 'an enthusiastic correspondence' during Rive's prolonged absence and after his return. Nakasa had been refused a passport to take up a fellowship in journalism at Harvard and was then forced to leave on an exit permit, preventing him from ever returning to his home country. Nakasa's letters to him, Rive observed, became 'more and more pessimistic and more despondent'. They vowed to meet up in 1965 as Rive had applied for a Fulbright Fellowship to study in the United States. But Rive was never to see him again.

His memoir is silent on what was happening at this time in his day-to-day existence on a more personal level beyond his life as a writer, claiming that not much happened between the previous and the looming trip. He continued to teach at South Peninsula High and would do so for another decade before moving to a lectureship at Hewat College, and persevered with the work in sport coaching and administration. He had finally completed his BA part-time studies at the University of Cape Town (UCT), after a ten-year slog, and graduated in December 1962 just before his departure on his trip. His ex-student and now good friend George Hallett took a number of photographs of him looking pensive in his graduation gown and sash. It was, after all, his first graduation from a world-renowned university.

Back home after the trip, Rive must have given a lot of thought to what he wanted to achieve next in terms of his formal education and research what was a primary influence on his writing. African-American writers was clearly high on the list of options. Ideally this had to be done in the United States and

Richard Rive, graduation photograph, December 1962
(photographer: George Hallett)

preferably in New York near Hughes and Harlem. He believed his brashness got him the Fulbright funding he needed to do this work, as he replied in typical cocky fashion to an aggressive academic on the interview panel about what he would do if he did not get the award: 'I'd then like to see who does.'[86]

Rive departed for New York in August 1965, having been awarded the Fulbright Fellowship and Heft Scholarship to study, according to his account in *Writing Black*, African and Afro-American Literature under Robert Bone at Columbia University. A transcript of the components of his master's degree from the Magdalen College archive shows that, in fact, the emphasis in the degree was on education, not literature, but the latter is clearly what most excited him.[87]

He had been extremely anxious that he might not be granted a passport, in which case he vowed not to go on an exit permit (official permission to leave the country on condition you could never return) as 'no one was going to deprive me of my country'.[88] Despite the dispiriting situation in South Africa, Rive had clearly made up his mind that his own future now lay not as an exile, but as a writer inside the country. Unlike the dilemmas he had faced when on his previous trip, he now seemed certain that he would return to South Africa after his stay in New York. The effect of exile on Nakasa was still a fresh and disturbing memory.

In 1965, while Rive was studying for his master's degree at Teachers College at Columbia University, he once again met up with Hughes and, through him, other prominent Americans, such as Arna Bontemps, Jay Wright, LeRoi Jones and Arthur Spingarn. At a party at Hughes's apartment, Rive was struck by the writer's incredible energy. Hughes invited Rive to his house in Harlem one evening to discuss poetry and then to go out for supper. The dinner with Hughes and Bontemps at Frank's on 125th Street near 3rd Avenue in New York is described by Rive in 'Taos in Harlem: An Interview with Langston Hughes'

(1967).[89] This article is an imaginative recreation of their meeting and discussion, using bits of Hughes's poetry and Rive's previous encounters with him. One clearly senses Rive's admiration for Hughes and his life of commitment to writing and to the struggle of black people in America and the rest of the world. What struck Rive was the humility of the man. And, like Hughes, Rive could not resist engaging in witty talk with all sorts of people, suggesting their intense curiosity about and keen interest in the lives of others. Yet both had bouts of loneliness that could only be fought by feeling that their work and lives were somehow inextricably connected to the struggles of their community.

For Rive, Hughes's life must have had strong resonance with his own: both so-called coloured in hostile white worlds; both determined to be writers, experimenting with a range of genres and always willing to nurture and support younger writers; both from poor, troubled families centred on the mother, yet each feeling different, spurned by the rest of the family; active sportsmen when young; both choosing to lead lives as single men; and both intensely closed about their sexual lives.

Rive's insistence on keeping quiet about his sexual life might have been simply that – a choice he made about what in his life was private and what was public. The repercussions of the gay uprising against police brutality at Stonewall bar in New York in 1968 and the permissive late 1960s were only really felt in South Africa in the post-1994 period.[90] The climate in the country was not conducive to coming out before then. Still, many individuals did have the courage to live more openly gay lives. One of the factors that possibly influenced Rive to remain silent about his sexuality was his strong desire to fit in and be accepted by wider society. Hughes was always tight-lipped (often called a 'clam') about his sexual relationships. It was at the supper with Hughes and Bontemps that Rive posed a veiled yet pointed question about Countee Cullen: 'And the tragedy of his personal life? ... Did it influence his writing?'[91] This question was presumably about Cullen's rumoured homosexuality and the way it influenced his poetry. The question was probably also probing Hughes about his own sexuality. Hughes politely dismissed the question, saying he did not know. It was the first more or less overt reference to homosexuality in Rive's writings and only one of two in his whole body of work.[92]

The silence on questions of sexuality in Rive's work is intriguing. It was not only that he remained silent about his homosexuality, both in his public life and in his fiction and non-fiction, but also that this obvious silence coexisted with the loudness of his protests against inhumanity and racialism. The very silences in both real life and fiction on this matter are in themselves exemplary of a not uncommon Jekyll-and-Hyde existence forced upon, or chosen by, gay men who were young in a highly repressive and Calvinist South Africa. It would have been unthinkable for a biographer to write about this aspect of Rive during his lifetime, not because of the predictable resistance from Rive himself, but mainly because it would have been viewed as diminishing, even betraying, his recognised contribution to the fight for freedom.

Rive's fiction as a whole portrays, according to Lee, 'the oppressed, the downtrodden and the dispossessed'.[93] To what extent is Rive's preoccupation with the marginalised not only political but also linked to his own sexual repression? Contradictions in his sense of self are evident in his ambivalence towards homosexuality. When did he begin to sense that he was homosexual? The Manuels are amongst the very few, it seems, in whom Rive confided about his sexual orientation. They were living in Port Elizabeth during the late 1960s, and Rive often stayed with them when he visited the city. On one of these visits, they remember him speaking in confidence to them about his homosexuality.[94]

While evidently having recognised his own homosexual impulses by the early 1960s at the latest, *Writing Black* nevertheless expresses disgust at the sexual advances of a male Greek owner of a publishing firm in terms Rive must have known could easily be read as thinly veiled homophobia:

> *The owner took my hand and held it for an embarrassingly long time. He spoke in a melancholy tone and said … that he loved the Negro race; he admired Blacks; he was a friend of my people; he would personally translate all my works into Greek. He was a bachelor and would invite me for dinner that very evening at his flat … There was something repellent about his fawning and his over-attention … Once in his apartment, he suggested I stay for a week … 'You indulge in erotica?' I left without the promised dinner.*[95]

The unwanted advances, while clearly repulsive to Rive, were nevertheless written in such a way that reinforces the very attitudes that kept him from being more open about his orientation and he must have known this would be the case. Why mention this incident at all? Was he rhetorically positioning himself as heterosexual in the public eye by enabling a reading which seemed to align him with homophobia? Was he once again demonstrating the pervasiveness of racial typecasting, only this time with the black man as sexual exotic object to the European?

It was not only sexuality that was an unspoken subtext at the supper with Hughes at Frank's. There was also tension between the two writers' views about distinctiveness in black American writing and life, about Hughes's belief in the 'black soul'. Rive, on the other hand, using his own non-racial ideas about black literature in South Africa, assumed that integration of black writing into a national corpus was necessary. Rive's views as a black writer differed from those of Hughes in distinct ways. In his essay 'The Negro Artist and the Racial Mountain' (published in 1926), Hughes takes issue with the view of Countee Cullen, who wanted to be 'a poet – not a Negro poet'.[96] Cullen's non-racial view, Hughes claims, results in the equation 'I would like to be a white poet' and adds that 'within the race toward whiteness, the desire to pour racial individuality into the mould of American standardisation' is the outcome. This non-racial attitude is 'the mountain standing in the way of any true Negro art in America'. Hughes believed in the black race. Rive's non-racialism meant his views on culture and race were closer to Cullen's.

Despite the emblazoning of 'Black' in the title of his auto-biography, Rive continuously contested the idea of a separate black race and the very notion of 'race'. His questions to Hughes in 'Taos in Harlem' are meant to engage on this point: 'Do you think that American Negro Poetry will finally be completely integrated into American literature? … And lose its ethnic qualities? … And would such a state be desirable?'[97] In the preface to his memoir, Rive emphasises his 'strong belief in non-racialism', which leads him to say, 'I will look forward to the day when it will not be necessary for writing in my country to be tied to ethnic labels, when the only criteria will be writing well and writing South African'.[98] Hughes, even from Rive's account, was clearly irritated by Rive and the position that underpinned these questions. Hughes made fun of them and changed the subject. Years before this meeting, the correspondence between them, from roughly the early 1960s, reveals a cooling of relations. Perhaps the honeymoon of the initial exchanges was over, or perhaps they realised how different they were. Perhaps Hughes found Rive's non-racialism inimical to his own interests in the black soul. Perhaps Rive had now made it as a writer and Hughes was no longer central to his advancement. Or perhaps Rive in the latter half of the 1960s suffered the effects of the increasing and suffocating repression in South Africa, choking his creativity and his drive.

Despite these differences, which crystallised during Rive's

time in New York, Hughes remained a major influence on Rive
as a writer. Like Hughes, and maybe to some extent because
of him, Rive's work is about the lives and struggles of ordinary
oppressed people. Rive's main vehicle was prose, but, like Hughes,
he also explored a range of genres. His short story 'Resurrection',
first published in 1963 and chosen by him to represent his work
in the anthology *Modern African Prose*, invites comparison with
Hughes's short story 'Father and Son', published in 1934 in *The
Ways of White Folks*. Both have as their theme the dilemma of
a mulatto child from a white father and a non-white mother.
In 'Resurrection', we experience the funeral of the dark-skinned
mother from the viewpoint of the 'coloured' daughter, Mavis.
Rive's story begins on a dramatic note and while it captures the
trauma and bitterness of those in the family who are ostracised
by the fairer, bigoted relatives, the inexperienced writer lays it
on too thickly with the obvious symbolism of hymn fragments,
the pain Mavis unrelentingly shrieks at us and the unconvincing
repetitions of the ending:

> *Mavis felt hot, strangely, unbearably hot. Her saliva turned to
> white heat in her mouth and her head rolled drunkenly. The
> room was filled with her mother's presence, her mother's eyes,
> body, soul. Flowing into her, filling every pore, becoming one
> with her, becoming a living condemnation.*
>
> *'Misbelievers!' she screeched hoarsely. 'Liars! You killed me!
> You murdered me! Don't you know your God?'*[99]

Hughes's 'Father and Son' carries the reader along with the
passion and courage of the mulatto son, Bert, in his battle to
be recognised by his all-powerful white, racist father, Colonel
Norwood. Hughes refracts his politics through character and
story, but also occasionally uses his narrator to preach. In the
following extract, we find the narrator pontificating (and one
hears Hughes here) on the effect an individual can have:

> *In the chemistry lab at school, did you ever hold a test tube,*

pouring in liquids and powders and seeing nothing happen until a certain liquid or a certain powder is poured in and then everything begins to smoke and fume, bubble and boil, hiss to foam, and sometimes even explode? The tube is suddenly full of action and movement and life. Well, there are people like those certain liquids or powders; at a given moment they come into a room, or into a town, even into a country – and the place is never the same again. Things bubble, boil, change. Sometimes the whole world is changed. Alexander came. Christ. Marconi. A Russian named Lenin.

Not that there is any comparing Bert to Christ or Lenin.[100]
Rive avoids such authorial intrusion in his short story narratives. However, the way he refracts his message through character is, at times, jarringly obvious. It is as if Rive insists on his indignation being written into the narrative. These somewhat divergent approaches reflect their different views on the role of the writer. Although never a member of the Communist Party, as claimed by the McCarthyites, Hughes gave visible and active support to the American left at critical moments in the country's history through his writings. Up to the period of the McCarthy hearings, writing and fighting were, to him, inseparable. In 'Father and Son' he makes direct reference to the Scottsboro trial and Camp Hill shootings. Rive, never as closely involved in political organisations and their polemics, believed that while the black South African writer had a dual function – 'as a Black he storms castles and as a writer he defines the happening' – as writer per se, 'his main function … is to define and record. He is an articulate memory of the oppressed people.'[101] There should be a distance, Rive asserts, between writing and fighting. This insistence on writer as witness, even angry witness, rather than revolutionary, is indicative of his more conventional, less politically radical notion of the role of the writer.

Rive derived the battle metaphor for his argument about

the nature of the writer's domain from one of his favourite South African poets – Arthur Nortje. The final line of Nortje's poem 'Song for a Passport' reads: 'O ask me all but do not ask allegiance!' To Rive, the line exemplifies the call for the writer to be allowed to define his own voice, while yet remaining, like Nortje, and like Hughes in his last decade, party to a much broader struggle against bigotry and tyranny. Perhaps it was the very early and seminal influence of Jack Cope's outlook and the way he insisted on the absence of propaganda from literature that helped lay the bedrock for Rive's own strong assertions, in literature and in life, of individualism, albeit an individual voice that believed it represented the voice of the oppressed mass.

The most important contact he made in New York was with Hughes and with those to whom Hughes introduced him. The chapter in *Writing Black* dedicated to his time at Columbia recounts numerous other meetings with ordinary Americans. Rive is most scornful and dismissive of those who see him as an African curiosity and associate Africa with the primitive and wild animals. On the other hand, he is constantly curious about the attitudes and politics of black Americans, arriving in the United States at a time when the influence of the Civil Rights Movement and black power movement were growing. He taught at a school in East Harlem during the university break in order to get closer to the black youngsters he saw on the buses and on the streets of Harlem. While he found the lack of discipline and unruly behaviour in the classroom impossible to handle, he was affectionately tolerant of their naive questions about Africa, accounting for their militant attitudes towards whites as a legitimate response to the 'American refusal to accept the Black into the mainstream of its development'.[102] In all probability, the experience in the school must have made him reflect on the respect for teachers back in Cape Town and on his own high standing at his school as well as in the broader community.

The return to South Africa in June 1966, after an absence of a year, was once more marked by a sinking feeling at the depressing realities of home. Despite having a master's degree from an internationally acclaimed university, it made no difference to his second-class status in his own country. The five-year period between Rive's return from Columbia and his departure for Oxford in August 1971 is covered in a mere three pages in his memoir, and is remembered by him as a time of dearth and death. It was, after all, the period when National Party government hegemony seemed to be beyond challenge and the struggle for a new order was at its nadir. Stephen Gray eloquently calls this most difficult period in the life of the country 'the deep freeze of high apartheid', contributing to 'the despair, darkness and disillusionment that set in on Richard from the mid sixties'.[103]

During 1967, Rive half-heartedly studied for a Bachelor of Education degree at UCT, but he was completely disillusioned with the institution, as it bowed to pressure from the Extension of Universities Education Act of 1959 to exclude all black and most coloured students and those who did attend had to have special government permission. He seemed to find comfort and purpose, however, in his teaching and the lives of his students, as well as in his involvement in sport during this time: 'I felt very close to my pupils and experienced with them the same hopes and despairs.'[104] His genuine concern for the well-being of some of his students was exemplified by the way he was touched by the tragic drowning of a young boy from his school. At the news of the death, brought to his attention by another boy at the school, he rallied to give what practical help he could. He and the boy drove to the scene of the death, an hour outside of Cape Town, so as to find out what he could. He counselled the distraught youngster along the way, and then drove all the way back to the home of the deceased to assist and console the parents. The tragedy was deepened when the boy who brought him the news of his schoolmate's death was himself killed soon thereafter in a motorcycle accident. On the death of his old patron Hughes in the same year, 1967, Rive is, however, strangely silent.

The other death that stung him was that of Arthur Nortje, in 1970. Rive had first met Nortje at Trafalgar High, where Nortje had matriculated in the same year as Rive. He was to meet Nortje again at a gathering of aspirant writers over food and wine at the Hazendal home of Cosmo Pieterse in 1963.[105] Pieterse and Rive had been at Trafalgar High at the same time and both became teachers. Pieterse, who was himself a poet and actor who later left the country for London, encouraged young aspiring writers to visit his home. Nortje was in the final year of his BA at the University of the Western Cape (UWC) and Rive's impressions of Nortje were that he was 'a squat, somewhat untidily dressed young man with a heavy and laboured accent'.[106] It was typical of Rive not only to notice the accent but to ask Nortje, almost as a put-down, if he were Afrikaans-speaking. Nortje took offence to the question and retorted: 'But I write in English. Why must you ask?' It seems, however, that the two got along and Nortje consulted Rive about some of his poetry. It is quite fascinating that Rive assumes, and seems to relish, the roles of established writer and forthright but also pedantic mentor in the relationship, doing to Nortje exactly what Jack Cope had done to him:

> We went through [the poetry] in fine detail and I was hard on him, forcing him to substantiate the use of every word he had written. Finally he threw down the sheets in anger and demanded, 'Are you for me or against?' I tried to explain that I was neither for him nor against. I was for good poetry and against bad poetry. Much of what he showed me was good but he was as capable of producing weak lines. He refused to accept my reasoned argument … to be critical of his poetry was to be critical of the man himself. He was his poetry.[107]

Rive drove Nortje home after this session and it was Nortje, not Rive, surprisingly, who spoke most of the time. As was the case with Jonker, Rive recalls that Nortjie was a very 'intense' person. There is a hint in this description of their encounter that Rive is underplaying the awe and admiration he had for Nortje's poetry, particularly by 1980, when he was composing his memoir. On a number of occasions Rive was to quote lines from Nortje in his articles and essays, in order to articulate the solitude and expectation that he felt burdened the South African writer at home and abroad.

Rive's own descriptions of his encounter with Nortje also reveals the missionary zeal with which he assisted younger writers. There were dozens of aspirant writers who showed him their fledgling attempts and he was unselfish in giving of his time, perhaps also enjoying the sense of being big brother that accompanied the exercise of mentoring. Wannenburgh testifies to this aspect of Rive as writer and friend:

> Richard ... was enthusiastic about my writing and was prepared to guide me. Whenever I completed a short story, I took it to him, and we would sit at his kitchen table while he went through it in fine detail, asking questions and making suggestions, sometimes for hours at a stretch.[108]

The years after Rive's return from Columbia were also marked by a dearth of creative work and he remarks that 'I continued writing although my output was a mere trickle'.[109] He managed to write three articles for *Contrast* in 1967, but nothing after that until much later, in 1972. Part of the reason for the block he experienced in the late 1960s must have been the suffocating air generated by the rule of terror, which banned both the possession and/or distribution of local and international writing that was even vaguely critical of the regime. The deaths of Jonker and Nakasa were metonymic of these dark times. Also, Rive's own feeling of being firmly in his middle years, of having achieved much yet often being acutely lonely, were surely debilitating factors which prevented him from working productively. If there were any stage when Rive might have regretted not going into exile, it was probably in these few trying years. In an interview with Chris van Wyk, Rive comments on this period between 1966 and 1971:

> *1966 was the moment of truth in South Africa for black literature when all writers in exile were banned ... And no objection from anybody in South Africa ... South African Literature became White by law. Now between '66 and '71 nothing happened. There were exactly two writers left in the country – black writers – James Matthews and myself. The rest had gone into exile or into prison. And James was not writing and I was so disillusioned – books banned, surveillance and all the pressures that work on one in South Africa – that I went into the academic stream and I kind of collected degrees and lectured and wrote books about writers instead of writing myself you know, not books actually, articles. I did a lot of polemical writing more than anything else. This might have gone on indefinitely if it weren't for 'Sounds of a Cowhide Drum' ... In '71 the breakthrough came with Mtshali's not very good poetry and Nadine Gordimer's over-flattering introduction to it ... '71 was the end of the protest school of writings.*[110]

While Rive and Matthews might not have been writing in this difficult period, they were as engaged as ever with the world, with other writers and their times, finding ways of keeping their minds alive through getting together, laughing, smoking, drinking, arguing about ideas, books and their own work. Often younger writers and artists were initiated into the world of ideas and books at these gatherings. George Hallett's photograph of the two writers at one such session at Selous Court in the late 1960s captures a spirited and animated moment. Hallett recalls:

> *I witnessed long passionate debates about the characters that*

James Matthews and Richard Rive at Rive's Selous Court flat in Claremont, Cape Town, late 1960s (photographer: George Hallett)

appeared in their short stories. James would accuse Richard of creating characters that were simply mouth-pieces for Richard, and therefore not authentic. Richard on the other hand would respond by trouncing James' lack of knowledge of the English language. After much mud-slinging over glasses of red wine, we would finally depart for the Cape Flats in a festive mood.[111]

This period was filled with both despair and hope. It was about this time that Rive felt the need to 'round off [his] formal education',[112] which would lead him to apply to do a doctorate. Initially he applied to King's College, Cambridge, which turned him down, and then to a number of colleges at Oxford, with Magdalen College being his first choice. Clearly piqued at being turned down by Cambridge, Rive's letter of application to Magdalen is overly assertive and melodramatic in tone:

Because I am a brown South African … to get the qualifications I have has been no mean feat. I grew up in the slums, won

*scholarships from the age of twelve, won awards to continue
further studies and finally received an American Fulbright
Fellowship. It is out of the question I think to receive direct
assistance from the state, as my colour excludes me ... Thus I will
be doomed to spend the rest of my life eking out a meaningless
existence here trying to teach a bit of literature at grade school
whereas I know I have the ability (and proved it) not only to
do meaningful research, but to play an important role at any
university ... where African Literature will be taught.*[113]

In his application form to Oxford University, he stated that his
area of research was to be 'trends in contemporary novels or
poetry in Africa in English'. He listed Philip Segal, professor in
the department of English at UCT, as one of his referees. Segal
wrote in his reference that Rive had not achieved brilliant results
in English but he studied while teaching and showed tenacity in
his academic work.[114] A more interesting and personable report,
with very astute observations about Rive's character and ability,
was by Lindy Wilson, who headed the South African Committee
on Higher Education (SACHED). SACHED at the time was a
reputable, liberal anti-apartheid institution that worked to get
non-white scholars access to higher education. Wilson wrote:

*He would be an excellent person to do a post-graduate degree
... he is obviously very knowledgeable on African writing:
possibly an even better critic than a writer (that's only my very
own opinion). He gave a lecture to the SACHED students some
time back, and it is certainly one of the best lectures I've heard
... he's someone with a good sense of humour and tells some
very funny stories against himself ... he is an unusual person to
meet in South Africa these days. But he stays because he says
he belongs.*[115]

Lindy Wilson also suggests in her report that the senior tutor
at Magdalen write to Jack Cope and Uys Krige for more information on Rive.

Magdalen offered him the position of a junior research fellow, which enabled him to fund his studies there. It is not clear, from his own account, why he made Cambridge and Oxford his first choices for the doctoral degree. The University of Leeds was then the leading institution for the study of African Literature but it did not seem to be an option. Was it the iconic reputations of Cambridge and Oxford that attracted him and would, by association, lend him the prestige he sought but was perpetually denied in his own country? As he was not certain about the specific topic of his research before he left, knowing only that he wanted to focus on African Literature, the choice of Oxford was clearly not because of the particular expertise it offered but more likely because of the iconic status of Oxford as the quintessence of a university and of Englishness. It was also close to London, where he had numerous friends and which he regarded as a second home. Still an underpaid teacher struggling to make ends meet, Rive had to appeal to the Oppenheimer Trust to cover the cost of his boat trip to England. After more than a year of working at getting into a university in the United Kingdom, he finally departed Cape Town for Southampton on the *Pendennis Castle* in the spring of 1971. It had been only nine years since he boarded a ship in the same dock to embark on his first trip overseas as a fledgling writer bursting with ambition and hope. Now he was departing as an established literary figure both in South Africa and abroad, keen to round off his formal education with one of the highest possible qualifications and at one of the world's most prestigious universities; yet he remained a mere 'non-white', an *Untermensch* in the land he was leaving.

Part III: *1970 – 1980*

Chapter 5

By 1970, Rive's last major output of short stories had been in 1963, with the publication of *African Songs*. He published a short story called 'Andrew' in 1968,[1] but it was ineffectual and really an extract from his novel *Emergency*. In 1969, the short story 'Middle Passage' was published in *Contrast* magazine. A few years later, Rive turned the story into a play, under the title *Make Like Slaves* and it was selected by Wole Soyinka, Lewis Nkosi and Martin Esslin for first prize in the 1971 second BBC African Service competition for new half-hour plays. Together with the eight other finalists, chosen from more than six hundred entries, it was included in Gwyneth Henderson's *African Theatre: Eight Prize-Winning Plays for Radio* in 1973. *Make Like Slaves* was produced as a BBC radio play and aired before the end of 1972. Perhaps this work reached the greatest number of Africans on the continent and around the world, given the popularity of radio and the BBC African Service at this time. English-speaking listenership for the BBC External Services (then the World Service) was, in the early 1970s, around 28 million listeners who tuned in at least once a week, and possibly half that number was in Africa.[2]

The play was a two-hander, with the main characters called 'He' and 'She', and set in Cape Town, where a white woman is rehearsing a play about slavery in the black township of Nyanga. The play is intended for an international audience and repeats the stereotype of the African as exotic primitive. The woman feels she is not getting through to the black cast and seeks the help of the coloured writer, whom she feels would be closer to their world. He is irritated by the bleeding-heart liberalism of the woman but reveals his own isolation as a 'brown' man from the black community; he is more familiar with London and Paris than he is with his neighbours in Nyanga. Soyinka had this to say about the play: 'It's a study of relationships, not only between the two characters, but between each character and the social reality each thought He or She understood. And the process of continuous shifting of this relationship I think was very subtly handled.'[3] Even Lewis Nkosi seemed to be in a generous mood, complimenting the quality of the writing and talking of the vivid and vivacious language.[4] Rereading this play more than twenty years after the start of the transition to a new order in South Africa, one is struck by how hackneyed the theme of the impenetrable external and internal apartheid boundaries has become on the one hand, but on the other how frighteningly pertinent and present these divisions still are for most South Africans.

Rive had been interested in the theatre and dramatic script form from his student days at Hewat. All four of his student pieces in the Hewat magazine of 1951 were dramatic dialogues. Critics have noted the dramatic quality of his short stories and his frequent use of dialogue and music to convey character and situation. He was also an amateur actor, as a 1962 letter to Langston Hughes delights in recounting:

> *Did Sylvia Titus write to you that she played Lady Macbeth in a Drama Centre production in which I played Ross? It was great fun and we crowded the city hall with Whites who came to hear Non-whites who spoke impeccable English and even knew what they were speaking about. We found it amusing. One critic said that after 5 minutes one accepts these dusky Scotsmen as genuine. I ask you.*[5]

Rive loved being on stage and he constantly performed off stage.

The success of *Make Like Slaves* was only to emerge once Rive was at Oxford. At home in 1970, while making his initial approaches to study overseas, he wrote a story which won him the *Argus* newspaper's Writer of the Year award. 'The Visits' was the first new short story Rive had published since the early 1960s. It was far more muted in its protest than any of his previous works and much more reflective in tone. Like his novel, it was clearly semi-autobiographical. While the short story can be read as a protest at the manner in which apartheid dehumanises, divides and alienates, it is also possible through a queer reading to see it as an intensely personal reflection on frustrated, unspoken desire and unresolved inner turmoil. The story marks a turning point in Rive's writing life – it marks the end of his protest writing and sees a shift towards greater interiority in the main character. It is also one of the last short stories he was to write, suggesting he felt the need to explore other genres such as the novel and dramatic scripts, as a new mood started to take hold of South Africa.

'The Visits' tells of a teacher in his forties who shares his flat with a male student. A black woman beggar visits the flat a number of times to ask for food. The protagonist is wracked by a sense of intrusion and the need to get rid of the woman but also feels guilty about his hostility towards the indigent woman and begins to empathise with her and her plight. The woman finally stops coming after the young student, who is more often than not away from the flat visiting his girlfriends, frogmarches her from the property. The story is marked by a pervasive sense of loneliness and an inner emptiness in the life of the protagonist that verges on despair. It ends with the student once again disappearing and the protagonist alone in his study 'slumped down at the desk. He felt like crying but couldn't … [and] sat at his desk just staring in the dark.'[6]

Two aspects of the story are striking: firstly, the social chasm between the world of the teacher (who can be read as either 'coloured' or 'white' but who is clearly not 'black') and the alien and impoverished world of the black woman. This existential gap becomes a moral dilemma for the protagonist, who largely resists her presence but also at times desires to help her, strikingly like the relationship between the two characters in *Make Like Slaves*. The teacher is confronting his internalisation of the divisions wrought by apartheid and exploitation, but is impotent to effect any change to inner or outer relations, except to offer fleeting yet finally ineffectual charity. Secondly, unlike any of the earlier short stories, which in varying degrees ended with some measure of hope or redemption, here there is only 'a staring in the dark'. This would be the more conventional reading of 'The Visits'. There is another possible interpretation of the story, one that is about intense loneliness and unspoken homosexual longing, about the silences in the text.

Queer readings of many of Rive's texts assume that there is something in the work that could not be said directly. Such readings often rely on such symptomatic reading, speculating about textual patterns or gaps that seem to be indicative of deeper psychological conflicts in Rive, which he suppresses and deliberately obscures or, perhaps, (un)intentionally encodes into a story.

In an alternative symptomatic reading, along the lines suggested by Allon White in *The Uses of Obscurity*,[7] the story becomes a self-inscribed narrative of the utter loneliness and near despair at the loveless existence Rive feels he leads at this point in his life. The protagonist, like Rive in 1970, is middle-aged (Rive was by this time forty, the teacher in the story is forty-five) and filled with a weariness about his aging, about his work as a teacher and the meaning of literature in his life. He is, in his eyes now, 'Mr Chips. Old at forty-five.'[8] The South African poetry anthology he is reading elicits the comment 'what a boring bore'. However, there is an unspoken dilemma running parallel to that of his concern for and alienation from the black woman – the relationship between the teacher and the student lodger.

Like 'The Woman', initially the student is not given a name but merely called 'The Student', and the very first sentence of the story inextricably entangles the two characters, inviting comparisons as to their various meanings in the life of the protagonist: 'It was on the evening The Student had gone out that The Woman had first arrived.'[9] Unlike the woman, though, the student is never named and, even more than the woman, becomes a presence by virtue of persistent withdrawal and erasure by the seemingly dominant theme of the woman's visits. It is thus arguably the young man's absence, more than the presence of the black woman, which leads to the feeling of despair in the teacher at the end. The numerous arrivals of the woman beggar are paralleled by the numerous departures of the student from the flat. The teacher is 'annoyed' by the woman coming to the door and is equally 'annoyed' at what seems to be the sudden and loud departure of the student. The sound of the student departing on his motorbike is on one occasion referred to as 'the tortured whine as the Honda gathered speed up the driveway'. 'Tortured' is quite possibly the unspoken emotion of the teacher, for the young man, whether present or absent, is the real cause for the protagonist's unspeakable emotional abyss:

> How vacant the place sounded without The Student. How empty when he wasn't there. How empty when he was there. A different kind of emptiness.
>
> Impossible to speak to him any longer. He was too … too physical. Throwing his weight and looks around. Girls, the telephone and the Honda. Looks and muscle.[10]

In this passage, the ambiguous placing of the fragment

'throwing his weight and looks around' more evidently refers to the student's relation to girls, but also possibly refers to his relation to the protagonist. And, how could he use his 'looks' to manipulate the teacher without there being some suggestion of homoerotic meaning? But this 'different kind of emptiness', the notion that there is some unfulfilled homoerotic attraction towards the student, is left unexplored, merely hinted at again in a similar fashion at later points in the story. This reading of 'The Visits' thus suggests that, in addition to the more obvious subject of racial and class divide and attendant moral dilemma for the protagonist, there is a narrative of thwarted homosexual desire and despair encrypted in this story.

On his departure by ship for Oxford in August 1971, Rive must have felt enormous relief at the prospect of respite from the conditions at home. He describes himself as 'overwrought' and had been given a large number of pills and medicine by a doctor friend to help him through the next few months.[11] His first two months at Oxford, September and October of 1971, were, however, filled with a yearning for home and depression associated with dislocation and the ever-present burden of the demanding doctoral work that lay ahead. To combat these feelings, Rive worked on *Make Like Slaves*.

Rive lived in rooms at Longwall Annex in Oxford, adjacent to Magdalen College. He soon took to the customs and aura of Oxford in a way that many other students from South Africa, feeling alienated from the town and institutional ethos, did not.[12] He delighted in being part of Oxford's arcane, dramatic rituals and eccentric characters:

> *I took quite easily to most Oxford customs. I enjoy eccentricities and eccentrics, and Oxford had enough of both. I liked the don who mumbled Latin to himself on his cycle as he creaked down the High [Street]. I enjoyed the sight of the don who hurried past me near Queen's, his gown flapping while he exclaimed to*

*all who cared to hear him, 'They nearly all failed palaeography
again.'*[13]

One reads in these affectionately satirical depictions of the eccentric academics a possible reflection of Rive's own playful yet
authentic vision of himself as the witty, wise and unconventional
teacher – the stereotypical Oxford don. While often he gently
parodied the convoluted and euphemistic idiom of Oxford, he
loved to use this register himself. By adopting the idiom, he
became a habitué of Oxford and an embodiment of Englishness.
But because of the overly performative nature of his mimicry,
he could also simultaneously be mocking the selfsame idiom,
knowing that he would never be entirely accepted as 'English' or
'Oxford' because of his skin colour.

Rive immersed himself in life as an Oxonian because he was
finally able to study at an institution where, he assumed, he
would be seen as a student, rather than as a black student. Yet
one of the most striking memories of his stay in Oxford, which
he highlights in detail both in his memoir and in an article called
'Four South Africans Abroad', reflects on the manner in which the
resistant subjects of a racist social order internalise the colour-
conscious mindset and value-laden assumptions of racism. The
incident that he reflects on in both these texts occurred when he
felt himself treated shabbily by a young female English waitress
at an expensive restaurant he had wandered into by mistake. He
assumes the cold treatment is because of the colour of his skin,
but it turns out that she sees him as just another 'Oxford toff'
who 'speaks posh' and she is tired of her treatment at the hands
of his 'class'.[14] Even armed with his obdurate ideology of non-
racialism, Rive was not immune to the insidious infiltration of
racialised assumptions.

While this frank self-critique is quite dramatically revealing
of the toxicity of racism, what is as interesting about Rive's
accounts of this incident is the existential ambivalence about

belonging and exclusion that he does not himself comment on, but which is evident in the texts. He senses on entering the restaurant that it is in a league beyond his means, but he stays and deliberately orders the most expensive items – a retort to any notion that he might be out of place. He also raises his voice to object to the young waitress's treatment of him, but does so 'adopting my most Magdalen College accent', which, given that Rive arrived in Oxford with his already pronounced Oxbridge accent, must have verged on the melodramatic. The use of this accent is again an assertion, both for the sake of the listener but perhaps equally for his own sense of self, of being an intimate, an insider, not, as his colour might suggest, an 'alien'. He desperately wanted to belong, but belonging always remained elusive.

During Rive's stay at Oxford he often made trips into London, staying with friends. He most often slept at the Camden Town residence of Albert Adams and his partner Ted Glennon. Adams had immigrated to London in 1953 and had subsequently made a name for himself as a South African artist living abroad. He remembered that it was during Rive's period at Oxford that they consolidated their friendship. According to Adams, Rive had many acquaintances in London whom he often visited. He recalled a particular incident about Oxford related to him by Rive, which illustrates the latter's pretensions to being a 'gentleman of culture', but also shows his uncompromising sense of right and wrong. It also reveals the way in which those close to him tell such anecdotes – with great affection for Rive and a simultaneous shaking of the head in disbelief:

> *We saw him fairly often. In fact I think it's that time when Richard had friends, he often met them here ... he had many acquaintances and friends in London and he used to invite them and we used to have a meal together here ... and I do remember one occasion, this difficult Richard ... Richard came down, and he was in such a mood, he was so angry, and*

he said that he had been to a restaurant in Oxford and had ordered fish, and they brought him the fish, but the cutlery wasn't fish cutlery ... and Richard would not eat ... and I remember the little argument between the two of us, and I said, 'Well Richard, today they don't really use fish cutlery anymore.' The reason was the metal which [the] cutlery had been made of in the past, you know, somehow retained the smell of fish. So that's why they did have some cutlery or other. 'Oh no,' Richard said, and he [went] into [a] scream and how he, you know, told the waitress where he comes from this is not the practice – they had separate cutlery for fish! 'I would not eat the meal!' and he stormed out of the restaurant. But that was typical of Richard.[15]*

Rive's application to King's College, Cambridge, had not been successful because the college claimed it did not have the expertise to supervise research on African Literature. Rive's acceptance by Magdalen College was not without qualification either. The college was concerned that, like King's College, it did not have the expertise to supervise Rive's proposed research in the area of African Literature. It felt he might have to work under the rubric of 'twentieth-century literature', which he was reluctant but not unwilling to do. The college administration had received a number of references (besides those from Philip Segal and Lindy Wilson) about Rive's abilities, including a very favourable one from Mary Renault (who signed using her real name, Mary Challans). However, possibly because Rive's master's degree from Columbia was in Education rather than a research degree in Literature, Magdalen recommended that Rive register for a Probationary Bachelor of Literature (Prob B Litt) and not a PhD, which is what he finally did.

Under the initial supervision of JL Fuller, Rive embarked on his research in 'twentieth-century literature'. Fuller's progress report on 15 December 1971, however, indicated that Rive

had clearly by then embarked on a very specific study of Olive
Schreiner and was making good progress. Rive was guided by
what he initially thought was a precondition at Oxford for doing
literary research – the writer needed to be long dead. He then
considered working on either Olive Schreiner or Pauline Smith,
but in the end chose Schreiner. It is clear that Rive came to Oxford with no clear idea of what he wanted to research within
the general area of his interest, African Literature. Nine years
later, reflecting on the choice of Schreiner in an interview with
Chris van Wyk, Rive responds to Van Wyk's question, 'And your
passion for Olive Schreiner?' in the following forthright terms:

> *Ah, there's no passion at all! I had to get a degree so I decided
> to do Olive Schreiner. She was a remarkable woman, absolutely
> out of her time. I was also interested in that period of South
> African politics and the period in England when she was
> writing. It was the Oscar Wilde, George Bernard Shaw kind of
> pre-Bloomsbury. My favourite period in literature.*[16]

Rive was possibly tailoring his reply to fit the more radical and
less traditional audience of the magazine *Wietie 2*, which Van
Wyk had just launched. He probably had a genuine interest in
Schreiner's work and ideas and greatly admired her novel *The
Story of an African Farm*. As Stephen Gray has argued, there
were affinities between the two writers:

> *Like Olive Schreiner … with whom he empathized sufficiently
> to devote the middle years of his work to her, he was a subtle
> public manoeuvrer, steering conference agendas and literary
> gossip circles alike back to basic issues: human rights; integrity;
> down with deception.*[17]

In late 1971, Rive explored the holdings on Schreiner at various archives and wrote to numerous institutions, including
the Jagger Library at the University of Cape Town (UCT),
the South African Public Library, the Cory Library for
Historical Research at Rhodes University, the University of the

Witwatersrand Library and the Cradock Municipal Library, to ascertain what resources they had on Schreiner. He made good progress in these initial stages of the research and on 1 May 1972 he was admitted to the full B Litt. This was under the temporary supervision of Terry Eagleton of Wadham College, who had taken over from Fuller. Eagleton would continue in this capacity until someone with the appropriate expertise on Schreiner could conduct the supervision.

On 19 June 1972 Eagleton was replaced by Ridley Beeton, who was based at the University of South Africa (Unisa). Eagleton's hand-over report suggests that Rive was working well and making progress: 'He has an interesting topic and is researching it assiduously. Apart from some minor stylistic problems . . . there is no reason why he shouldn't produce a useful piece of research.'[18] One of Beeton's first suggestions to Rive was that he look into the Schreiner holdings at the University of Texas and he recommended that Rive contact Professor Bernth Lindfors there.[19] Lindfors was a founding member of the African Literature Association (ALA) and also founding editor of the *Journal of African Literature*. He was to become a useful adviser to Rive on his Schreiner research and also a good friend.

In preparation for the research on Schreiner back in South Africa, Rive wrote to Guy Butler at the department of English at Rhodes University. Butler replied with some very useful suggestions and invited him to visit the department. Butler pointed Rive to Schreiner's early diaries, which could not be traced and which Cronwright Schreiner had used in his biography of his wife. He also suggested that Rive visit the municipal library at Cradock (Rive had already written to the library in November 1972) and that they should climb Buffelskop to Schreiner's grave together, which they did when Rive went to the Eastern Cape during his research visit to South Africa. Rive had put on quite a bit of weight by this time and was also smoking a lot. One of the first things he did once they reached the tomb was to light up a cigarette. They were accompanied on this pilgrimage by Athol Fugard and Don Maclennan. Butler told Rive he had discovered that the Albany Museum had 'a whole cupboard full of Schreiner material, as yet unlisted'.[20]

Rive was given leave of absence for the last term of 1972 and the first term of 1973 to return to South Africa to do research. Magdalen gave him a generous £300 to support the visit. He left Oxford for the Cape as early as June 1972 and was to return only in April 1973.

When Rive was researching the Schreiner holdings at the Cradock library in 1972, a quintessential South African incident occurred. A curious farmer, obviously disturbed by the anomalous black presence at the whites-only municipal library, engaged in a conversation with him and asked where he was from. The farmer's assumption was clearly that Rive was an Englishman and Rive of course picked this up. Rive then deliberately switched to Afrikaans to claim his local District Six (and thus obviously non-white) identity, despite what his accent signified. He was able to assert distinct identities of himself, some of them quite contradictory, when and where he deemed it strategic and desirable, either for his own imaginings of who he was, or to skew the way others should perceive him. It is remarkable and certainly not out of character that he had the guts to enter the library in the first place! But it was not at Cradock he was to make the breakthrough that was to come.

While on leave from Oxford to do his archival work, Rive also took on a temporary teaching position at Athlone High School for a few months. The extra money he earned was welcome. He had taught at the school for a very short stint in the early 1960s. The reason for the brief change of high school then and his subsequent return to South Peninsula is not clear, however. On this occasion, there was probably a need for a senior English and

Latin teacher at Athlone High at that time and he offered to fill the gap. One of the students in his Standard 8 class at Athlone High, Clive Slingers, had Rive as his class teacher as well as for English and Latin. Slingers remembers Rive for his 'pomposity, his foibles, sense of humour and imposing character'.[21] He says Rive made one of the boys translate a Latin piece on the board, knowing the boy was fumbling and making up the translation, but forcing him to continue, while passing sarcastic comments such as 'Your mother doesn't love you' and 'Have you no ambition?' Slingers says Rive read aloud numerous passages to them from classics such as works by John Steinbeck and from his own stories and novel. He distinctly remembers Rive reading them his story 'Resurrection'. Slingers claims that of all the teachers he had, Rive is the most memorable. He had clearly not lost his touch while away studying.

His field trip had yielded a fair amount in quality and quantity, so in a letter dated 18 March 1973 he confidently suggested to the tutor for graduate studies that the title for his PhD should be 'Olive Schreiner (1855–1920): A Biographical and Critical Study'. In Beeton's supporting letter of 13 April 1973 he testifies to the quantity of material but says he has not seen much of Rive's writing yet.[22] Finally, on 27 June 1973, with only a year to go at Oxford, Rive succeeded in changing his registration to a PhD.

It was only after Rive returned to Oxford in April 1973 that he made a breakthrough in his research on Schreiner. In the section of his memoir where he talks about this work, he frames it by making reference to the large amount of luck that came his way, allowing him to make an important contribution to South African literary historiography. 'While I was doing my research in England and South Africa,' he wrote, 'there occurred, luckily for me, a series of propitious and serendipitous events.'[23] While visiting Rive at Oxford, Jack Cope mentioned to him, as Beeton had done, that Schreiner archival material was said to be found at the University of Texas. In response to Rive's query to the University of Texas, Bernth Lindfors sent him microfilm copies of the hundreds of Schreiner letters, which included letters between her and Havelock Ellis. In 1972, during his South African research visit, another chance meeting with Cronlyn Cronwright (daughter of Schreiner's husband Samuel from his second marriage after Schreiner's death) allowed him to gain access to more information and documents. But the most significant find, a result of the series of uncannily lucky breaks he describes in his memoir, he considered to be the access he gained to the personal correspondence between Schreiner and Karl Pearson, with whom Schreiner had had a close relationship. Pearson's daughter had perchance heard Rive's BBC play on radio, which she liked, and also read about the author and his research on Schreiner in the BBC *Radio Times*. She decided to write to Rive, inviting him to visit her in Hertfordshire to examine the Pearson-Schreiner letters she had in her possession. These letters added valuable new knowledge to Schreiner scholarship, especially about the envisioned ending to her unfinished novel, *From Man to Man*, and about her life in London between 1886 and 1889. It was this find that helped Rive to get his doctorate.

A number of other close friends and acquaintances visited Rive while he was at Oxford, tempering his initial feelings of being homesick and depressed, and also giving input into his work. The Manuels visited him at Magdalen College, where Rive smuggled Hazel into his rooms, much to her amusement. Businessman Latief Parker and Non-European Unity Movement (NEUM) stalwart Hosea Jaffe, close friends and comrades of Victor Wessels, spent much time in discussion with Rive. According to Parker, Jaffe's in-depth knowledge of South African history, from an anti-colonial and anti-imperialist perspective, helped Rive to develop his critique of Schreiner's liberalism.[24]

Historian Bill Nasson, together with his friend and fellow South African Dinesh Ramjee, also visited Rive in Oxford in 1973 or 1974. Ramjee had been a student of Rive's at South Peninsula High and remained good friends with his old high school teacher, who had asked his ex-pupil to come and spend a weekend in Oxford. Ramjee had immigrated to the United Kingdom, and Nasson, who had been at Livingstone High School, was a student at Hull University, reading English Literature and History at the time. Nasson had, in fact, met Rive before at some of the Saturday lunches at the Rouwkoop Road home of Lindy and Francis Wilson in the Cape Town suburb of Rondebosch. The Wilsons were liberal intellectuals and anti-apartheid activists associated with UCT. Nasson had, in the early 1970s, been a student at the South African Committee for Higher Education Trust (SACHED) where Rive had also done some part-time teaching. Lindy Wilson – later a film-maker – had been its director at the time. The College was a post-school correspondence education centre that provided an alternative education through the University of London and external qualifications for black students who wished to avoid segregated government university education in South Africa at the time. At these lively lunches, Nasson recalls Rive 'holding forth' as they ate their Royco soup and bread, and drank the cheap wine that was a common staple in those days.

When Nasson and Ramjee visited Rive at Oxford a few years later, the older man was still holding forth. Rive arranged their accommodation in the Annex at Magdalen College. It was winter and cold, and Rive, draped in his Magdalen scarf, in the car that he had bought, took them on a day tour to Warwick Castle and to Churchill's birthplace, Blenheim Palace. He insisted they also see Holman Hunt's famous painting *The Light of the World*, which Rive greatly admired and which was housed in the splendid chapel at Keble College. At Keble, Rive continued to hold forth in his usual serious and mocking tone, making disparaging comments about the red-brick, late-nineteenth century architecture (clearly nothing like the wonderfully medieval Magdalen was, of course, the implication). As they were walking in the grounds, Rive spotted fellow South African and Rhodes scholar then at Keble, Willem Landman, who approached them and said to the visitors, '*Jirre, Keble is 'n kak plek*' (Jesus, Keble is a shitty place), to which Rive responded reprimandingly, in that fulsome affected manner he loved to perform, that Landman should *not* be speaking in Afrikaans in that place.[25]

On 18 February 1974 Beeton submitted a progress report that indicated substantial progress with the writing of sections of Rive's dissertation and, by the end of the same month, Rive wrote to the tutor, saying he would complete the work by March. He also requested financial help for typing and binding and was given £75 to this end. Working furiously, he eventually finished by 21 April, which was when he submitted his dissertation for final examination. The crucial viva (the oral examination) took place only a month later, in May.

On hearing he had been awarded his PhD, Rive was ecstatic, reaching the zenith on the trajectory to educate himself, a path that he had embarked on when he was still a teenager in the District, against daunting odds. In his 'dark suit, gown, mortarboard and white bow-tie', he immediately called on friends John Khan and Willem Landman to celebrate with him, shouting, 'I'm coming in for sherry. I'm a bloody Doctor of Philosophy now.'[26]

On his return to Cape Town later in 1974, again by ship, he went to see his sister Georgina to proudly proclaim (as he would to many others), in the typical Rive pose when he was pleased with himself – his thumbs tucked under his armpits and fists campily limp in front of his strutting chest, lips pouting – that he was 'a doctor of literature, *not* of medicine'.[27] His pride at his Oxford achievement would also be reflected in the way he peppered his Selous Court flat with Oxford memorabilia and in frequently wearing his Oxford T-shirt. But as on every other sojourn out of his home country, his elation at what he had achieved and his determination to go back home were deflated by the dispiriting reality of the situation in South Africa:

> *I was returning to South Africa because that was where I belonged. I had no idea what to expect, whether there had been meaningful changes or not. I certainly did not expect any preferential treatment. In spite of my achievements and qualifications I was still an unenfranchised Black suffering under a policy of racial discrimination, born and nurtured in a notorious slum in a beautiful city in a bigoted country.*[28]

Despite this, returning as a doctoral graduate of Oxford, he could use his educational status and defiantly see himself as 'a member of one of the largest, most exclusive and influential old-boy networks in the world'.

Chapter 6

The South Africa Rive found when he disembarked was markedly different in mood to the one he had left three years earlier. The iron grip of the Nationalists had started to weaken and the first signs of a widespread resurgence of both organised and spontaneous resistance to the state had appeared on a number of fronts. Armed resistance to colonial and imperial rule had intensified on the southern African subcontinent and elsewhere – America was in retreat in Vietnam and armed struggle, particularly in the Portuguese colonies, was intensifying in Africa. In South Africa, the working class, consolidated by the rapid industrialisation of the 1960s, solidified into a number of militant union formations that began to rattle the cage of National Party rule.

On the literary front, the new mood of defiance and self-assertion was expressed through the work of a new generation of poets who came to be known as the 'Soweto poets' – Mbuyiseni (Oswald) Mtshali, Mongane Wally Serote, Sipho Sepamla and Mafika Pascal Gwala. Rive describes their work in a way that both connects them to his generation but also recognises their independent contribution: 'Their writings were as strident and declamatory as those of the Protest School of the 1950s and early 1960s, but this time the form was different, poetry as opposed to prose.'[29] *Writing Black* recounts his meetings with each of the Soweto poets in terms that reflect his admiration for their work, particularly for Sepamla and Gwala, as well as revealing his sense of excitement at the growing family of black writers in the country. The title of Rive's memoir is an echo of both the assertive mood of the work of these poets and the growing influence of the Black Consciousness Movement.

After resuming his normal working life, Rive continued to be active in school sports and it was in this regard that Alf Wannenburgh contacted him during this period. As a journalist for the *Sunday Times*, Wannenburgh had been asked to edit a page reporting on 'coloured' sport, as the newspaper had until then depicted only white sporting events. Rive agreed to help and, according to Wannenburgh, organised a number of his former pupils to gather sporting results and match reports. However, Rive insisted on having a weekly column that often raised questions of sport and politics, which the conservative editors disliked. They put pressure on Wannenburgh to cut Rive's column. This caused a break in their friendship, recalled by Wannenburgh in his memoir of Rive:

> *Inevitably there was a showdown with Richard, who arrived at my home one Sunday morning, demanding to know why I hadn't used his column. Naïve about the workings of newspapers, he brushed aside my explanations and, insisting that it was a case of interfering with editorial independence, broke with the* Sunday Times *– and with me.*[30]

What to Wannenburgh was naivety was to Rive a matter of principle. Rive could be a formidable adversary in an argument or conflict, not baulking at confrontation, standing by what he believed to be right and just, even if it meant ending a friendship. But on occasion 'principle' was imbricated with ego and self-promotion. Having agreed to write for such a 'separatist' sports page, Rive must have strategised that he could use the opportunity to make comments on sporting issues and, inevitably, on the political aspects of sport at the time. His profile as a writer and columnist would, at the same time, be raised in the most widely read newspaper in the country.

During late 1974, his final few months at South Peninsula High, he became mentor to a UCT student-teacher, Maeve Heneke, who was doing her teacher training at the school. He had previously met Heneke through Daphne and Victor Wessels. Both Rive and Heneke used to visit the fiery and articulate Victor to keep him company during his banning and confinement to his house in the early 1970s, as did many other young intellectuals fascinated by Victor's razor-sharp political acumen and his astounding knowledge of history, culture and politics, as well as his articulation of NEUM positions on current affairs. Heneke had first met Rive at the house of another set of his friends, Waxie and Tooti Daniels, when she was a fifteen-year-old teenager. Waxie Daniels used to teach with Rive at South Peninsula High and, like Rive, was noted for his interest in literature and amateur theatre and for his affected manner of speaking. What Heneke remembers quite vividly of this encounter was how Rive responded to her polite and conversation-making question to him about a new novel by a writer called Wilbur Smith, 'Have you read *When the Lion Feeds*?' His reply came swiftly: 'Yes, and it's complete rubbish!'[31] This lack of decorum, especially to a teenager, was a manner not unlike that of Rive's high school guru and teacher, Ben Kies, who would be ruthlessly honest, no matter what the feelings of the recipient of the comment. Yet, at the same time, such grandstanding and comments made a lasting impression on those who encountered him. Despite her initial put-down by Rive, Heneke, who became an impressive teacher herself, grew to be a close and admiring friend. She remembers the camaraderie between Richard and Victor, noticing that 'he seemed a very different person when he was around Victor and Daphne'. During these visits to the home of Daphne and Victor Wessels, Rive 'always had to leave at I think it was quarter to eleven, as there was someone he used to go and fetch, and he was to leave bang on the dot'. Who was Rive fetching at that hour, and so regularly?

During her practice-teaching stint under Rive's tutelage,

Heneke had the chance to observe closely and critically his engagement with his students:

> He took pride not so much in the achievements of the very bright students he taught, but he was over the moon at about that time [because] he got a so-called gang leader, who was in one of his classes ... to write a poem, and he was so proud of this ... that's what made me warm even more to the man, the pleasure he took in one of his students' achievements.

Others have different memories of Rive, reflecting the very different reactions to him as a teacher. One of the students in his Standard 8 class, Val Preteceille (née Visagie), has very mixed memories of his influence and temperament, saying that he instilled in her a lifelong love of literature and the English language but she also thought he bullied certain children and she was angered by the way he treated some.[32] Heneke accounts for the perception some had of his being hard on certain children by saying that she was 'not entirely sure he would have been aware of how other people might be responding.'[33] Another of his South Peninsula students from the early 1970s claims Rive fondled and touched him against his will and, despite the fact that he told a few adults about the incident at the time, nothing was done about it.[34] The tenor of the times, which encouraged respect for figures of authority such as teachers, and the absence of greater legal standing for children's rights meant that adults, even parents, would often dismiss such claims by young adults. This claim, that Rive forced himself on young men or teenage boys, was not an isolated case, but seemed to have happened on at least one other occasion.

It is not clear whether it was this last incident – hinted at by Rive's close friend Albert Adams – or another one that almost got Rive into trouble. But from what Adams says, it is evident that Rive could be relentless if he liked a young man:

> He was interested in young men, and beautiful young men – that

was one criterion, that they had to be very beautiful. And he was very, very persistent because I know stories of his, you know, of his persistence in pursuing a young man that later on almost got him into trouble. In fact I think it most probably did get him in some kind of trouble. It was all kept quiet, it was all hushed up.[35]

Others who were taught by Rive found him, as Carol Abrahamse and Val Preteceille did, an inspiration. One such student was George Hallett, the now internationally renowned photographer. Hallett was a student at South Peninsula and it was Rive, he claims, that set him on the path to becoming an artist. He found Rive's love of the English language and of literature infectious and, coming as he did from an Afrikaans-speaking family, he wanted to speak English like Rive. Rive's pronunciation, while sounding affected to some, was to the young Hallett the model of Englishness, and he asked his teacher how he could improve his manner of speaking the language. Rive advised him to learn bits of *The Tempest* by heart, which Hallett duly did, speaking 'Full fathom five thy father lies' into the howling southeaster wind on the beach at Hout Bay, where he lived with his fisherfolk grandparents. The first photograph in Hallett's collection of striking images of writers, *Portraits of African Writers*, is of James Matthews and Richard Rive in animated conversation at Rive's Selous Court flat (see Chapter 4).[36]

After his return from Oxford, Rive took up a senior lectureship in English at Hewat Training College sometime in 1975. He was to remain at Hewat for the next fourteen years, until his death in 1989. Taking up a lectureship at his alma mater, where some of those who taught him were still on the staff, must have been cause for pride and excitement, especially returning there as *Doctor* Richard Rive. He was back in his flat at Selous Court and Gray teasingly talks of him at this time as '*Rishard* of *Saloo* Court'.[37] Gray continues in this satirical yet warm fashion:

The flat mispronunciation of his name stuck as an affectionate

joke and the block was named after the great white hunter, F.C.
Selous, no less. There, for the middle years of his existence, Richard
crouched, for Selous Court was in the 'white' area of Claremont,
off Rosmead Avenue, near the racecourse in Kenilworth. He did
live in daily dread of a Group Areas Act bureaucrat knocking on
the door. When the knock came, after all of twenty years, it did
provoke a most restrained short story, 'The Man from the Board',
his only one in years, and then about the suaveness of his eviction
on the grounds of the colour of his skin. On principle he defied
discriminatory laws, and on principle he suffered.

Rive taught English Literature and Teaching Methodology at
Hewat. When he could, he continued writing, albeit haltingly,
and continued to play an active role in sports administration.
Michael Chitter's wonderfully insightful biographical vignette
of Rive traces his recollection, as a young school athlete, of a
trip to Johannesburg in 1975 under Rive's supervision. The piece
captures the fascination and the fear Rive induced in the minds
of his young charges:

> *[Rive] was part of the teacher contingent that accompanied*
> *about one hundred Western Province athletes to the national*
> *South African Senior Schools Sports Union Athletics Cham-*
> *pionships. I was walking alongside him and five other fourteen-*
> *year-old Western Province athletes … The rule was always to*
> *remain obscure in his presence. I was always trying to prevent*
> *becoming a victim of his often stinging insults and disparaging*
> *remarks.*
>
> *He had a way with words and most of the youngsters could*
> *not avoid hanging around him – even at the risk of becoming*
> *targets. He entertained them with his vocabulary. Any feature*
> *along the wayside that reminded us of the Cape Flats would*
> *make for entertaining comedy. The secret was to remain*
> *relatively obscure, but within earshot of his antics.*[38]

He made it known and those around him felt it – he was at the top of the ladder of educational achievement; he was *Doctor* Richard Moore Rive. At Hewat, among colleagues and students alike, he became affectionately and respectfully called simply 'Doc', which mostly replaced the old 'Chokka'.

While relishing the respectability, he continued to oppose racial inequality in his work as a writer, teacher and sportsman, and relentlessly continued to undermine white superiority wherever he could. Gray tells the story, with obvious relish, of how Rive used his influence to get Gray's anthology of southern African stories, *Writers' Territory*, prescribed to schools under the Department of Coloured Affairs:

> *Thanks to Richard's influence, Coloured schools were setting it, as it was the only reader to include work by a 'non-white' South African (to wit: one of Richard's own stories – banned!) Such was the courage of educational publishers then that Richard's was the* only *Black South African writer in a heavily traditional sequence from David Livingstone through Trollope and Haggard to Kipling and Plomer. Heady, apartheid-breaking stuff in those days.[39]*

While Gray's tone exposes the conservative and compliant ethos in institutions of the time, he is also demonstrating that what, from the vantage point of almost twenty years later, seems like a puny and token gesture was in fact a radical and courageous challenge in pre-1976 South Africa. Rive continued to dare – and, at the same time of course, promote himself.

Milton van Wyk became acquainted with Rive when he was a young student at York Road Primary School and his mother, a primary school teacher, had enrolled at Hewat College in 1975 to do further in-service training. She was in one of Rive's classes and, like many older students who came to Hewat as in-service teachers doing part-time studies, she was impressed by and in awe of this accomplished, highly educated, articulate and well-travelled writer-teacher. Milton van Wyk recalls:

My mother enrolled as a student at Hewat College of Education
in Athlone to upgrade her qualifications in January of 1975
and this is where she had contact with Richard Rive ... With
the fondness for holding a captive audience, Richard would
tell his class stories of his travels and his meetings with famous
writers. I do suspect the stories were embroidered with the
Rive penchant for exaggeration. He admitted later that while
being a guest lecturer at Makerere University in Uganda he
'nearly discovered Ngũgĩ'. These stories filtered through to our
supper table, where I took an interest in this man who could tell
enchanting stories of far-away travel and interesting people.[40]

As a consequence of Van Wyk's fascination with Rive on hearing
his mother's supper-table stories, he began to read all of the
writer's work he could lay his hands on. He talks of this as his
'second acquaintance with Richard' and records his response as
follows:

It made me think about my own situation in a rather fractured
society. Through his books I learnt to read widely and critically.
I could identify with his writing because it was concerned with
events, places and characters familiar to me. Through Writing
Black *... I learnt about African and American authors like*
Luis Bernardo Honwana and Richard Wright. These authors
articulated circumstances not too unfamiliar to mine which
prompted questions concerning duplication of situations
despite physical distance.

While at Hewat in 1977, Rive made an application to become
a member of the Claremont branch of the Teachers' League
of South Africa, the branch in which his old friend Victor
Wessels was a leading member and to which another NEUM
stalwart, Richard Dudley, belonged. Maeve Heneke, who was
a very recent recruit to the branch, remembers the meeting at
which Rive's application to become a member was considered:
'Without very much discussion the consensus seemed to be that

[Rive], because of his lifestyle, shall we say, as they put it then, he was vulnerable and therefore not really desirable as a member of the League, and his application was dismissed.'[41] I was present at that branch meeting and also remember that this was one of the reasons for not accepting his membership. I had become a student member of the Claremont branch of the League in 1977 while I was doing my postgraduate teacher's diploma at UCT and had been recruited to the branch by Heneke. Besides the veiled homophobia, there were also political reservations about his suitability as a League member. While on a research field trip to South Africa in 1973 to work on what was then still his B Litt, Rive accepted an invitation from Gessler Nkondo (now known as Muxe Nkondo), an English lecturer at the Turfloop campus of the University of the North, to address his students on the topic 'The Black Experience in South African Literature.'[42] Rive had met Nkondo the previous year at Leeds University, where Nkondo was doing his second master's degree and found himself in a series of tutorials being conducted by Rive. Speaking or lecturing at the 'bush colleges', a term the League used to point to the separatist and inferior nature of non-white universities, was a contravention of the principle of non-collaboration in those days. The fact that Rive had given a lecture at Turfloop, as well as his continuous contacts with liberals through his friendships with white writers, may also have militated against his becoming a member of the League, which advocated a boycott of bush colleges by academics.

Rive must have been tremendously upset at the way the door to membership of the League, political home of those whom he most respected and revered, remained closed to him. This did not affect his friendship with League members Victor Wessels and Ivan Abrahams, now a colleague at Hewat, nor did it diminish his support for the political line taken by the League on various issues throughout his time at Hewat; and he continued to be the main distributor of the League's mouthpiece, *The Educational Journal*, on the college campus.

He was at Hewat College when the 1976 student revolts erupted in Soweto in June and two months later when the protests exploded in the Cape province. While the initial spark for the revolt by students was the imposition of Afrikaans as the language of learning, Rive makes the interesting point that in the Cape 80 per cent of the coloured population spoke Afrikaans, pointing to a more fundamental cause for the uprising. The events of 1976 marked a turning point in the history of South Africa. For the next decade, non-white schools and colleges were sites of numerous protests that reflected a larger mood of civil defiance and the demand for a new social and economic order. 'Freedom Now' was to become a popular slogan. Hewat was as affected as the surrounding high and primary schools with which the college had a close and long working relationship. Rive was thrust into the cauldron of the events at the college, especially in the two arterial roads that flanked the college – Belgravia and Thornton roads – where demonstrations as well as anarchic lootings took place. James Matthews was detained indefinitely and held in solitary confinement. James's son and Rive's godson, Jason, was shot in the leg. Rive was shocked at the depths of the anger within him when he watched the police brutally tear-gas and charge innocent pupils in an upstairs classroom at the Alexander Sinton High School just opposite Hewat:

> *Pupils came stumbling out half asphyxiated holding their burning faces. They had to run the gauntlet of flaying batons. I reacted in a manner completely irrational for me. I found myself screaming loudly. Part of me was divorced and amazed at this manifestation of hysteria which was completely foreign. I grasped the wire mesh of the fence and screamed abuse. I had no idea how I could have lost such complete control of myself.*[43]

These protests by school students continued in one form or

another until the advent of the new order in 1994 and punctuated the everyday life of black students, teachers and parents from 1976 onwards. Rive continued to be active in non-racial sport, helping to organise inter-school sport, as Hewat College was also a participant in the inter-school athletic championships in which high schools participated. He says of this period:

> After the events of 1976, I settled down into a steady routine for the next two years. I lectured in English ... wrote short stories and articles when the time and inclination allowed and worked desultorily on preparing my thesis on Olive Schreiner for publication.[44]

Rive is referring here to the publication of the first volume of Schreiner's letters, which was only to materialise almost ten years later.[45] The second volume was never published. But perhaps the description of his work as 'desultory' was an accurate reflection of his overall mood and inability in this period to produce anything that fired him or that was new. In 1977, he published with Ad Donker *Selected Writings*, a collection of already published stories from the late 1950s and early 1960s, as well as critical essays published between 1964 and 1977 in *Contrast*, *New Coin Poetry*, *The New Classic* and *English in Africa*. The collection also contained his most recent story, 'The Visits', written seven years earlier.

The publication of *Selected Writings* came, significantly, after the uprising of 1976, which ushered in an era of renewed hope for the achievement of freedom in South Africa. This publication, together with his doctorate from Oxford, cemented his reputation as a writer, critic and scholar. It was during this period of the late 1970s, according to Gray, that Rive 'repeatedly refused comfortable job-offers at the then mostly segregated University of Cape Town, feeling its Department had as yet hardly acknowledged the existence of South African authors'.[46]

Selected Writings served to consolidate Rive's achievements as a writer after a very trying period in his life and the life of South Africa, and was also perhaps symptomatic of his irrepressible drive to keep himself alive as a writer. The collection reproduced the earlier short stories such as 'Rain', 'No Room at Solitaire', 'Street Corner' and 'African Song', all first published in *African Songs* in 1963. He made very minor changes to these stories for the new publication, occasionally altering formatting, paragraphing or punctuation as well as more archaic terms to make them slightly more coherent and contemporary. 'Dagga Smoker's Dream', first published in *New Age* in 1955, was also included.

Rive's critical essays formed the bulk of *Selected Writings* since this was the form he had been working on most in the preceding decade. Unfortunately, he did not date these texts in *Selected Writings*, nor did he identify their provenance. In this regard, Jayarani Raju and Catherine Dubbeld's bibliography has been indispensable.[47] Rive had first begun publishing critical essays in 1962, writing then on ' "Colouredism" and Culture' in *Fighting Talk*. 'No Common Factor', the first of dozens of essays to appear in *Contrast*, was published in 1964. In this essay Rive takes issue with the editors of the recently published *Modern Poetry from Africa*, Gerald Moore and Ulli Beier, who define African writers as being only black African. Rive counters this with his view that 'merit, not anthropological and political interests' should be the criterion for deciding who constitutes 'African writers'. Rive claims that by ignoring the work of white African writers such as Alan Paton, Nadine Gordimer, Doris Lessing, Pauline Smith, William Plomer, Uys Krige and Jan Rabie, 'the African literary experience is incomplete'.[48] He feels that there can never be a definition of 'African Literature' as there is no common factor between African writers, all of whom are unique individuals. Anticipating the argument that all African writers are the products of the clash between colonial and anti-colonial forces, Rive responds in the essay by declaiming: 'I am certainly not the product of a clash of cultures, rather a synthesis of all experience, and the boundaries are more comprehensive than Africa and Europe.'[49] His position here reveals Rive's aggressive humanism, which asserts individual achievement beyond the limits of skin colour or historical place. His thinking demonstrates the influence of non-racialism in opposing 'race' as in any way defining identity and, as he shows in later essays, his antipathy for this reason to the ideas associated with *négritude* and with the rise in influence of black nationalism in post-independent Africa. He was, however, to rethink these ideas of the relationship between non-racialism and black subjectivity as the influence of Black Consciousness increased in the post-1976 period.

In the essay 'Senghor and Negritude', first published in 1975 in *The New Classic*, Rive traces the rise and decline of the literary phenomenon of *négritude* and focuses on the work of its main proponents, Aimé Césaire, Léon Damas and Léopold Sédar Senghor. In his assessment of its influence, hallmarks and contradictions, Rive drew heavily on the work of Es'kia Mphahlele, who, in his first and very influential edition of *The African Image*, was critical of *négritude* both as philosophy and in its literary expression. Rive's assessment of the poetry of Senghor was remarkably empathetic, more so than the view of Mphahlele, who was at that stage more condemnatory of the romanticism he identified in the work.[50] Rive, however, attacked what, from the point of view of his non-racial beliefs, he saw as the innate racism of *négritude*:

> *Négritude is by definition racist, no matter how hard Sartre tries to rescue it from this charge by means of verbal sophistry such as 'non-racist racism' … That which divorces itself accentuates difference … It implies status and hierarchy. Therefore the Black who abstracts himself and seeks protection*

within race, no matter how valid his reason, is a racist racist.[51] Rive's polemic here reveals how his belief in non-racialism and his experiences in South African literary circles guided his attack on *négritude*. However, it also reveals the limitation of his critique in that, while the essay correctly points to the colour-conscious elements of *négritude*, it overlooks the fact that non-racial thinking could not offer a way of privileging the African/colonised over the European/coloniser, for by constantly imagining a single human commonality, it downplays the attendant intersections of power that inflect these categories of race and space and presupposes a level playing field for logic to prevail in this centuries-old contest.

Another interesting feature of a number of Rive's critical essays in *Selected Writings* ('Arthur Nortje: Poet', 'Taos in Harlem' and 'Four South Africans Abroad') is their reliance on personal, autobiographical narrative to carry an argument. His superlative gift as a storyteller makes these essays often more interesting than the more conventional ones written in academic register. Rive creates a form that combines autobiographical anecdote with critical reflection and which makes such critical work both readable and personal. This combination anticipates the form of *Writing Black*, the memoir to be published four years after *Selected Writings*.

In 1978, the year after the publication of *Selected Writings*, Rive was awarded a second Fulbright Fellowship to undertake postdoctoral work at the Humanities Research Center at the University of Texas in Austin, as well as to conduct a series of lectures across the United States. In addition, he was given a British Council scholarship to give a series of lectures at universities in the United Kingdom on the return leg of his visit to America. Two months prior to his departure, something prompted him (a growing sense of aging? a need to rekindle old acquaintances in a time of national ferment? simple nostalgia?)

to write to his old friend Mphahlele. He had, quite inexplicably, made little effort to keep in touch with Mphahlele after their time together in Paris on his trip to Europe in 1962. There had been a few businesslike letters after that meeting, until 1964, after which the break in direct communication began, until Rive writes the following letter fourteen years later, on 31 October 1978. It is warm and familiar in tone, peppered with witty and cutting remarks that were so typical of the man. Rive is clearly keen to re-establish contact and brings his dear friend up to date with what has happened in his life since their last encounter:

Dear Zeke

No doubt this will come as a major surprise. The intention is to shock you out of your wits. Yes, it is Richard Rive writing after years of silence. Actually I have been in purdah for longer than I care to remember. Somehow I have kept abreast of your movements, so have not been cut off entirely. Since last I saw you (in Paris?), I went to Columbia for an MA, returned to Cape Town, taught and did a B.Ed, then to Oxford where I did my D. Phil. I am at present head of the English Department at Hewat Training College (where incidentally I qualified as a teacher initially).

I was unwilling to go to UWC [University of the Western Cape] when I returned as feeling is very strong down here about staff joining the university. I share this. Cape Town University wanted me to teach Middlemarch *and* Lord Jim *to white first-year coogles [sic] from Constantia, a fate worse than death. No African or South African literature. The same old fight. All literature died with Hardy. Hoe sê hulle? 'Dieselfde ou parcels net different labels.'[52] So I opted for Hewat where I took over the Department after two years. I teach a healthy course in African Literature. My students are superb, not very bright, but on the ball. We have had sit-ins every year since I have been here, and of course they were amongst the initiators in 1976. During a period of three months I tried to teach 'L'allegro' and every day was interrupted by something being burnt down, or tear gas or police taking pot shots. It wasn't much fun and played havoc with Milton, but he'll survive.*

I am supposed to rewrite my Olive Schreiner thesis and edit the letters for Donker, but have no stomach for it. Olive was fine while she lasted and strangely enough fitted in well with the twilight of Oxford, but she is somewhat out of place in robust, 1978 Cape Town. Also Donker is as tight-fisted as anyone I have yet encountered. He has reduced this to such a fine art so that no writer is safe. I wonder whether Sipho [Sepamla] is on the dole already. I must wriggle my way out of his clutches. Be careful of cultivated accents, even Dutch.

How's the family? I read The Wanderers *I think in England and wondered as it wandered. I presume that you are writing at the moment. I have written two short stories this year, a helluva output for me, one I sent to* Drum *(remember? It was a magazine once) and the other to* Staffrider. Contrast *has gotten too precious for me.*

Incidentally I have a grant (still getting them at ripe old senility) to do research at Texas. I presume your ghost still breathes there and they speak of Mphahlele in muffled terms. (This is no joke. I have met people who feel that you must have died decades ago as you've become a legend. You know, Shakespeare, George Eliot and Zeke.) Don't worry, it is rapidly happening to me. People ask, have you met Achebe, Soyinka and Okigbo and you're still living? Be that as it may, I am going to America in January–July, to do some research at Texas and then a helluva lotta traveling in the States to the African literature departments wherever they are, bringing a breath of oppression and much goodwill.

I hope that when I return in July, I can come via Johannesburg, and then maybe we can have a reunion. 'And when that time comes which is the beginning of our end …' In either case, desultory as it is, I am extremely glad that I have renewed my correspondence with you. I am not married yet and now unlikely to be. The last before one, married while I was at Oxford (thank God, what a close shave) and the most recent, a buxom wench who cooks well, is at the time hoping to get political or marital asylum.

When next I write I shall be in a more serious vein. By the way, where is Cosmo [Pieterse] teaching? And Dennis [Brutus]. If you have addresses I shall appreciate them.

Love to Ribs, whatever kids are still at home and most of all yourself.

Richard Rive[53]

This letter begins by Rive clearing the air on a matter of difference between the two writers on the question of teaching at the apartheid 'bush colleges' such as the University of the Western Cape and, by implication, the University of the North, which had offered Mphahlele the position of chair of the English department on his return in 1976 from exile, and which he was keen to accept, until 'Cabinet-level interference forced the homeland authorities and the University of the North to buckle, blocking his appointment'.[54] Once this is out of the way, the letter, as David Attwell notes, 'assumes solidarity on several fronts'.[55] Attwell also speculates that the criticism Rive levels here against the publisher Ad Donker, who had just published *Selected Writings*, led to Mphahlele withdrawing his *In Corner B and Other Stories* from the publisher a week later. Another very interesting feature of the letter is the section in which Rive feels the need, albeit in a flippant manner, to maintain the facade of heterosexuality, reaching the ridiculous when he styles a prospective wife in archaic English terms of 'a buxom wench'. Since Rive's first acquaintance with the Mphahleles in the mid-1950s, Rebecca, or Ribs as she was affectionately called, continually raised her concern that Rive should marry. In this letter, he is perhaps playing to that pressure.

When Rive left for his six-month stint in the States in January 1979, he was approaching his 49th birthday, but as always was keen to travel, explore and engage with others about writing and the politics of race. His host in Austin was Bernth Lindfors, who housed him for a few days until he found accommodation for the two-month stay at the university. The research he intended to do at the Center was on the letters of William Plomer, but Rive's memoir suggests he was even more interested in finding out about racial attitudes, especially amongst ordinary Americans in the South, given the extent of the coverage on this topic in this section of *Writing Black*. He never did publish anything on Plomer arising out of his research in Austin.

Rive seemed to be taken aback by the extent of the segregated urban configurations in both the city of Austin and at the University of Texas, even 30 years after the first black student had won a legal battle to be admitted to the previously all-white institution. He was also struck by the extent to which class and colour intersected in the South, noting in his memoir that 'Blacks and Mexicans are on the lowest rung of the socio-economic scale.'[56] He was contemptuous of and also irritated by the extremist views of certain black Americans, or those he calls 'Professional Africans', who idealised the African continent and whose virulent and self-centred essentialist assertions of black identity or African-ness Rive regarded as 'inverted racism' or sheer opportunism.[57] One such man, simply called 'Stewart' in the memoir, becomes the subject of Rive's wit used as invective, a form of insult he was particularly good at:

> *I was discussing Senghor with a shy Kenyan student when Stewart barged in [to Rive's office] and sat down. I maintained an annoyed silence.*
>
> *'I hope I am not intruding,' he said, knowing well that he was. The Kenyan looked embarrassed. Stewart realised that he had to add something.*

> *'You know, I love South African girls.'*
>
> *'Excuse me?'*
>
> *'I said I love Zulu girls.'*
>
> *I felt piqued. 'It's a trifle risky,' I replied dead-pan. 'They eat their partners after sex.'*
>
> *'No kidding!'...*
>
> *He left soon after.*[58]

The highlight of this trip abroad seems to have been the affirmation Rive received as a writer and intellectual at a major international literary conference. During his initial stay at the University of Texas, he had received an invitation to be a keynote speaker at the African Literature Association conference at the University of Indiana in Bloomington. His paper, entitled 'The Ethics of an anti-Jim Crow', was inspired by his reading of Richard Wright's *The Ethics of a Living Jim Crow*, whose life he found uncannily 'emotionally similar'.[59] His decision to style his address as an autobiographical narrative about his childhood in District Six and in a racialised society troubled him immensely in the days prior to the delivery, leaving him 'hesitant, uncertain and insecure', as he wondered to what extent this audience of experts and luminaries would find meaning in his particular story. He would be speaking to contemporaries such as Dennis Brutus, Mongane Wally Serote, Bernth Lindfors, Jean Marquard, Lenri Peters and Sheila Roberts, as well as three hundred other writers, publishers, politicians and academics. Gray describes what was to be a pivotal moment in Rive's career as a scholar and writer:

> *Few memorable moments occur in those so efficient and routine scholarly procedures, but evidently Richard's speech was one such. He was cajoled into jettisoning his slagged-out and now outmoded position paper, and so ... hauled forth the musty suitcase of childhood souvenirs instead. This was the very material he had relentlessly repressed in his thrust for respectability. This*

was Baldwin recovering The Amen Corner, *or Soyinka his* Aké.
This was Richard, funny and tearful and piercing, without grudges
and inspired, putting himself back on the world literary map. So
unblocked was Richard … that in the following decade no fewer
than five books would flow from that vein.[60]
The reception of his talk, as can be gauged from both Rive's own
account and that of Gray, was overwhelmingly positive and
he received a string of congratulations. It was this conference
paper fleshed out and extended that was to become his memoir,
Writing Black, two years later.

Before his return to South Africa, Rive took the short trip via
New York to Toronto to visit the Manuels and their two children.
They, like many middle-class 'coloured' South Africans in the
decade after Sharpeville, had emigrated to Canada in 1974, and
Rive was to visit them there a number of times. Their memories
of him are frank and filled with affection. He was adored by their
children and regarded by them as a 'grand-uncle'. The Manuels
remember him sitting with their four-year-old daughter and
her colouring book. He was caring and nurturing towards their
children. He used to write in longhand in exercise books and
would proudly point to one of his texts and proclaim, 'I wrote
this!' They remember his attachment to a grey Parker pen with
silver top and a fine nib, and his writing in his fine, diminutive
cursive script mainly in the morning or at night. He also
introduced them to Athol Fugard and to André Brink, whose
wife, they claim, was very maternal towards Rive.[61] Rive had
fond memories of the Manuels and some of the other émigrés,
many of them pupils he had taught at South Peninsula High.
But he was scathing of many others he met in Toronto, whom
he felt typified what he called 'the South African emigrant'.
This type of emigrant, unlike the exile, prefers Canada and
Australia to England and Africa and 'ekes out his dull, lower
middle-class existence in a kind of psychological limbo' and

feels 'comparatively safe from the Black South Africans he has left behind since they have neither the means nor inclination to join him'.[62] In identifying quite accurately the unspoken bias underpinning the lives of many of these emigrants, Rive is also styling his own cosmopolitanism as patriotic and pan-African.

After four months in America, Rive arrived in London and stayed in Camden Town with Albert Adams and his partner Ted Glennon before he commenced a lecture tour that took him to the universities of Sheffield, Leeds, York, Sussex, Loughborough and Kent. He made a nostalgic trip to Oxford and was flattered to find that he was still remembered by the staff at Magdalen; much had changed, but many aspects of Oxford life remained as he had experienced them. Oxford, London and Cape Town, he claims in his memoir, are the three places that he could envisage as being home.

On his return to South Africa, he was met at the airport by some of his close friends – Gus and Mabel Jansen, Tony Eaton (they were together at Oxford and Rive was godfather to Eaton's son, Tom), Victor Wessels, Ian Rutgers and Leonard du Plooy. Rutgers and Du Plooy, in their twenties, were students whom Rive had supported through their education, and to whom he was emotionally close and, perhaps, physically attracted. Rive had met Rutgers in the early 1970s, when he had coached Rutgers's brother and became a close friend of the family. It seems that Rutgers became Rive's ward when he was in Standard 8 and lived with him for a time at Selous Court.[63]

But despite this warm and fraternal welcome back home, he was once again reminded of the fact that he could not say 'I am a South African'.[64] However, his sense of Cape Town as his first home must have taken on an added dimension when, in December 1979, he signed a contract to have his own house built, in the suburb of Windsor Park not far from South Peninsula High. No doubt it was an amusing irony to him that he had finally come to live at such a quintessentially English and also 'regal' address. According to Albert Adams, Rive accused him of being 'a queen' when he asked Rive to take his feet off the antique furniture in his London home. Richard, in his private moments or when with dear friends like Albert, could clearly also talk of himself in the mock-serious camp register gay men sometimes use. He was now surely the 'queen' in his Windsor Park palace. His self-parody most certainly did, on rare occasions when he did not feel compelled to perform the conventional man, extend to his sexuality.[65]

Rive submitted his paper from the Bloomington conference to *Staffrider* magazine and had encouraging responses from fellow writers Chris Mann, Stephen Gray and his old mentor Es'kia Mphahlele, who had by then decided to return from exile. They urged him to turn it into a book. He entered the 1980s as a well-established and leading member of the community, in education and in the literary world. He was no longer the 'Chokka' of years gone by, but to many he had become 'Doc', an affectionate and reverential nickname that was just one of the many spin-offs from his success at Oxford. Rive was entering the second prolific decade of his writing life.

Part IV: *1980 – 1990*

Chapter 7

The student revolts of 1976 were the most dramatic and visible sign of the manner in which the balance of power was starting to shift from the apartheid state, which had held firm control of the nation since the Sharpeville crisis of 1960, to the forces opposing it. In the aftermath of the 1976 crisis, the apartheid rulers devised new strategies to attempt to maintain control: the creation of independent homelands was intended to allow black people to hold 'citizenship' and a measure of administrative power; the 1983 Constitution Act established a 'tricameral' parliament, in which Indians and coloureds would have their own legislative houses and which was to replace the all-white legislature. For public service professionals such as Rive, one of the consequences of this strategy to divide and co-opt was that salaries suddenly increased dramatically at the start of the 1980s. But while this widened an existing class divide within oppressed communities – between professionals and skilled workers on the one hand and the mass of semi-skilled and unemployed workers on the other – it failed to buy the allegiance of most intellectuals and activists. The majority of leaders of the oppressed remained implacably opposed to the government's offer of sham citizenship and power sharing.

By the early 1980s there was widespread mobilisation of workers, students and activists in South Africa against the various policies of the state. Among the liberation movements at home and in exile there was a simultaneous increase in confidence. In the Cape, the Federation of Cape Civic Associations (FCCA), a broad front of neighbourhood civic organisations that were resuscitated or established in the late 1970s and early 1980s, was founded by Victor Wessels and his comrades early in 1979, the same year as Wessels's untimely death. Rive made numerous contributions to the activities of a number of FCCA affiliates in the early 1980s, often presenting talks on poetry or literature for high school students. He used to have his notes inked on small, ruled index cards and used these as prompts during these talks. The formation in 1983 of the United Democratic Front (UDF), an internal federation of organisations broadly supporting the African National Congress (ANC), was the most popular and visible manifestation of this increasingly organised opposition. This new surge in organised rebelliousness was the beginning of the end of the old regime. Rive's upbeat determination and spirit of defiance in this post-1976 period were a reflection of this larger social mood and he could say in 1980, unlike when *Emergency* was banned just a month after publication, 'Now I couldn't care two hoots about whether they banned something or not. But then it was quite frightening.'[1]

Rive turned fifty in March 1980 and soon after his birthday, in June of that year, took formal transfer of his newly built house 'Lyndall' at 31 Windsor Park Avenue, Windsor Park, where he was to live until his death nine years later. The imagined 'Buckingham Palace' of District Six now became a real home in Windsor Park. Group Areas legislation was of course still in place and the suburb was one of the smarter middle-class coloured residential areas, populated by professionals and their families. Michael Chitter, an artist and ex-high school student of Rive's, insisted that the area should really be called by the more generic, less elitist 'Heathfield', to which Rive retorted: 'I do not live in "Heathfield"! I live in Windsor Park!'[2] However, Rive did give Heathfield and not Windsor Park as his address on a copy of his CV (dated 1989), showing how he could adopt highly rhetorical positions to argue a point in particular circumstances but not necessarily hold to that view in other contexts.

Nadine Gordimer was more critical of what she saw as Rive's material aspirations. According to Gordimer, Rive was intent on 'middle-class comfort, its status of swimming pool and fine car, and took unashamed if not defiant pleasure in getting physically as far away as possible from the ghetto, although his best writings remained rooted there.'[3] Gordimer here exaggerates Rive's distance from 'the ghetto' and reveals something about her own mistaken assumptions about the ways in which black writers inhabit their different worlds; throughout his life Rive taught in segregated and impoverished residential locations and assisted students from these location-ghettos. His desire for suburban comfort and his love of mod cons and gadgets was combined with a contrary impulse to re-immerse himself continually in the life of the oppressed through education, in the civic and sporting arenas, and in the realm of ideas and imagination.

Stephen Gray was also critical of what he saw as Rive's quite 'flashy' lifestyle and describes his new house in a somewhat exaggerated and unfair manner:

> ... old Rishard of Saloo was no longer. He was now Dr Richard M. Rive of 'Lyndall' ... Named after Schreiner's heroine, his high-tech custom-built villa nestled in the reeds of a bird sanctuary, a splendid fortification in Cape Town's permitted elite 'coloured' area ... There his life-style was conspicuously flashy. One fellow 'coloured' writer, to show his scorn for Richard the sell-out, drunkenly pissed through his study window and over the word-processor.[4]

Rive's house was by no means a 'villa', but an ordinary, middle-class, three-bedroom home with quite an unattractive grey, face-brick finish. Gilbert Reines, who only saw the outside of the house after Rive had died, thought it looked grey and 'severe.'[5]

It was on a conventional single plot of 594 square metres, quite close to the road and the neighbours on either side, with no front fence. The sanctuary Gray speaks of, the edge of Princess Vlei, was a row of houses away and was (and still is) not properly conserved or visible from his house. The fellow writer who reputedly 'pissed through his study window' was none other than the iconoclastic James Matthews, who was always critical of Rive's pretensions from their first acquaintance in the 1950s, but who remained firm friends with him to his death.

Around this time Rive also bought a new, fairly large Toyota sedan, the acquisition of which Gray again quite disparagingly spoofs: 'Richard drove, in his new air-conditioned Toyota Cressida, and what with head-rests and piped Vivaldi, I suppose he did resemble some new African big spender.'[6] In fact, Rive's car, in contrast to the BMWs and Mercedes-Benzes driven by others in the area, was unflashy and pedestrian. Gray's exaggeration is partly to make his subsequent punchline work. At a restaurant where he and Rive were dining, it turned out that fawning waiters had mistaken Rive for Joshua Nkomo (a politician from Zimbabwe) rather than recognising him as a prominent writer. As a portly and bumptious, dark-skinned, middle-aged man, Rive bore a strong resemblance to Nkomo, who was often in the news in the late 1970s and early 1980s. But, like Gordimer, Gray's dig at Rive's lifestyle does not take into account the manner in which many oppressed intellectuals at the time were able to combine fairly comfortable living conditions with a full and selfless commitment to the struggle for a liberated South Africa.

The front door of 'Lyndall' opened into a spacious lounge and dining room. The walls that greeted the visitor were covered with original artwork: linocuts by Peter Clarke, sketches by Tyrone Appollis, prints by Gregoire Boonzaier and graphics and paintings by Cecil Skotnes and others. Rive was most proud of

Richard Rive next to the Cecil Skotnes woodcut on the front door of his Windsor Park home. The woodcut depicts 'the bird of wisdom', inspired by Olive Schreiner's story 'The Hunter'. © The Estate of Cecil Skotnes (photographer: Philip de Vos)

the large, painted woodcarving that formed the inside panel on his front door – a specially designed work by his artist friend Cecil Skotnes. Albert Adams claims that Rive got the idea for a carving on his front door from Irma Stern, who had a Zanzibari carving etched onto her front door.[7] When Chitter visited the house he was struck by the works of Peter Clarke, whom he had just discovered at an exhibition in Ocean View. When he shared his excitement with Rive, the latter was quite dismissive of Clarke's work, saying, according to Chitter's re-imagined dialogue, 'Peter never developed over the years. Township Art they call it. I call it, Stagnant Art ... Pure art and the exploration of finer elements of art is what should prevail. Now look at my Skotnes collection ...'[8]

An illustration of the carving in this photograph later formed the cover of the programme for the memorial service for Rive at Hewat College. The programme claims the following about the carving:

> [Olive Schreiner's 'The Hunter'] tells of a man who sought the
> bird of wisdom all his life and at the end one feather gently
> fluttered down and dropped on his breast. This woodcut was
> the theme of the decoration on the door of Richard Rive's home
> 'Lyndall', carved by Cecil Skotnes at Richard's request.[9]

The quest for knowledge symbolised by the motif was what held so much resonance for Richard – and also, of course, that it was a genuine Skotnes artwork. Rive was good friends with Cecil Skotnes and his wife Thelma and visited them regularly either on his own or accompanied by friends. Skotnes composed woodcut illustrations for the cover and interleaving illustrations for Rive's collection of short stories *Advance, Retreat* (published in 1983). This continued Rive's tradition of illustrating short stories with original graphics, initiated in his very first edited collection, *Modern African Prose*, with illustrations by Albert Adams. In fact, even his earliest *Drum* stories were accompanied by large and often lurid, hand-drawn pictures graphically illustrating the human drama as was the convention in *Drum* at that time.

Off the lounge at 'Lyndall' was the kitchen, stocked with modern gadgetry, and there were two bedrooms and a sizeable study opening out onto a patio and swimming pool area. Ian Rutgers, then a student at Hewat College being supported by Rive, moved in with him and had a room in the house until 1982, when Rutgers moved out to set up his own home. It was in this entertainment area next to his pool that Rive often had sessions of chatting, strategising, laughing, drinking whisky and soda while braaing with his closest male colleagues from Hewat College, where he was by then a senior member of staff and head of the English department. It was in his study or on the pool patio where he chatted to young men like Chitter whom he had invited into his home. He was now markedly overweight, with a protruding belly, which made his shabbiness of dress more noticeable. Rive often wore clothes that he liked until they took on an air of being worn out. He was noted for wearing, at one time or another, for example, a cream Aran wool jersey, large tracksuit pants, his Oxford tie and a navy blue blazer.

In its comforts and ambience, this suburban home was a far cry from the dilapidated and overcrowded Caledon Street home in the District. However, like Eaton Place – regulated from the late 1940s onwards by apartheid authority – it was still an area reserved for a particular 'race group'. The comfort of 'Lyndall', where Rive was composing *Writing Black* during 1980, did not diminish the stridency of the voice protesting against racism and inequality. And the socialising with friends and fellow writers that marked his life at Selous Court continued. At this stage in his life Rive was also very close to Skotnes's neighbours in the Cape Town suburb of Oranjezicht, Elsa Joubert and her husband Klaas Steytler. According to Gray,

> [Rive] was passionately enthusiastic about Elsa's success with Poppie Nongena *of 1978, the first novel in Afrikaans to carry a convincing black point of view. Much of Elsa's impetus derived from her reading of black African literature, including Rive's* Modern African Prose *so many years after the event.*[10]

He had also maintained his long-standing friendships with Jack Cope, Uys Krige, Jan Rabie and Majorie Wallace, all of whom he visited often. Except for Krige, who died two years before Rive, these older friends outlived him.

Turning fifty did seem to temper Rive's ambition, and in an interview in 1980 with Chris van Wyk in the magazine *Wietie 2*, Rive sketches, in a rare tone of modesty, his writing plans in the years ahead:

> I haven't got the kind of view, the wide kind of vista that the novelist requires in terms of consistency. The short story is fine, that I can manage. And I would feel that I should go back to

my forte, which is short story writing essentially. I'm going to
try another novel to see if I can break the voodoo. But I am
sufficiently modest to realize what my limitations are.[11]

In 1981, the publication of *Writing Black* by David Philip must
have seemed to Rive like the realisation of a dream he had been
nurturing for the best part of the last fifty years – he had indeed
become a prominent writer nationally and internationally and
the story of his life mattered. The publication of a memoir
could not have been an uncomplicated decision, for to recall
names and relationships and actions in a police state could have
meant exposing individuals and organisations to the scrutiny
of the security apparatus and thereby endangering the lives of
particular individuals or their family members and associates.
This was certainly one of the reasons why the bulk of the memoir
recounts exploits overseas and why perhaps reviewers such as
JM Coetzee found it 'superficial'.[12] Another reason it does not
delve as deeply into what would have been a fascinating glimpse
of the interconnectedness between a private world and a public
writing life was Rive's own deep-seated antipathy towards
writing overtly about his inner emotional and creative life. It is
possible that if Rive had written a memoir from a vantage point
post-1994, he would have produced a far fuller account of a
writing life and of struggle inside the country. It is also likely,
given his determined silence on the matter, that an exploration
of sexual orientation would have remained equally absent from
this work.

Alf Wannenburgh wrote a review of *Writing Black* for the
Sunday Times newspaper soon after the book was published.
He was, he says, careful to give a favourable review, hoping
it would help to restore the friendship that had been broken
off by Rive a few years earlier. However, what seems to have
struck Wannenburgh about the book was Rive's conscious
identification with the Western and the European, as opposed

to his dis-ease with Africa, which in his own thinking at least, was the geopolitical location of his home:

> *Something that struck me quite forcefully, however, was that in his account of his travels he seemed to be so ill at ease in Africa beyond city lights and modern plumbing. Flying across the Mediterranean, leaving Africa for the first time, he felt the severing of the umbilical cord, but in a sense it was more of a return to the intellectual womb. Away from the dust and flies and other discomforts of Africa, there was greater lyricism in his writing ... When writing about Africa, the only tree he mentioned was the noxious alien Port Jackson, but in Sweden he travelled 'through pine, fir and silver beech forests interspersed with quiet farmhouses and an ice-blue lake'.* [13]

Wannenburgh, as an intimate friend who later became an antagonist, has an insider-outsider perspective on Rive and his ideas, which often leads to insightful observations. However, Wannenburgh's claim of Rive as a Europhile is reductive and does not capture the complex tensions that constituted Rive the man. Rive's cosmopolitanism no doubt had one centre in western Europe and England, but this was entangled with imagined roots in Harlem and black America, and in Africa as well as, above all, his very own local origins in the crossings that constituted urban Cape Town.

Chitter's 'Richard Rive: The Man' captures the paradoxical amalgam of traits that marked Rive and which is almost always highlighted in more frank and sharp-eyed depictions of his character. Chitter met Rive again by chance on UCT's campus in late 1983 or early 1984. In his prose descriptions of Rive and his recreated dialogue between the two of them, Chitter displays a remarkable ability to capture physical aspects of Rive during those years, his standard attire that many have come to remember, as well as his spoken idiom and attitudes:

> *I called out to him, 'Dr. Rive?'*

Somewhat startled, the Writing Black [sic] author,
surprisingly returned, 'Hello ol' chap ...!'

... 'Are you studying here?!' [Rive asks Chitter]

'I'm an art student at Michaelis.'

... 'Where do you stay?' [Rive asks Chitter]

I tried to answer the question, but was abruptly interrupted.
He continued with his barrage. By the next question he had
already invited me to his home in Heathfield. We waved
goodbye.

Left standing, I watched him from a distance striding down
University Avenue in a faded blue tight fitting tracksuit, books
held under the arm in typical fashion ... I could not help but
notice that he had grown older. Judging from his extended gut,
he had also outgrown the faded blue tracksuit he had worn
in 1975. Watching him throw back his head and strut along,
I could not help but conjure up the vision of an English Fairy
Tale Classic. Beatrix Potter's Mr Toad was marching merrily
down University Avenue. The University of Cape Town as an
institution for the privileged and educational elite perfectly
matched the vision. He owned the world and the world owned
him. I could not imagine him other than as a 'grand academic'
– and he surely acted the part.[14]

Chitter's piece is often gentle and kind-hearted towards Rive,
but at other times also scathing and cutting, identifying Rive's
less desirable traits in terms that will make many nod in
recognition. Chitter succeeds in portraying the compound of
clashing qualities that constituted both Richard Rive and the
reactions of people towards him.

Chitter also recalls a number of visits he made to Rive's house
in Windsor Park. The young man never addresses the question
of Rive's homosexuality, clearly not of interest to him, but of
which he was undoubtedly aware. There are times in Chitter's
text, however, when one could read the silent presence of Rive's

homosexuality in tangential suggestions in and between the lines. Besides the possible wordplay in the phrase 'Fairy Tale', the intriguing account of Rive eating sausages evokes extraordinary appetite and monstrous gorging:

> *The air was heavy with the pleasant smell of roasted Frankfurters ... and his arrogance. They were the largest sausages I had ever seen! He served me one on a plate ... he sat down and started hacking at three of the sausages ... It would be impossible to find such large, meaty and tasty sausages on the shelves of any of our local supermarkets ... He gobbled at the meat ... slurped, gobbled and gulped, audibly.*

Chitter's descriptions of the two men deep in conversation on Saturday nights beside the pool oscillates wildly between narrative distance and narrative empathy between author and subject. The last few paragraphs of the portrait reveal an intense moment of sharing that nevertheless remains veiled to the reader:

> *... He was self-righteous and his years of experience as a teacher and lecturer stood between me and him. He needed to make that distinction. However I refused to be intimidated and though at first decided not to take him seriously, later visits proved that he was not joking. With the stroke of a wand Richard Rive declared his place of residence to be 'Windsor Park', no matter where people might believe it to be in the Western Cape. He spoke of Buckingham Palace. He led me to his study. I was impressed. The relevance now permeated my mind as I listened to the mention he made to 'Buckingham Palace, District Six'. The title as a by-the-way-matter-of-fact, referred to a book he was busy writing. The information he shared with me concerning this book filtered out of my saturated mind, leaving no lasting impression. The wall-to-wall bookshelves greeted me. An English study, perhaps? I am not too sure. He was in his element. This was Richard Rive at his best.*

> *He shared absolutely everything with me. His thoughts, his*
> *emotions and experiences. He did it in a dignified manner.*
>   *'My God, he was lonely ...!' I realised for the first time. I felt*
> *sorry for him.*[15]

'I'm writing like hell now' was how Rive characterised his work at the start of the 1980s.[16] After the publication of *Writing Black*, he continued chipping away at the Schreiner book but also started compiling *Advance, Retreat*, a selection of his short stories for David Philip, as the interest created by the memoir probably provided a new publishing opportunity. He dedicated this new compilation to Candice Rutgers, Ian's first child, who had then recently been born. With *Advance, Retreat* (1983), Rive recycled his earlier published stories such as 'Moon over District Six', 'Dagga Smoker's Dream', 'Rain', 'The Bench', 'Resurrection', 'No Room at Solitaire' and 'The Visits'. Two new stories were also added to the collection.

In *Selected Writings* the short stories were reproduced almost exactly as they had appeared in their earlier versions. In *Advance, Retreat*, however, Rive was asked or seemed to feel the need to make certain changes to the earlier versions, given the markedly different socio-political context of the early 1980s. Some of the stories were now almost thirty years old. In 'Rain', for example, the 'Malay' of the original now becomes the 'Muslim'.[17] Solly, the Jewish shopkeeper in 'Rain', in the original unashamedly blurts: 'You coloured people are worse than Kaffirs.' In the new collection this is replaced by Solly's nondescript 'You also live in a blerry tent?'[18] These changes reflect a language and consciousness more in keeping with that of the 1980s, when the hard divide of white/black, master/servant of the 1950s had been undermined and challenged as a result of long resistance and also as a result of the more recent impact of Black Consciousness. However, these changes have the effect of diminishing some of the raw, visceral antagonisms that marked social relations in the 1950s

Part IV: *1980–1990*

and early 1960s, the portrayal of which gave these early stories
their anger and power. The changes unfortunately then also rob
them, to some extent, of their value as refractions of sociological
and linguistic realities of their time.

The two 'new' stories included in *Advance, Retreat* were 'Riva'
(first published in *Staffrider* in 1979) and 'Advance, Retreat' (first
published as 'Black Macbeth' in *Contrast* in 1980). Both stories
seem to extend the new direction evident in Rive's stories, first
apparent in 'The Visits'. This new inflection entails an overlaying
and muting of the protesting voice with reflection on the
inner suffering of protagonists who were even more evidently
autobiographical than the character-driven early stories. These
later stories were also often more satirical and parodic.

The title 'Riva' refers to the character Riva Lipschitz, a Jewish
woman of about forty, whom the Rive-like narrator, Paul, recalls
encountering twenty years earlier when he was a first-year
university student climbing Table Mountain with two school
buddies. Initially the story seems to cover the familiar ground
of colour prejudice and race politics – the three young coloured
hikers have to occupy a separate mountain hut to the white Riva,
who is overbearingly friendly and assertive, at least to Paul, but
not to his two friends, who find her entertaining and friendly,
making a genuine attempt to break barriers. We seem to be in
the same territory as in the story 'Middle Passage' or its play
version *Make Like Slaves*, where the protagonist encounters a
guilt-ridden white female liberal whose patronising politics and
views rile him but about whose zealousness and chutzpah he is
strangely curious. It soon becomes clear from Paul's descriptions
of Riva, and of his acute irritation at her appearance, manner,
voice and laugh, that the intense dislike coexists with a
simultaneous lurid fascination for this woman. Months later he
decides to visit her in her jewellery shop in Long Street, Cape
Town, accepts an invitation to her decaying tenement flat for

169

tea, but then is overcome by the same initial repulsion for her overbearing and eccentric manner and abandons the offer of tea, walking out on Riva. Margaret Daymond, in a review of *Advance, Retreat*, compliments the story as one of the more successful in the collection, and one that demonstrates Rive's ability as a writer to 'attain a many-voiced power to reveal otherwise undiscoverable truths'.[19] Daymond states that the reasons for Paul's dislike of Riva 'are not articulated but ... are all there in the action'.[20] She accounts for the strange relationship in the following terms: 'Rive has captured the meeting of two kinds of racial suffering and their competing claims so well that the story has the power to disturb beyond words.'

The closest Paul comes to accounting for his distaste for Riva is when he finally gets himself ready to refuse the tea she is busy making in her dingy Long Street flat by thinking to himself: 'I must leave now. The surroundings were far too depressing. Riva was far too depressing. I remained as if glued to my seat.'[21] But this vague explanation is completely unconvincing to the reader, who has to decode the paradox by reading beyond this explanation and between the lines of Paul's story. What was it about Riva and her flat that was depressing? He describes her home:

An old triple-storied Victorian building with brown paint peeling off its walls. On the upper floors were wide balconies ringed with wrought-iron railings. The main entrance was cluttered with spiralling refuse bins ... We mounted a rickety staircase, then came to a landing and a long dark passage lit at intervals by solitary electric bulbs. All the doors, where these could be made out, looked alike ... Next to the door was a cat-litter smelling sharply ... I entered, blinking my eyes. A large high-ceilinged, cavernous bedsitter with a kitchen and toilet running off it. The room was gloomy and dusty ... There was a heavy smell of mildew permeating everything ... Nothing was modern ... Dickensian in a sort of nineteenth century way.[22]

The detail in this description makes Riva's flat sound remarkably like Rive's own childhood home, Eaton Place, in Caledon Street. The abhorrence and simultaneous entrancement, as reflected in the minutiae of the description and his very presence there combined with his inability to leave, are a symmetrical reconstruction of his own ambivalent sense of the place he imagined or remembered as his childhood home. Perhaps the sense of displacement felt in Riva's space was a symptom of how far Rive imagined he had moved from the decrepitude and disarray of his origins to suburban respectability, modernity and orderliness.

A queer reading, also identifying what is 'not articulated', might account for Paul's attitude in a less obvious way. Perhaps Riva represented an unspeakably dark side of his being, a Hyde to his Jekyll, which he now fleetingly, yet nevertheless more dramatically than ever before, confronts in the story but cannot endure for more than an instant. The name 'Riva' itself is possibly a feminised version of 'Rive'. The way she is described when he first sees the 'newcomer' on the mountain invokes the image of an aberration and androgyne:

> *A gaunt, angular white woman, extremely unattractive, looking incongruous in heavy, ill-fitting mountaineering clothes …*
>
> *I took in her ridiculous figure and dress. She was wearing a little knitted skullcap, far too small for her, from which wisps of mousy hair were sticking [out]. A thin face, hard around the mouth, grey eyes and a large nose I had seen in caricatures of Jews. She seemed flat-chested under her thick jersey which hung down to her stick-thin legs stuck into heavy woollen stockings and heavily studded climbing boots.*[23]

In addition to this bizarre picture created by the narrator, Riva is seen to act in a remarkably camp fashion – seeking attention through provocative repartee and insults, indulging in wordplay and exotic self-inflation, exaggeration and ritual, and constantly styling herself as 'a queen' – strengthening the reading that it is her overt claiming of alternative, atypical and transgressive camp identities that both repels and attracts Paul.

This must be one of the few times in his stories where one sees a Rive-like protagonist lose the position of social dominance, control or the moral upper hand. Riva beats Paul/Rive at his own game and her self-assured presence and volubility silence and displace him from centre stage. She has the last, disparaging laugh as he departs, for the story ends with no verbal retort or attempted reclamation of dignity from Paul. He can only say, like one who is dumbfounded and defeated, 'I stumbled into Long Street'.[24] Reading Riva as an alter ego of Rive, there is in the story his sense of himself as aberrant and consequently self-loathing, so remarkably refracted through Paul's loathing of the freakish Riva. The reaction of the narrator to Riva is similar to that of the aging scholar Aschenbach in Thomas Mann's *Death in Venice*, who is disgusted by whom he perceives to be repulsive older men he encounters, but who could be interpreted as representing his own latent homosexuality and marginalisation that he could not name and confront.

'Advance, Retreat', the other recently written story in the collection, is also symptomatic of the new emphases in Rive's style. The bulk of his published stories in the 1950s and 1960s had been written in a style of gritty realism, with compact description of character and place, and pithy, Hemingway-like dialogue, all infiltrated by the constant presence of the protesting voice. With 'Advance, Retreat' we see Rive moving into a more extended burlesque and satirical mode, not primarily concerned with protest, but more with wit, humour and parody.

In this story, the principal of the coloured Retreat Senior Secondary School is a reactionary buffoon who insists on playing the lead in every annual Shakespeare production put on by staff and students. It is his turn to play Macbeth and Rive uses the character names from Shakespeare's play to refer to teachers who challenge the backward politics of the principal when he wants the play to be staged under permit in the whites-only area of Fish Hoek. His main political rival is the senior English teacher, none other than Duncan, of course (sounding very much like Rive himself at times), who rallies support to resist the principal's 'racial Macbeth' in favour of a 'non-racial Macbeth'. Both sides of this political spat are ridiculed and laughed at through the very successful play on the relationships between characters in Macbeth and the tensions between them, as represented by staff members of the school. While Rive obviously revels in the literary witticisms, irony and Wildean humour that arises – at times hilarious but on a few occasions somewhat forced – the story mocks both the politically opportunist and the politically progressive positions on racialism, non-racialism and culture hotly debated at that time. This indulgent, burlesque style was to characterise large parts of the novel *'Buckingham Palace',* *District Six*, which Rive was soon to write.

It is also noteworthy that about thirty years prior to writing 'Advance, Retreat', Rive had made his amateurish attempts at pieces that played with Shakespearean style in one of his student pieces in the Hewat College magazine. Now his intertextual narrative succeeds with the flair of a slick and experienced writer. Rive is here an African writer working in English, but one who continues to draw on and pay homage to the great figures in the English and American canons.

The waves of popular opposition to apartheid rule in South Africa continued to grow in the 1980s; by 1985 the trade union movement had established itself as a major force in resistance politics locally and nationally, the exiled resistance movements had established internal presences and the ANC-inspired UDF was launched with widespread support in 'coloured', Indian and African areas. More socialist-oriented groups, such as the New

Unity Movement and the Cape Action League, had also started to emerge. The organisations with which Rive was associated, the New Unity Movement (a reincarnation of the Non-European Unity Movement) and the South African Council on Sport, had garnered widespread support within civic and sporting associations, and amongst teachers in the province through the ongoing influence of the Teachers' League of South Africa. Both organised and spontaneous resistance had reached such a pitch by mid-1985 that the government declared a state of emergency in July in an attempt to quell the tide. Despite the perception that the military might of the ruling class was unassailable, there was an intense optimism and a confidence that the balance of forces had shifted in favour of the struggles of the oppressed in the country.

A conference on culture and resistance, held at the University of Botswana in July 1982, was a cultural event symptomatic of this frenzy of oppositional activities at the time. The conference was an ANC initiative organised by writers in exile in the Medu (Roots) Art Ensemble. Poets Mongane Wally Serote and Keorapetse Kgositsile were key figures in Medu and the conference brought together about six hundred writers, musicians and artists in often-heated discussions about literature, culture, commitment and politics. Peter McDonald captures one aspect of the gathering's intense and hard debate when he states: 'James Matthews gave a paper defending the ongoing importance of Black poetry, while Gordimer ... returned to her earlier reflections on the distinctiveness of the literary.'[25]

Rive was fifty-two at the time of this photograph, starting to show a few grey hairs and looking somewhat tired here. I have been unable to find out what the topic of his presentation was. The tenor of his recently published memoir suggests that he might have walked a tightrope somewhere between the positions of Matthews and Gordimer.

Richard Rive presenting a paper at the conference on culture and resistance at the University of Botswana in July 1982 (Photographer: George Hallett)

Hewat College, where Rive had been lecturing for twelve years by 1985, was surrounded by primary and high schools, and the contacts between the schools and the college were particularly strong because the schools were used by the student-teachers from Hewat for their practice-teaching sessions. In addition, the college, moved from its original premises in District Six to a site on the Cape Flats in 1956, was strategically located between Thornton and Belgravia roads, which lead from central Athlone, the heart of the Cape Flats, down to the townships in the south. When the schools erupted during the protests in 1985 and 1986, Hewat was also affected. Like the schools around it, Hewat faced a series of student actions, such as sit-ins, marches, refusals to write final examinations and demonstrations against retaliatory actions of the state, including the closing of the schools. Rive and some of his colleagues at Hewat played a critical role in helping to support, redirect or defend the actions of the students and the wider civil actions that the surrounding communities and political organisations had initiated.

Apart from the school protests, two historic events of this period occurred on or just next to the Hewat campus. The callous shooting of three children by Security Force members concealed in wooden crates on a railway delivery truck (what came to be known as the Trojan Horse incident) took place in Thornton Road in October 1985.[26] In August 1986 a march from Athlone stadium to Pollsmoor prison, led by the Reverend Allan Boesak, to free Nelson Mandela, who by then had been moved to the mainland prison from Robben Island, regrouped on the Hewat College campus.

Rive used this volatile period and these events as the backdrop for what was to become his last novel, *Emergency Continued*, and also for the last short story he would publish, 'Mrs Janet September and the Siege of Sinton'. The female narrator, Janet September, an old woman who inadvertently joins the protests of students against closure of their school, verges on a caricature of the old 'coloured' 'auntie', very similar to the comic persona created by the contemporary Cape Town comedian Marc Lottering. It feels as if Rive had great fun writing the story, filled with the vividly drawn narrator and her quaint idiom, homespun philosophy and naive yet not inaccurate political views. As is also clear in the short story 'Advance, Retreat', Rive has moved from prose in which race politics and protest are pervasive to pastiche, weaving serious political protest with comic, semi-burlesque character portrayal verging on caricature, gentle parody and melodramatic plot structure. All these elements are also present in *'Buckingham Palace', District Six*, making it a distinct departure from Rive's earlier major work. It is his best novel.

The sharp rise of interest in District Six as a locus refracting the intensifying conflict between the apartheid state and the resistance to racial oppression is accounted for by Vincent Kolbe, himself a child of District Six and a founding member of the District Six Museum:

> *There was immense internal and external pressure on the apartheid order during the 1980s. These were the UDF years.* District Six, the Musical *by Taliep Petersen and David Kramer had a tremendous impact. The more moderate 'Friends of District Six' gave way to the Hands Off District Six campaign. HODS held a historic meeting at Zonnebloem in 1988 that mobilised and re-energised a whole range of people.*[27]

The year 1986 was the twentieth anniversary of the official declaration of the District as a white area under the Group Areas Act, and was seen by Hands Off District Six as an opportunity to intensify resistance against the government. Rive was an active supporter of the Hands Off District Six campaign. Siraj Desai, a central figure in the campaign, remembers chatting to Rive at one of the organisation's protest gatherings in the derelict remains of the District in 1986, and recalls Rive's witty response to the pamphlets being distributed (calling for 'Hands Off District Six'): 'Aren't you chaps twenty years too late?'[28] Symptomatic of the surge of interest in resistance, heritage and reclamation, *'Buckingham Palace', District Six* appeared in the same year as Adam Small's *District Six* and Jansje Petronella Wissema's photographs of the area. It was the same year in which David Kramer and Taliep Petersen were conceptualising the enormously popular and influential *District Six, the Musical.* The album of the music was launched in November 1986, before the staging of the musical itself in April of the following year.[29]

It was probably at the opening of the Wissema exhibition and the launch of the Small book in the city that Bill Nasson and his colleague in the History department at UCT, Vivian Bickford-Smith, encountered Rive.[30] Nasson had recently joined UCT in 1982 and recalls that Rive was at a distance, 'holding forth' to a group of older women, whom Rive liked to call 'the blue rinse brigade', the kind of audience who would also attend his lectures in the extramural programme at UCT's Summer School. He spotted Nasson and Bickford-Smith and called them over, introducing them to the group as 'the men from the other place', both having got their doctorates from the University of Cambridge. As the women's attention turned away from Rive to the younger men, Rive, taking back the centre stage, loudly announced to all: 'By the way, do you know that I am only the second coloured man in history to graduate from Magdalen?' After a brief silence, when no one asked the obvious question Rive was clearly soliciting, he added, 'The first was Sir de Villiers Graaff!'[31] The women, Nasson says, politely but quickly moved away. Rive then proudly said to the two men who remained behind: 'Oh, I enjoyed that, didn't you?'

All his adult life Rive had been campaigning against one or other form of racial injustice. By the mid-1980s he had achieved a reputation as a leading and flamboyant literary and civic figure in local and national anti-apartheid struggles. He continually insisted, in both his novels and his critical essays, that the struggle for District Six was to be seen not as singular but as representative of all forced removals around South Africa. His fiction and critical works influenced and were influenced by the ideas of fellow activists and intellectuals trying to re-conceptualise memory, space and identity. Rive's refrain in *'Buckingham Palace', District Six*, often mouthed by the hero/gangster Zoot but clearly authorial in voice, that District Six 'was never a place – that it was a people',[32] is a rhetorical articulation of his position that physical space and human dignity are inextricably interconnected. Artist Peggy Delport, for example, in her work on aesthetic memorialising of District Six, quotes as an epigraph Rive's notions of the dynamics between space, people and perception:

> *A sense of place must also be a sense of people or lack of people. If you attempt to destroy a place you also attempt to destroy a people ... In literature place ... is a locale, a circumscribed area or stage on which something is to happen. To have a sense of place is to have an empathy and identification with that place, a mental attitude towards and appreciation of it.*[33]

David Kramer also read and was inspired by *'Buckingham Palace', District Six* as he prepared his musical for the stage. His biographers, Dawid de Villiers and Mathilda Slabbert, explain how he and his wife Renaye came to meet Rive and use his work:

> *The Kramers had ... befriended Rive, whom they met through Abraham de Vries and Elsa Joubert, both Oranjezicht residents whom Rive would occasionally visit on Sundays ... The reference to the area [District Six] as 'fairyland' was used by Kramer and Petersen in the 1991 musical of the same name.*[34]

Rive, in turn, was so inspired by *District Six, the Musical* that he saw it eighteen times and it must have seeded the idea he had for turning his own novel into a play over the summer of 1987.[35]

The 1980s had proved to be a very good decade for Rive. He was appointed as a visiting professor at Meiji University in Tokyo and also at Harvard University, where he went to teach. In the late 1980s he felt the need to take the next step in his professional career and applied for a professorship in the English department at the University of the Western Cape. Unfortunately, it was at the time when literary theory was high fashion in local English departments and he thought his lack of interest in the kind of theory prevailing at the time lost him the appointment.

His novel *'Buckingham Palace', District Six*, published in 1986, and the play version staged in 1989 were to restore him to centre stage as a South African writer. After the initial publication of the novel by his old champions David and Marie Philip, it went on to be published by Heinemann in London and Ballantine (1987) in New York, and in translation in Dutch (BPDS-Novib/Ambo) and French (Belfonds) in 1988. And, in 1987, his *Olive Schreiner: Letters 1871–1899*, published by both David Philip and the prestigious Oxford University Press, finally saw the light of day after a labour of more than a decade. His contribution to scholarship on Schreiner, however, did not go much beyond finding and compiling these important letters. Why the second volume did not appear as planned is unclear.

In 1987 Rive started work on what was to be his only attempt at a biography – on the early life of Pixley kaIsaka Seme, lawyer, intellectual, politician and founder of the ANC. Tim Couzens, a long-standing collaborator and friend, who eventually helped to complete and publish the work that Rive left incomplete at his death, describes the genesis of the work: when Rive was visiting professor in the department of English and American Literature at Harvard University in the spring of 1987, he was invited to examine the archives at Northfield Mount Hermon School in north-western Massachusetts, which Seme had attended when he studied overseas as a young man. As was the case with his research on Schreiner, Rive discovered a series of letters and other documents, which formed the basis of his initial work on Seme, which he wrote up in 1987. Couzens completed and added to Rive's biographical essay for *Seme: The Founder of the ANC* by Richard Rive and Tim Couzens, published in 1991.

The book begins with Rive's biographical piece on Seme called 'The Early Years' and one immediately encounters, in the very opening paragraphs, Rive's dramatic narrative flourishes and his keen endorsement of Seme's vision of 'black unity':

> During 1911, a thirty-year-old black lawyer with a growing practice in Johannesburg, South Africa, took the major initiative in organising a nation-wide congress of black representatives. This was an idea that had already germinated in his mind eight years before while he was still an undergraduate student in New York. His name was Pixley kaIsaka Seme. He was a Zulu barrister-at-law, practising in the Transvaal as an attorney of the Supreme Court of the Union of South Africa.
>
> In this historic call, he emphasized the necessity for black unity.[36]

Rive traces Seme's biography from his birth in 1881 and his early years in Natal to the time at Mount Hermon, his student days at Columbia University during his BA studies and his law studies at Jesus College, Oxford, both these latter institutions being fortuitously Rive's own alma maters. Seme's poor leadership of the ANC from 1930 to 1937 is touched on and his death in 1951, Rive concludes, marked the end of the 'old, conservative, passive African National Congress'.[37]

The fact that Rive did not get to do much work on this biography beyond 1987 was in all likelihood due to the frenzy of other creative and editorial work in which he was immersed. In 1987 he was also completing his compilation of Schreiner letters and in 1988 he was rewriting his well-received 1986 novel as a stage play. These heady years of 1986 to 1989 must have been exhilarating for him, recalling no doubt that other zenith in his writing life, the period between 1962 and 1963.

Chapter 8

The novel *'Buckingham Palace', District Six* has become Rive's best-selling work. It was a prescribed work for matriculants in the Western Cape from 1997 to 1999 and is still set by teachers at various high school grade levels throughout South Africa. It has been published in the Netherlands, the United Kingdom and the USA, and translated into many languages including Italian, French and Spanish. It is Rive's most successful work of fiction, both in terms of sales and its impact and popular reception. Unlike his previous work, though, the novel has received minimal serious critical attention, with only a few references to the work by scholars such as Zoë Wicomb and Brenna Munro. Wicomb, in a chapter in Derek Attridge and Rosemary Jolly's *Writing South Africa: Literature, Apartheid and Democracy, 1970–1995*, addresses the question of shame in the formulation of coloured identity. She finds 'neither the place nor the affectionate portrayal of characters is sentimentalized; the autobiographical text is marked by the ethnographic' in descriptions of generalised life in the District. Wicomb also finds moments in the novel that 'covertly or uneasily refer to shame.'[38] In contrast, Zakes Mda dismisses the work as marred by nostalgia.[39]

The novel started life in 1984 as a commissioned newspaper story about childhood and Christmas in District Six. In an interview with Mark Bowman in *South* in 1989, Rive says: 'Five or six years ago a local newspaper asked me to write something about a child's Christmas in District Six. I tried to start something every June for a few years until, in 1986, I got stuck in and it just took off. I realised it had become a novel.'[40] The novel is about colourful, memorable characters in a row of houses called 'Buckingham Palace', a fictionalised version of Rive's first home in Eaton Place, in Caledon Street in the District. The row of houses is inhabited by Zoot, the petty gangster, bouncer and poet; Mary, the madam of the Casbah; the conservative Mrs Knight, her husband, the barber, and their three daughters, Faith, Hope and Charity; a Muslim family called the Abrahamses; and a young Rive and his family. Katzen, a Jewish shopkeeper in the District who escaped from Germany during the Holocaust, is the landlord of 'Buckingham Palace'. The vivid and often witty descriptions of the characters and the place are filled with affection, humour and a strong sense of irony. Eaton Place and District Six have now lost that overriding sense as places of despair that coloured their depictions in the earlier fiction and even in 'Riva'. They have become places that assert alterity and resistance, and are marked by renewed hope for reclaiming them, against all odds, as the spaces of an imagined homeland.

Spanning a period of fifteen years, the novel traces the effects of the forced removals of people from District Six, which had been declared a whites-only area in 1966. It is both a humorous reconstruction of character and communality in the District and a hard-hitting critique of the destructive and dehumanising nature of the Group Areas Act in particular and the apartheid system in general. The villain of the novel is in fact the Group Areas Act and those functionaries and beneficiaries who enforced and colluded with it. The forced removals that ensued after 1966 destroyed the homes, lives and friendships depicted in the novel. The narrator recalls: 'We fanned out in many directions like the spokes of a cart wheel … Everyone died a little when it was pulled down.'[41] Like the rest of Rive's work, *'Buckingham Palace', District Six* reflects his unflagging opposition to racial oppression. What was initially conceived of as a story about a child's Christmas in District Six became a protest against forced removals.

The episodic story is told in three parts, set in 1955, 1960 and 1970. This span of time allows Rive to create a sense of the community prior to the ravages of forced removals, and then to depict the destructive effects of racial tyranny as the community is fractured by forced dispersal. The triptych structure, which allows the fate of the community to be mapped from organic integrity to imminent threat to tragic fragmentation, is symbolically reinforced with the fairly obvious naming of the three parts as 'Morning', 'Afternoon' and 'Night'. Each of the three parts is introduced by an italicised narration that is clearly styled as a personal, largely autobiographical reminiscence of people and places: 'I remember' is how the novel starts. The narrator is also called Richard.[42] Most of the details of place, character and plot in the italicised interludes are a fictionalised account of Rive's own experiences in District Six. The main narrative in each part is more patently a fiction, drawing on Rive's encounters in the District and based on characters he had known, observed or imagined. The narrator in these main narratives is not Rive himself, as promised in the interludes, but a nameless, anonymous narrator who is equally intimate with the area. The main stories are thus embedded within strongly autobiographical memory, yet at the same time assert a distance and independence from Rive that allow the characters and the locale to become a reconstruction of a past that is concurrently egocentric and nostalgic, eccentric and parodic, as well as generic and emblematic. The nostalgia is a strategic nostalgia, invoked not for mere sentimental reasons but as a narrative ploy to expose the final destruction of the vibrancy and humanity in the District by the dastardly actions of the apartheid government.

In 1955, Rive was twenty-five-years-old, but in order to convey a sense of a child's experience in the District, the narrator becomes a ten-year-old at the start of the novel in that year. While this juggling with autobiographical and fictional time leads to a few anachronistic details, the mix helps to create an impression of vibrant and imaginative verisimilitude. Robin Malan, in his 1996 editorial notes to the David Philip educational edition of the novel, points out that the comics the young Richard claims to read were outdated for a fifteen-year-old in 1960.[43] This does not detract from the poetic, lilting quality of the narrator's reminiscences and, for this musical quality, Rive has clearly drawn on the style of one of his favourite poets, Dylan Thomas.[44] Rive was fond of playing recorded readings of Dylan Thomas's work, such as the paean to his childhood years, *Under Milk Wood*, and poems such as 'Fern Hill'. The opening lines of Rive's novel, with phrases such as 'the ripe, warm days … split tree stumps and wind-tossed sand … when I was a boy and chirruping ten', echo Thomas's alliterative musicality in 'Fern Hill'. These narrative interludes in Thomas's style provide some of the most strikingly lyrical passages. Alf Wannenburgh also points to the influence of John Steinbeck, another favourite of Rive's:

> *Reading the novel, and seeing the play, I was, however, struck by how little Richard's perception of his subject matter had changed in a quarter of a century. When we talked late into the night at Selous Court, the literary format we visualised for District Six was greatly influenced by Steinbeck's* Cannery Row, *and Richard still hadn't shed that influence when he eventually wrote the novel.*[45]

I suspect that rather than trying to 'shed' the influence of Steinbeck, Rive would have consciously drawn on the works of Steinbeck and Thomas, two of his favourite writers.

The structure of the novel – three italicised authorial reminiscences about District Six at the start of each of the three parts, followed by a fictional recreation of those periods –

suggests that the preoccupation of the work is the contestation over memory: official narrative and state propaganda are counterpoised with the notion of popular memory as a weapon against tyranny. Both the quasi-autobiographical sections as well as the fictional sections ring with refrains such as 'And I still clearly remember the characters and the incidents' and 'We must never forget'. Rive was writing this novel in the mid-1980s, a time when apartheid, although still firmly in place, was in fact crumbling because of heightened local resistance and reconfigurations in global power relations. Rive was asserting memory coloured in a particular way, contesting what the racist authorities would want remembered or forgotten. At the end of the novel, as the final forced removals from the District take place, we hear Zoot (whose sentiments are clearly those of Rive at this point) using sharply polarising deictic terms to proclaim:

> We knew that District Six was dirty and rotten. Their newspapers told us so often enough. But what they didn't say was that it was also warm and friendly. That it contained humans. That it was never a place – that it was a people. We must tell how they split us apart and scattered us in many directions like the sparks from this fire. They are trying to destroy our present but they will have to deal with our future.[46]

As in much of black literature under apartheid, here we find the strongly contrastive 'they' and 'we'. In Rive's counterpoint, the dehumanising racism of the apartheid regime is contrasted with the humanising resistance by asserting integrity and commonality. In one of the last interviews he gave before he was stabbed to death, Rive spoke to Evelyn Holtzhausen about what the novel, and the play based on it, meant to him:

> I want people to remember what happened to District Six so that it can never happen again. I want people to be proud of the past they have been denied by official decree. It's not the

> *rubble of their homes that's important to remember but what*
> *it symbolises – an ideology that allowed the destruction of lives*
> *and homes and attempted to wipe out a people's past.*[47]

In *'Buckingham Palace', District Six* Rive's non-racial beliefs are refracted through the assertions made by the narrator and the characters. Morality and history, for example, are not on the side of the racists, according to the rhetoric of the narrator: 'What men,' he asks, 'have the moral or political right to take away a people's past?'[48] We are constantly reminded through the pluralising of place and character that the story of the District we are witness to is emblematic of a wider South African and international struggle against racist tyranny. Zoot, in his farewell speech to Mary, the matriarch of the group, declares: 'We are not eight. We are eight thousand, more than eight million. We are all those who suffer in this sad land.' And later he says, 'They can never destroy our Marys.'[49] Katzen, the Jewish landlord who owns the row of houses the characters inhabit, aligns himself with the group in their resistance to the removals despite being classified as 'white'. He invokes his experiences as a Jew in Nazi Germany to draw parallels and point to ironies that further damn the racism of the National Party and lauds the antithetical alternative of non-racialism as the envisioned social matrix – a place which is home to all, irrespective of colour, class, origin or religious belief. The fiction is attempting to imagine a new world beyond race and racism.

A correlative of Rive's non-racial outlook was his attitude towards the use of dialect in his fiction and the theatre version of *'Buckingham Palace', District Six*. Unlike writers such as James Matthews, Adam Small and Athol Fugard, Rive consciously refrained from using full-blown dialect for characters who would have spoken in a distinctive working-class patois sometimes called *Kaaps*, that mixture of English and Afrikaans and invented expressions. Rive's brand of non-racialism insisted that

Kaaps was a debased and demeaning language, as was Cape 'Coon' culture, encouraged by the apartheid authorities and writers such as ID du Plessis in order to assert the ethnicity and distinctness of the 'coloured race'. As Wannenburgh suggests, 'Richard was suspicious of any concession to the vernacular of the Cape Flats, regarding it as a compromise with "colouredism".'[50]

Rive refused to use this local dialect in his fiction, even when the characters he sketched would have spoken it. Characters in *'Buckingham Palace', District Six* such as Zoot, Pretty Boy and Oubaas speak nothing near the full-blown dialect such gangster characters would have used in District Six. Rive finds it sufficient to hint at such dialect through the Afrikaans nicknames (such as Oubaas and Moena Mooies) and through occasionally using Afrikaans nouns such as *koeksisters*, *kinderfees*, *stoep* and words such as *onder kuffiyeh*. These lexical suggestions of a dialect, together with other details of place and character, succeed in giving the novel a strong sense of local colour. Rive's own joy at playing with words and his penchant for quoting and showing off his large vocabulary give rise to the wit, irony and humour at times but also detract from the authenticity of character as we hear gangsters engaging in very Rive-like talk. For example, when Zoot addresses the barber Last-Knight as 'my worthy tonsorial friend', we can hear Rive himself ostentatiously mouthing these overly literary words.[51] Wannenburgh also finds the 'educated speech' in the District Six characters inauthentic:

> There is something of the sympathetic outsider in [Rive's] writing about the District. The words mouthed by his characters are often studied simplifications of educated speech – as in the American proletarian fiction, written by non-proletarians, in the thirties – homogenized and lacking the colour and rhythms of the vernacular.[52]

'Buckingham Palace', District Six has been read largely as an

imaginative reconstruction of life in District Six, which con-comitantly serves as political protest against the destruction of the community. But the novel can also be read as the imaginative recreation of alternative family structures. Rive's new location, comfortable yet alone in his Windsor Park home in the 1980s, made him, in all likelihood, reflect more deeply about the nature of family.[53] Perhaps the inscription of alterity in the novel is not a conscious encoding on Rive's part but a subconscious subtext that lurks beneath the surface of the text dominated by authorial intention of protest and reclamation. Or, these 'alternative readings' are creations of readers with an eye to unveiling alter-native meanings that would otherwise have remained hidden by heteronormative and pre-1994 discourse.[54]

Mary's family is constituted by the women of her bordello, the Casbah, and Zoot creates an all-male home with his fellow outcasts Pretty Boy and Oubaas – both marginalised groups yet the most caring and humane social structures in the book. These two gendered families are separate yet joined together in a row of units in the same physical structure, and there is constant movement between the two. It is Mary who most often provides the real maternal care and refuge. She takes in the young Moena Mooies when she has been abused by Mr Wilkens, and it is to Mary whom Faith turns, and not her mother, Mrs Knight, when she has been molested by Elvis. Zoot tries to date the upper-class Jennifer, but the relationship fails and Zoot realises he is happier and more comfortable living with Pretty Boy and Oubaas. All families in the District, including these reconfigured ones, are destroyed by the apartheid bulldozers. It is from these alternative families, though, that the primary resistance to the forced removals originates. Zoot and Mary play leading roles in organising the resistance to the removals. Rive's childhood home at Eaton Place, filled with trauma and alienation, has been reinvented in this fiction as an ideal form, where the marginalised are at the centre and where love is defined by communal compassion rather than conventional heterosexual relationships.

In 1987 I started work as an English lecturer at Hewat College of Education, seconded from my high school as a temporary replacement for Rive, who was away for six months and teaching at Harvard. On his return, I acquired a permanent position at the college and he resumed his role as head of the English department in which I was working. Colleen Radus, a colleague in the department, and I decided to stage a Bernard Shaw play with the students. Rive overheard this and berated us for clinging to the canon, for not doing something more local. Rive remembers this incident in an interview in *South*: 'In a moment of rashness I said I would re-write *"Buckingham Palace"*, *District Six* from book form into a play. It took me about seven weeks of writing morning and night and then it still had to be cleaned up.'[55]

Rive spent his summer vacation of 1987–1988 transcribing his novel into a play for the Hewat production in September 1988. He then reworked this adaptation in collaboration with Fred Abrahamse into a script for the professional Baxter Theatre production in 1989.

Grand but perhaps not inaccurate claims were made in the programme notes about the import of the production at the college: 'The play could claim to be the first entirely indigenous drama production in the history of College theatre in this country. Members of the Hewat staff and students are responsible for everything from the script to the designing of the sets.'

The production lived up to the hype and a committed cast with huge amounts of energy made the play a resounding success. The other dimension that made the play work so well was the use of period song, as well as original music composed by music lecturer Alvin Petersen and two of the students. This achievement and the tremendous enthusiasm unleashed in the lead-up to and during the production were primarily a result of Rive's vision that we should foster local literature. The student cast was encouraged by the fact that the play drew on the very histories of their families, neighbours and themselves, and the experience generated a great deal of interest in local history, musical tradition, literature and politics.

Two aspects of the script reveal how Rive worked and thought. For the student cast at Hewat, director Colleen Radus and I split the large chunks of narration by the narrator into two parts, for a male and a female, mainly to help create some variation in voice in what were often lengthy speeches. Rive seemed merely to have transformed huge chunks from the italicised interludes in the novel into monologues for the character-narrator. This would have resulted in long, undramatic periods in the play and slowed down the pace of the production enormously. His one-act play, *Make Like Slaves*, based on his short story 'Resurrection', and his Hewat script for *'Buckingham Palace', District Six* reveal the work of a prose writer who, while often producing dramatic and striking dialogue, was not really a playwright by instinct.

The other intriguing feature of Rive's script was that he refused to use dialect in the dialogue of the District Six characters. For the Hewat production, Colleen Radus and I encouraged student actors to introduce local Cape dialect into the play. Rive was not happy with the way we altered his script for the Hewat production, not only cutting the lengthy narrator's speeches but also changing some of the standard English lines of the characters into dialect. He was infuriated when we claimed that we needed to create authentic speech for the characters and retorted: 'I write so that people all over the world can understand.' In the professional production at the Baxter, the actors conveyed a sense of dialect mainly by inflecting Rive's standard English dialogue with local accents.[56] While

Richard Rive in 1988, backstage at the Hewat College of Education production of his penultimate novel, *'Buckingham Palace', District Six* (photographer: unknown)

the characters in Rive's fiction were often drawn from the local poorer classes, he saw his readership as being a broader, more intellectual and international one. On the use of popular dialect, he differed from his mentor Langston Hughes, whose lifelong use of the language of the blues in much of his poetry and plays was an indicator of his desire as a writer to write constantly about and for 'his' people. Rive felt he could do exactly the same by using largely standard forms of English with mere hints of dialect. Unlike Hughes, Rive, the cosmopolitan humanist, was not a proponent of 'the blues' – the idiom of the 'black soul'.

This photo is a most telling image of the contradictory elements of the composite that was Richard Rive. The photo shows a much older, avuncular man in a formal but loose jacket, with the overlong tie resting on his protruding belly. His lips are half smiling, eyes at an angle looking reservedly, comfortably, at the camera. On his head is the Cape 'Coon'/'Coloured' minstrel straw hat with red band used in the Hewat staging of his play. The hat, worn by the protagonist Zoot, the District Six gangster-poet, is iconic of Cape 'Coon' revelry, a phenomenon which Rive in his more idealistic youth regarded as a debased ritual revitalised by the apartheid authorities to affirm a segregated identity. The Coon Carnival, such a view insisted, was born out of a condition of colonial slavery and reappropriated by apartheid to establish a tribalised coloured identity. Yet here is Rive wearing the hat. But the hat is also an image of him in his Oxford University boater – that quintessence of educated Englishness, the place that made him, 'Dr Rive' or, as many called him, 'Doc'. Strangely, for a writer who doggedly sat it out in South Africa through the dark years of apartheid, Oxford was where, Grant Farred claims, Rive desired eventually to retire.[57]

Rive quite liked the student Rowan Esau, who played the part of Zoot in the Hewat production, and Esau in turn paid due obeisance to Rive. Esau's cousin happened to be Milton van

Wyk, who then finally got to meet Rive when he accompanied Esau and Rive to a play at the Baxter, at Rive's invitation. Van Wyk tells the story of this meeting and of Rive's response:

> *The first time I met Richard he unceremoniously boomed: 'Do you know who I am?' I was really in the fortunate position not to be humiliated, so I responded in the affirmative: 'Yes, you are Dr Rive'. One dare not call him anything but Dr Rive. 'And have you read any of my books?' was the next salvo. I explained to him that I had read everything that he had published thus far and we became immediate friends. I became known to him as 'that good UCT student'.[58]*

One sees here Rive's slipping into a role – that of the celebrity/ writer – and thoroughly enjoying the game he is playing. He plays this role so slickly and predictably, so self-consciously, that the performance begins to have the feel of parody or even farce. Yet, at the same time, he seems to be taking himself seriously and is truly thrilled at the idea that his works are known to the young man. Parody and self-inflation become indistinguishable to the reader and perhaps even in the mind of the performer.

Van Wyk continues his account of the night out with Rive, and his story quite accurately captures the role Rive often played in company, where he ruled the roost, but also aptly depicts the talent of the raconteur able to spin his experiences into memorable tales. The account also conveys a particular kind of behaviour, vocabulary and manner Rive adopted when in company where he felt completely at ease and able to be over the top:

> *After the theatre production he would always insist that he buy the penurious students supper. I vividly remember a meal at 'La Grotto' seafood restaurant in Plumstead. I thought it impolite to impose on Richard even though he had thrown a brace of impressive-looking credit cards on the table while trumpeting: 'Order anything, I'm rich!' I suspect it was not so much a gesture of magnanimity as much as a wordplay on his name. I ordered*

the smallest item on the menu and when it did arrive, dwarfed by his portion of Lorenço Marques king prawns, he rolled his eyes and in a belittling way bellowed: 'You ordered that?' An evening out with Richard always meant ending it at his home for coffee and a heated discussion/argument on the merits and demerits of African writing. He would entertain us with stories of writers coming to his home and ending up physically fighting with other writers. The famous story was about James Matthews bringing then unknown poet and author Pascal Gwala around to meet Richard. After drinks James and Pascal got into a heated argument which ended up in fisticuffs all around Richard's library. Richard meanwhile sat back, as he was prone to do, and surveyed the fracas, mildly punctuating the brawling duo with: 'Mind the computer! Don't break my table! Put that chair down, James!' Apparently while driving the two home later that night the scuffle broke out again and Richard was forced to stop the car as the duo resumed their fisticuffs on the pavement.[59]

The Hewat version of 'Buckingham Palace', District Six was such a success that the Baxter Theatre decided to stage it. The Baxter production, under the direction of Fred Abrahamse, took place a year after the one at Hewat and was the first fully professional performance of a stage play written by Rive. That it was to be held at the Baxter must have given him an even greater sense of both cultural and political achievement. A UCT-affiliated theatre, the Baxter was boycotted by Rive and those aligned to non-collaborationist principles in the 1970s as a result of a government permit it had to have to allow for 'multiracial' audiences. Because of his involvement in school and college sport in the 1970s, Rive was a member of the South African Council on Sport, the most popular expression of non-collaborationism at the time. From being a protesting voice outside the bounds of the Baxter to taking centre stage in its largest theatre just a decade later was a crowning achievement of his writing and, as he would have styled it, his 'thespian' life. Like his early hero Hughes, he was now short story writer, essayist, novelist and also playwright. And as he worked with Basil Appollis, who was playing Rive, in preparation for opening night and the run, Rive surely felt the ironic echoes of thirty-six years earlier, when, as an aspirant writer, he accompanied Hughes to the Strand Theatre in London to see *Black Nativity*:

> *I arrived first and soon afterwards a taxi pulled up and a beaming Langston alighted. Overhead, neon lights flickered 'Black Nativity – Langston Hughes*. Black Nativity – *Langston* Hughes'. *He beamed more broadly … Langston grinned at the ticket clerk and said conspiratorially, 'I would like two tickets for Dick and myself. I am Langston Hughes, I wrote the book.'*[60]

Rive was not to see the opening night of 'Buckingham Palace', *District Six* at the Baxter Theatre on 19 June 1989. Appollis claims that 'on the afternoon of his death, Richard left a dress rehearsal at the Baxter Theatre saying: "Now I can die" '.[61] Rive died in the early hours of Sunday morning on 4 June 1989.

The opening night of the play was one of the strangest theatrical experiences of my life. There was such a pervasive sense of absence, of death, yet such a searing sense of presence, of ghostly reincarnation, as Appollis, so much like Rive in looks, voice and manner, became Richard in his absence, as if Rive had refused to die. Reflecting on the experience, Wannenburgh recalls:

> *Basil Appolis [sic], who portrayed Richard, the narrator, wandering through the scenes of his childhood, played him so true to the original in appearance and manner of speech and movement that it was difficult to shrug off the feeling that the portly figure in blue blazer, grey flannels, black shoes and outsize cricket jersey – the uniform he wore when we first met and was wearing still when I last saw him a month before he died – was in fact Richard.*[62]

Rive, it seemed that night, was not going to let us forget.

The UCT production of *'Buckingham Palace', District Six* at UCT's Little Theatre in 2000 was based on Rive's Baxter script but with a few more cuts, more varied narration and a few newly scripted scenes. Under the direction of Basil Appollis and a cast of drama students, the characters were given a vibrant, larger-than-life quality through the use of vivid and changing lighting and imagined rather than real spaces. Unlike the previous productions, the emphasis was on the theme of memory and the necessity for telling and retelling stories. The set was not the conventional realistic depiction of a District Six row of houses; instead, the angled walls were bare and the floor space had plain platforms at various levels. Both lighting and set reinforced the interpretation that the play was about memory, nostalgia and imagination; it was obviously about District Six and forced removals yet also not confined to a particular time and place. It has been, for these reasons, the most subtle and striking production of all versions of the play that I have seen.

The 2002 Artscape production of the play was the second large-scale, professional production since the first one at the Baxter thirteen years earlier. The cast included well-known South African actors such as Soli Philander as Zoot, Shaleen Surtie-Richards as Mary, Royston Stoffels as Father Rowland and Denise Newman as Moena Mooies. Basil Appollis directed it and again played the role of the narrator. The performances drew packed and appreciative houses but the critical reviews were mixed. Many felt that the play went on for too long – a problem common to many of the various stagings as they tried too hard to trace in detail the storylines of various characters. The production would have been improved by making cuts to the script. The play won a Vita Award for best ensemble performance, reflecting how it succeeded in conveying the sense of community that is at the heart of the work. The production captured a wide range of the emotions and tensions in the novel, including what, for Appollis, is at the heart of Rive's work about living in District Six: 'You learn, if you reject [racial segregation], how to feint, how to dodge, how to mask your resentment, how to insulate yourself against hurt by laughing too loudly or shouting too wildly.'[63]

In contrast to this reading of the work as a complex and nuanced dramatic fiction, Zakes Mda dismisses it as purely nostalgic when he criticises it as typifying the wave of 'removals theatre':

> *[These works are] of varying merit that look nostalgically at life in the townships and where people are forcefully removed. These include* Sophiatown *by the Junction Avenue Theatre Company,* Kofifi *by Sol Rachilo,* Buckingham Palace, District Six *by Richard Rive, and* District Six: The Musical *by David Kramer and Taliep Peteresen [sic].*[64]

It is not clear to which particular production of the play Mda is referring or if he is making this criticism of the actual novel, but all four major productions as well as the two school productions I have seen, while varying in quality and also in the emphasis placed on realistic interpretation of place and character, inevitably combine nostalgia with wit, parody and, unavoidably because of the original plot and ending, political protest.[65]

Sensing renewed interest in Rive's work in the wake of the publication of *Writing Black*, the pending work on Schreiner, and the great success of *'Buckingham Palace', District Six* from a publisher's point of view at least, David Philip also republished Rive's first novel, *Emergency*, in 1988. It is likely that Rive had at about this time agreed with David Philip to do a sequel to his first novel and republication of *Emergency* would thus make sense. Of Rive's creative energies in the 1980s, Stephen Gray says: 'He could not stop writing, and rewriting, his past, feeling the future close.'[66] The period of creativity and productivity Rive had just come through seemed set to continue into the 1990s as he had a number of projects on the boil – he had to complete the second volume of his book on the letters of Schreiner; he was to compile a comprehensive history of black writing in South Africa about which he had written on a number of occasions; and he was working with other writers such as Sipho Sepamla on a project to get local writing published at prices affordable to local readers.[67]

It is a strange twist that one of the last recorded pronounce-ments we have from Rive reflecting on his writing was a passing acknowledgement of the very writer who was his first writing mentor and champion, Jack Cope. In the week before he died, Rive commented to Holtzhausen that he was working 'on something' and that 'it was Jack Cope who told me always to leave something to go on with and I have made a habit of doing that … It was the best advice, as a writer, that I have ever been given.'[68] He was most likely referring to *Emergency Continued*.

Emergency Continued, as the name implies, suggests that the novel is a sequel to Rive's earlier novel *Emergency* (1964). Set during the apartheid government's state of emergency of 1985, it is a continuation of the story of Andrew Dreyer, now a middle-class deputy principal who lives with his wife Mabel, son Brad-ley and daughter Ruth in suburban Elfindale, Cape Town. Abe Hanslo has become a professor of African Literature at York University in Toronto, Canada, and Justin is an ex-Robben Island prisoner and United Democratic Front (UDF) activist living under house arrest in the working-class suburb of Manenberg. Like the prequel, and like *'Buckingham Palace'*, *District Six*, the novel is structured in three parts, each part centring on a day of intense political and student protest in late 1985 – the march to free Nelson Mandela from Pollsmoor prison (Wednesday, 28 August); a day of protest to reopen schools in the Western Cape closed through emergency legislation by the state to prevent protest (Tuesday, 17 September); and the Trojan Horse incident

(Tuesday, 15 October). Like the earlier novel, the main character in age, profession and creative output bears some resemblance to Rive. One of the main preoccupations of the writer Andrew Dreyer in the 1990 novel is with the interchangeable, slippery notions of fact and fiction.

The heady days of protest in 1985 were marked by the leading and often fearless role played by young school, college and university students, not a feature of the earlier 1960 emergency, in which workers and activist intellectuals played the leading role. *Emergency Continued* is primarily about the crisis of identity experienced by Andrew Dreyer, who is torn between, on the one hand, continuing his comfortable and mediocre life at work and in his home, disengaged from active political struggle, and, on the other hand, like his activist son Bradley and his girlfriend Lenina (Justin's daughter), becoming a committed part of the social movement to resist apartheid. The claim made by Andrew at the end of *Emergency*, 'maybe I've been running away from myself', becomes the main existential angst of the older Andrew in *Emergency Continued*.[69] In the first part of the novel he begins to go to political rallies in search of Bradley, who has gone missing. He writes to Abe, speculating about his attendance at one of these meetings:

> So, Abe, after two hours of haranguing and rhetoric my ears were ringing. All the time I was trying to work out why I had really come. There must be a complexity of reasons both conscious and subconscious. Of course I wanted to find out what these meetings were all about. I wanted to find Brad. I wanted to find myself. And I ended up mentally confused and incoherent. My intellectual self rebelled against the apparent disorganisation, the sloganising, the political clichés, and the populist nature of the meeting. But my gut reaction was that this was all me.[70]

By the end of the novel Andrew has taken an active stand. This is revealed most dramatically by his paying tribute to the slain

Justin at the funeral rally, where he establishes his own little-known credentials by pointing to his close association with Justin and the struggle in the 1950s. Andrew's alienation from his son Bradley, from school colleagues who often think of him as a sell-out, from Justin's world of popular struggle and, most importantly, from himself, disappears and he becomes an accepted member of the struggle family. In the closing pages, there is a somewhat sentimental rapprochement between father and son; the latter has now decided to stop running from the cops and return home. Andrew, also a writer of an obscure novel and a few short stories, opens his forgotten novel and reads to his son a passage that is also, of course, from Rive's *Emergency*:

> *You know, Abe, all my life I've been running away … Maybe I've been running away from myself. But that's all over now. I am determined to stay.*
>
> *'I don't know whether I am the one speaking, or whether it is the character in this novel, or whether it is you now, or the fictional character in my new book. Maybe we are all the same person saying the same things in the same voice.'*
>
> *'I never knew you like this, Dad.'*
>
> *'Yes, I am like this.'*
>
> *'You know, I am really beginning to understand you.'*
>
> *'I am at last beginning to understand myself.'[71]*

Self-actualisation seems to occur for Andrew by the end of the novel through a greater sense of his own place in history and through a new awareness of the power and relevance of his work as a writer. However, as a character in this novel, Andrew remains by and large unconvincing, far too absorbed in his own existential angst, which he seems almost deliberately to create at times by not talking about his past with family and colleagues, for inexplicable reasons. Whereas the younger Andrew in the first novel was inhabited by a searing energy, filled with what often seemed like convincing dilemmas, this older Andrew

faces what ultimately feels like an adolescent dichotomy recreated by Rive to match suitably the template of the earlier
novel. If Ursula Barnett felt that, in the first novel, 'the reader
never really becomes involved in Andrew's dilemma',[72] this is
even more of a shortcoming in the sequel. The last four lines
of the exchange between father and son quoted in the extract
above are not only feeble in the quality of dialogue, but what,
one asks, constitutes the father's self-discovery? When the son
claims to understand that his father is 'like this', he refers to the
extent of Andrew's political involvement; the son had not quite
realised how committed his father was and only now begins to
understand. But what is Andrew referring to when he claims
he is beginning to understand himself? Surely not his active
political past, which he has of course been aware of all the time?
Perhaps he realises that he has always been a part of the struggle,
rather than apart from it, as was the case with his life at the start
of the story. Yet this latter perception of being apathetic was the
questionable perception of others and not his own. It is neither
a convincing nor a momentous self-discovery, but rather a
formulaic one imposed on the character through this clichéd
claim of revelation.

   The events of 1985, especially with Hewat College becoming
one of the epicentres of the local struggles, catapulted Rive back
into protests that took to the streets. Unlike the much more
spontaneous student protests of 1976, the events of 1985 were
partially spearheaded by adult activists and intellectuals who
were based in emerging organisations. The caring teachers
could not help but become immersed in the battles between
students and police, naturally and instinctively in most cases
taking the side of their young charges but in a critical fashion.
Rive, with his keen writer's instinct, must have been moved to
capture the texture of those consuming and historic events of
1985, especially as Hewat and its surrounds were often pivotal

to the course of these events. As the refrain in *'Buckingham Palace', District Six*, 'we must never forget', keeps reminding the reader, the impulse of Rive the writer-activist is to record, fixing a historic moment in popular memory.[73]

For the first time since 1960, then, Rive became immersed in the events of mass struggle. Perhaps the dilemma of the older Andrew Dreyer in *Emergency Continued* was, to a certain extent at least, the dilemma of Rive, whose earlier work and political principles of non-collaboration and programmatic struggle seemed less relevant to this new phase of militant struggle. Perhaps the old dualities expressed by the younger Andrew, of being torn between notions of principled struggle and the actions of popular struggle, persisted in the older author himself, torn between 'my intellectual self', on the one hand, and 'my gut reaction', on the other.[74] But while the younger Andrew and his creator seemed to be using the work as a medium for a genuine exploration of these dilemmas, the older Rive seemed to be posing the problem more for the literary end of creating a formally interesting but neatly fitting sequel rather than exploring a considered, existential impulse.

Attempting to utilise a more reflective narrative form, so successfully employed for the first time in 'The Visits', *Emergency Continued* becomes too conscious of its own artifice, particularly in the sections relying on the epistolary narrative form. The supposedly autobiographical, italicised letters to Abe frame expanded, fictionalised constructions of the lived experience. The same device was successfully used in *'Buckingham Palace', District Six* in order to contrast italicised autobiographical reflection with the fictionalised transmutation of that autobiography. This distinction between intimate reflection and fictionalised engagement is seen by Daryl Lee to perform the following function in *Emergency Continued*:

The meta-discourse of the novel, in the form of Dreyer's letters

*to Abe Hanslo, provide [sic] a non-realist space in which to
deliberate upon the critical questions involved in historical
fiction which claims a political orientation and social role.
As such, Rive creates a structural tension in his text between
commentary and testimony, which might be redescribed as
between reflection and action, by which he hopes to reveal a
fuller picture of the pressures faced by progressive writers in the
state of emergency.*[75]

Lee provides an instructive account of what seems to be the
intention in this particular form of the novel, emphasising the
authorial view that the writer of historical fiction needs to be
involved and not disengaged – not writing from a position of
'seeming indifference'.[76] In addition, the narrator continually
emphasises his belief in a dialectic between fact and fiction,
asserting that truth can be told through fiction, but fiction
wrought from fact. As Andrew writes to Abe, '*I mean to tell the
truth through fiction, taking incidents directly from experience,
embellishing them a bit and then passing them off as fiction, or
faction.*' Wannenburgh considers this last work Rive's best
achievement: 'Andrew Dreyer ... is more perceptive, more introspective, more innovative; his talent has matured.'[77]

Rive remained committed to the struggle even in his last years,
despite being ensconced in middle-class comfort. Nevertheless,
he also believed that while a writer should not be indifferent,
he needed 'distance', even when writing socially relevant stories.
In *Emergency Continued*, Rive dramatises the strain that, in
his view, typified the position of the writer in apartheid South
Africa – tossed between the need to be committed and the need
to maintain a distance. Perhaps the events of 1985 renewed
the old tension felt by Rive in the early 1960s between what he
later came to call 'writing' and 'fighting', between the role of the
writer and that of the activist. *Emergency Continued* becomes
a reassertion of the position that the writer also needed to be a

fighter, a position that Rive never did finally believe, despite his pull to activism in times of crisis, such as the early 1960s and the mid-1980s. Rive resolves this tension by quoting and agreeing with Arthur Nortje that the two domains, while sometimes happening together, are of necessity separate:

> Like all black South African writers, because [Nortje] was both black and a writer, he faced the cruel dilemma of whether he should write, or fight, or do both: 'For some of us must storm the castles / some define the happening.' In those lines he seemed to suggest that although these functions may happen simultaneously, the different activities are performed by different people.[78]

Andrew's transformation in *Emergency Continued* is contrary to this stated position and perhaps the novel is, like *Emergency*, a reflection of how Rive's own dilemmas about positioning himself are explored in his fiction during times of social upheaval.

The ending is an extremely hopeful if tentative one – Andrew has established his reputation as comrade, writer, colleague, father and friend. The militant young, such as Bradley and Lenina, have become sensible without being cowed. Justin's lifelong heroism has been honoured. But in the home, however, the same 'seeming indifference' that marked Andrew's stance towards the struggle at the start has continued to be the tenor of the relationship between him and his wife, Mabel. Their clearly unsatisfactory marriage – she dissolves into a world of religious fervour, he into his work, angst and writing – remains that at the end. It is the one relationship not transformed by the crisis. Even Florence, Justin's wife, who has degenerated into prostitution and alcoholism, is redeemed by her appearance at Justin's funeral. More so than even his earlier relationship to Ruth in *Emergency*, Andrew's relationship with Mabel is all form and no substance.

Rive writes into Andrew's story his continued association,

started in *Emergency*, with Eldred, the young student who held some homoerotic lure for Andrew. In *Emergency Continued*, Eldred becomes Andrew's closest and most supportive colleague at the school, where they teach. At the height of the crisis at the school though, Andrew alienates Eldred's allegiance because Eldred finds his obstinate insistence that they teach for the school inspector, despite the abnormal conditions prevailing, a betrayal of the cause. Eldred initially refuses reconciliation and this pains Andrew:

> *The rest of the week he sat in his study and thought about Eldred and the snub at Rocklands. Andrew had looked on Eldred as his protégé. He had followed his career … He had been the master-of-ceremonies at Eldred's wedding reception in the Wynberg Town Hall. And when their first child, Chesney, was born, he was asked to be godfather. He was very pleased when Eldred decided to join the staff of Eastridge. And now this thing had come between them.*[79]

Andrew reminisces about their first meeting and Rive again chooses to describe the first moment he noticed Eldred in mainly physical terms, very similar to those used in the first novel: 'A bronze, athletic youngster with laughing green eyes'. Andrew and Eldred are both greatly relieved when they re-establish their old relationship, 'an old intimacy fully restored'. The character of Eldred seems to be loosely based on Ian Rutgers, with the Eldred-Andrew relationship reflecting the close bond between Rutgers and Rive. As was the case with Rive's fondness for Rutgers's firstborn, Candice, Andrew is said to be godfather to Eldred's son, Chesney. Andrew takes delight in the boy's presence as well as in the rapport between father and son. As in *'Buckingham Palace', District Six*, there seems to be more meaning and hope in unconventional, extramarital forms of familial and intimate relationships. At the end, Andrew has been accepted into the family of struggle, clearly more important to him than his lifeless marriage to Mabel, and he does not look to her for a reinvigorated family but to Abe, whom he hopes will be 'an additional father' to Bradley.[80] The failure of conventional marriage, the fraught nature of heterosexual love, the almost constant strains of family life, the allure of male friendship and the value imbued in alternative family configurations are a subtle valorisation on Rive's part of alternative relational and familial structures.

At the end of the novel, Andrew reflects on the possible staged nature of endings in fiction and muses: 'Real life is unpredictable and less dramatic.'[81] Rive's own death was of course unpredictable, but it certainly had the dramatic and tragic quality of imagined endings in film or fiction. Both Wannenburgh and Kathleen Hauke understand the tragic, ironic and dramatic qualities of his end and begin their narratives by reconstructing in distinctly dramatic terms the night of Rive's murder. That Rive died at the peak of his literary life and at the hands of two young men not dissimilar in social standing to his petty-gangster hero Zoot are sad ironies that all too often marked his life. Those of us who knew Rive during the build-up to the Baxter production in June 1989 remember his puckish, puffed-up pride at the fact that his creations, like Zoot and Mary and of course Richard-the-narrator, had finally become 'thespians', as he relished repeating in his posh accent.

Hauke's rough and incomplete draft of her biography of Rive, marked by blank spaces for information she had yet to ascertain, begins:

> *Richard Rive had not expected to die Saturday night. He'd had a good week and was riding high. By his wits he had raised himself out of the Cape Town slum of District Six and become the best educated 'coloured' writer in South Africa with a Ph.D. from Oxford. His mentor had been Langston Hughes and only the spring before he had taught at Harvard for a semester. They wanted him to come back for a semester every year …*

*The Friday before his death, he had attended the dress
rehearsal for a play based on his life at the Baxter Theatre,
University of Cape Town. Director ___ said, '___.'*

*Saturday evening he had invited a pretty boy, ___, age ___,
whom he had befriended to come for dinner, and bring a friend
if he liked. He fetched ___ and his friend, ___ . After dining
and enjoying a few drinks, Rive loosened up and told the boys
he might be able to get them parts in his play and that they
could earn money in 'blue movies' in Europe or America. As he
warmed to his subject, he stroked ___, and the boys, seeming
to have hatched a plan before they arrived, made their move.*

*With a kitchen knife, they stabbed Dr. Rive multiple
times. The once athletic but now out-of-shape Professor Rive
struggled, but his friends were stronger. Afterwards, his blood
was spattered over the living room, library and hallway of his
posh home in the Heathfield section of Claremont, an area only
recently integrated.*

*When Rive's housekeeper came in the morning, she discov-
ered his body.[82]*

Hauke drew on newspaper reports of the murder, particularly
Wannenburgh's, or possibly second-hand accounts told to her
through correspondence or interviews. While Hauke gets a
few details of identity, place and politics wrong, she sketches a
scenario that seems to be fairly accurate, gauging from a number
of accounts and court records.[83]

Wannenburgh also begins his *Mail & Guardian Review*
article with an account of the night of the murder, using it to
frame the rest of his critical, biographical narrative on Rive's life:

*On the evening of his murder, Dr. Richard Rive, a prominent
black South African writer and academic, picked up two
unemployed young men from lodgings in one of Cape Town's
poorest suburbs and took them to supper with him at his home
in an elite coloured suburb. He had no reason to suspect malice.*

The elder of the two, Vincent Aploon, 22, had visited him every weekend since being given a lift home from a nightclub by him six weeks before. The younger, Suleiman Turner, 17, whom Rive saw that night for the first – and last – time, accompanied him. Rive had suggested that Aploon bring a friend. Rive certainly had no inkling that shortly before he fetched them they had borrowed a meat knife from a neighbour.

On that Saturday evening, June 3, 1989, Rive was in a buoyant mood. He had just completed his third novel, Emergency Continued, *a sequel to his first,* Emergency, *written 25 years earlier. His first major play, an adaptation of his second novel,* 'Buckingham Palace', District Six, *was due to be staged in two weeks' time. He was, he and his peers felt, at the peak of his power …*[84]

Exactly what took place at Rive's home that Saturday night is blurred by the contradictory testimony that Aploon and Turner later gave at the trial for his murder. If, as Aploon claimed, he had on previous visits permitted Rive to achieve sexual climax by letting him kiss and fondle his chest, the two young men could hardly have been in ignorance about what to expect. It appears, however, that, while discussing the possibility of their getting parts in his forthcoming play, Rive said something that Turner interpreted as a sexual overture. Seizing Rive's car keys, he threatened to take the car if Rive would not drive them home. When Rive tried to retrieve the keys, there was a struggle in which a cut-glass whisky decanter was broken over Aploon's head. It ended with Rive lying dead in the passage, with twenty-two stab wounds. Any one of the six knife thrusts in his heart and lungs could have caused his death. The two then loaded Rive's valuables into his Toyota Cressida and drove off.

Rive's body, covered with blood, was discovered the next morning by Elaine Cloete, an acquaintance who had been contracted to do some catering for him. She went to his house on the Sunday morning to finalise the catering arrangements, only to find his body with the help of her son Christopher, who went round to the back of the house when Rive failed to answer the door. There were signs that he had put up a desperate struggle, with bloodstains in every room. Ten days later, nearly a thousand miles away in Johannesburg, Aploon and Turner surrendered to the police.

What exactly happened that night will never be known since we have only the untrustworthy accounts of Vincent Donald Aploon and Suleiman Turner. What is clear, from court records, Rive's diary entries, newspaper reports on the trial more than a year later, and from those who knew or sensed more about Rive's private sexual life, is that Rive knew Aploon and they had had sexual encounters, probably in exchange for promises and money, over a number of weeks. What is also clear is that the two young men had planned to rob Rive that night, having brought along a kitchen knife from a house behind the one in which they boarded in the working-class area of Bonteheuwel. That it was a sexual advance from Rive that sparked the violent retaliation as claimed by the men, and as sketched by Wannenburgh and Hauke, is perhaps a less likely scenario, invented by the accused to 'explain' the stabbing. It is unlikely that Rive would have made such an advance when *two* young men were present. Most other sexual encounters with young men, as suggested in court testimony or in photographs taken by Rive of young men, seemed to occur when he was alone with just one other person. Another possible scenario is that, as the night progressed and the real intention of the robbers became clear, Rive told them to leave but they insisted he drive them home. They provoked a fight and struck him down.

What is also evident from photographic and narrative accounts of the state of the rooms in Rive's home and the spread of blood was the ferocity of Rive's retaliation – he fought bitterly to the very end.[85] He might even have had a premonition that something was going to happen that night. His desk calendar, on which he noted forthcoming appointments, had an entry for 3 June stating 'change Aploon/friend?' One can perhaps interpret the uncertainty about keeping the date as ominous and presentient. Was he uncertain about this unknown 'friend' whom Aploon was bringing with him? Or did he simply need to change the date for some other inauspicious reason?[86] However much one might speculate in vain about the truth behind Rive's murder, in the final analysis, what matters is that it was a horrific way to die.

Rive's death made headlines in the *Cape Times* on the Monday morning of 5 June 1989 – 'AUTHOR RICHARD RIVE MURDERED'. There was an eerie silence in the staffroom at Hewat as we arrived for work and stood around in groups talking in hushed tones. Colleagues such as Ivan Abrahams had to cope with a barrage of questions from newspaper reporters about Rive's homosexuality in the week that followed. He refused to confirm or deny that Rive was gay.[87] The press that week was filled with numerous articles on the murder and tributes to Rive. JM Coetzee was quoted in the *Cape Times* article of 5 June, saying that Rive was a 'distinguished writer and critic, although not adequately recognised in South Africa'.[88] Since Rive had no next of kin to whom those who wanted to pay homage, and/or express condolences, could write, Hewat College took on this role.

A very small and private cremation and burial were arranged by some of Rive's closest and most loyal friends on 10 June and a memorial service was held at Hewat College on 13 June. Present and presenting tributes to Rive were Es'kia Mphahlele, Ivan Abrahams, Richard Dudley, Jan Rabie, Edward Pratt, Peter Meyer and Harry Hendricks. Obituaries and tributes by fellow writers in the form of poems and short recollections appeared in a number of publications. Typical of the anger and admiration that characterised many of these is poet Deela Khan's 'Man of Letters':

> Man of letters
> While you've sung your
> Life's song before noon:
> You laughingly swore you'd
> Sing again before dusk! Now – your
> Death's written Black, as papers display the
> Mindless brutality
> Endemic in our time.
>
> You fleshed the razed tenements with
> Bustle and tune in your ends to
> Chronicle the Lives who struggled
> Lived and Loved, in your
> Living Ghost-town.
>
> Spinner of yarns and dreams, it's the
> Hurting void that wounds. Yet your
> Voice and effervescence drums on.
>
> That you were hacked down in
> Ghetto-terror. It's this that
> Knifes the Gut.[89]

Khan interestingly foregrounds Rive specifically as a chronicler of District Six, as a storyteller and visionary, and as having a 'voice and effervescence', pre-empting the primary association that would be made with the writer and his works after his death.

The trial of Aploon and Turner more than a year later found that they had gone to Rive's home with the intention of robbing him, and when he resisted they attacked him. Aploon was sentenced to thirteen years in prison and Turner to ten. Glen Retief, in an article examining state repression of homosexuals under the apartheid state, highlights the trend in apartheid courts for judges to accept that the killers of homosexuals were sexually harassed by them and consequently acted in self-defence. Rive's case, Retief thought, was an exception in that 'evidence suggesting the murder was premeditated swayed the judge into finding the killers guilty'.[90] Both murderers, however, secured an early release, serving only five years of their sentences.

The police investigation also revealed that Rive had taken Polaroid photographs of more than two hundred young men whom he had asked to strip and pose naked or semi-naked for him, sometimes using the ruse that he was writing and illustrating a book on athletes.[91] A number of young men lured in this way were athletes he had met at training sessions. The sexual activities they participated in appear to be, from the photographs, affidavits and evidence at the trial, predominantly fondling, fellatio or pleasure-taking from piercing of nipples and scoring razor-sharp incisions on muscular parts of the body of the young men. Is there any connection between these sexual preferences and Rive's childhood experiences or to the condition of having financial and rhetorical power on the one hand and complete lack of power in the socio-political context on the other hand? Or is my very question a sign of how social diktats control how narrowly we imagine love and sex, their influence going far beyond merely enforcing a heterosexual monogamous norm, beyond the forcible separation of migrant husband and wife, the splitting of families and preventing marriages across lines of colour in our recent past, and infiltrate our innermost being, making us imagine only certain kinds of sexual relations as possible and conventional? To what extent did the preference for not only homosexual encounters but also for younger (and invariably coloured) men and for more risqué sexual practices prevent Rive from forming more lasting sexual relationships? What is clear from court records of the trial is that

Richard Rive's legacy: Basil Appollis (seated) and Shaun Viljoen at Artscape preparing for the dress rehearsal of *'Buckingham Palace', District Six* in 2001 (photographer: George Hallett)

Rive's sexual life was substantial, but deeply secretive. Would the post-1994 South Africa have provided him with more freedom to explore the kind of sex and pleasuring he desired and the very different ways of being human he hankered for? Or was the need for secrecy and privacy, marking a distance he so needed in both his emotional and sexual life (with the latter having strong associations with shame), so set by late adulthood that no matter what the changes in social context, his patterns of association and behaviour were indelible?

Within a year of moving into his Windsor Park home, Rive had drawn up a will that bequeathed all books autographed by him or by other writers, all personal copies of his books and all books on Olive Schreiner to the Magdalen College library. He left all his paintings, manuscripts, private papers and future royalties to his ex-student Leonard du Plooy. Du Plooy donated the manuscripts and papers to the UCT Library and Archive. The house, contents and car Rive willed to Ian Rutgers – Rive had in his last years become extremely devoted to Rutgers's two young children. Rutgers lived in the house for ten years after Rive's death, before selling it and moving elsewhere with his family. Rive now resides in the stories about him and in his many stories, in his creative and critical work – his living legacy.

A note in the programme for the 2001 Artscape production of 'Buckingham Palace', District Six says of Richard Rive:

I can hear his proud voice, almost but not quite parodying the Oxford accent, reciting lines from one of his favourite poems, Dylan Thomas's

> *Do not go gentle into that good night.*
> *Rage, rage against the dying of the light.*

Epilogue

As this work on Rive's life and work neared completion, I realised how many gaps there were in the narrative; how, like all
biography, it is but a partial account. I had not got around to
talking to some of Rive's closest friends who shared parts of
his life – for example, Wilfred King, in whose home he spent
many a Sunday, and Tony Kallis, who delivered a tribute at the
private funeral held for Rive on 10 June 1989. I had spoken
to John Ramsdale, but never finally captured the vivid and
detailed stories that this old friend and fellow thespian had to
tell of Rive's escapades as a young man. Nor did I capture the
tales some of the talented storytellers who worked with Rive at
Hewat College remember – those of Pieter 'Pikes' Smith and
Graham Paulse, for example. I delayed listening to and utilising
the wide range of interviews Kathleen Hauke did for the
research on her biography on Rive before she died, and which
her husband, Richard Hauke, so generously shared with me. I
feared I would be sidetracked from my own account, and the
plan to come to these interviews at the end of my own work
never materialised in the end. Grace Musila, a collegue of mine
at Stellenbosch University, grew up in Nairobi and recalls how
she and fellow Kenyan high school pupils had read Rive's short
story 'Resurrection' as one of their prescribed texts in the early
1990s and had been moved by it. She raised the question of
the impact of Rive's early work on a new generation of African
intellectuals and readers, which I had not been able to explore
more fully. Rowan Esau, the student who starred as Zoot in the
Hewat production of Rive's *'Buckingham Palace', District Six,*
generously gave me Rive's manuscript of a play script, which

Rive in turn had given to him as a gift from master to young, doting admirer. The manuscript, composed not in the laborious typewriter script he had used for his doctoral thesis and earlier manuscripts, but on what must have been one of his first computers, is called 'Dear Havelock'. It has only two characters, Olive Schreiner and Cecil John Rhodes, and imagines a series of exchanges between the two figures, as told by Schreiner in letters to Havelock Ellis. And so I could go on.

At the end of Rive's final work of fiction, *Emergency Continued*, the main character, Andrew, sits down at midnight to compose a letter, dated October 1985, to his friend Abe:

I have been steadily working at the novel which is very near completion. How will it end, or rather, how will it end itself? … It is quiet outside as only the suburb of a busy city can be quiet. One hears no cars screeching, no transistors blaring, no children screaming. It is far quieter than the midnight quiet of a Boland hamlet, where silence is a continuation of the sounds of day, not in contrast to it … I am metaphorically tired. I still have to end this chapter of my life. I do not know how to do so because chapters of one's life don't just end, they spill over into the next chapter, and the next and the next. Maybe the confusion of fiction and fact is a deliberate one … Maybe fiction does create a clearer insight into reality. Maybe life does, in its own peculiar way, imitate art.[92]

Notes

Preface

1   Milton van Wyk, written response to personal interview, 24 June 1999.

2   A list of recommended books 'dealing with multiculturalism and various cultures of our land in apartheid and post-apartheid times' for children and teenagers on the website of St Mary's School in Johannesburg includes Rive's *Emergency, Advance, Retreat* and *'Buckingham Palace', District Six.* Pupils at San Francisco University High School in the United States have set up a website on South African literature; their list includes Rive's *'Buckingham Palace', District Six.*

3   Speakers included writers (James Matthews, Deela Khan, Mark Espin, Gertrude Fester), academics (Crain Soudien, Vivian Bickford-Smith, Shaun Viljoen, Angelo Fick, Rustum Kozain) and publisher David Philip and his wife Marie Philip. André Marais, an ex-student of Rive's at Hewat College and an organiser of the event, made a video recording of interviews with those who knew Rive for the District Six Sound Archive.

4   Three close contemporaries and comrades of Rive's have recently passed away. Daphne Wessels (1928–2005) taught at South Peninsula High School when Rive started there as a young teacher and through her the friendship between Victor, Daphne's husband, and Rive developed. Irwin Combrinck (1926–2005) was a medical doctor and was Rive's doctor at one time. He was an intellectual and activist in the Non-European Unity Movement (NEUM) and like Rive grew up in District Six. Ivan Abrahams (1933–2006) met Rive as a fellow student at Hewat College; they became lifelong friends and were colleagues at Hewat for more than a decade. Abrahams was most generous in sharing his memories of Rive with me but I had not yet interviewed either Wessels or Combrinck, leaving me with a sense of their having taken aspects of the story of Rive with them to the silence of the grave.

5   The workshop of teachers held in 1998 at the District Six Museum focused on sharing ideas about teaching *'Buckingham Palace', District Six.* In response to a question of whether it was really 'literature', a debate ensued as to what constituted literature. An interesting feature of the debate was the polarisation of views – a few 'white' teachers felt that the novel did not qualify as literature, or that it was literature but not top-class material, while many teachers from schools in the poorer, 'non-white' areas hailed it

as a refreshing, valuable piece of literature which was a welcome antidote to all the Eurocentric works normally prescribed. This unexpected polarisation of attitudes, and the response of the 'non-white' teachers in particular, brought to mind the description by Rive of his very similar reaction when discovering works by the Harlem Renaissance writers: 'I could break with my literary dependence on White Folks who only describe the Ways of other White Folks', in *Writing Black* (Cape Town: David Philip, 1981), 10.

6   Since 1994, there has been widespread consensus in South Africa on the need to pursue the road of national reconciliation and building the 'rainbow nation', ideas embodied by Nelson Mandela and Desmond Tutu. Tutu, however, has on many occasions continued a tradition common in intellectual life in this country of critical irreverence towards aspects of popular national/governmental positions, while nevertheless subscribing to the general pro-capitalist direction of national reconstruction. For analyses of neoliberalism in post-apartheid South Africa, see, for example, Neville Alexander, *Thoughts on the New South Africa* (Johannesburg: Jacana Media, 2013); Hein Marais, *South Africa Pushed to the Limit: The Political Economy of Change* (Cape Town: University of Cape Town Press, 2011); and Patrick Bond, *Unsustainable South Africa: Environment, Development and Social Protest* (Pietermaritzburg: University of Natal Press, 2002).

7   Alexander, *Thoughts*, 13.

8   Cornel West, *Race Matters* (New York: Vintage Books, 2001), 8.

9   For a NEUM perspective on twentieth-century South African history, see Sarah Mokone, *Majority Rule: Some Notes* (Cape Town: Teachers' League of South Africa, 1982). See also Alison Drew, *Discordant Comrades: Identities and Loyalties on the South African Left* (Aldershot: Ashgate Publishing, 2000).

10   Desiree Lewis, 'Writing Hybrid Selves: Richard Rive and Zoë Wicomb', in *Coloured by History, Shaped by Place: New Perspectives on Coloured Identities in Cape Town*, ed. Zimitri Erasmus (Cape Town: Kwela Books, 2001), 157.

11   Crain Soudien, 'District Six and Its Uses in the Discussion About Non-Racialism', in *Coloured by History, Shaped by Place: New Perspectives on Coloured Identities in Cape Town*, ed. Zimitri Erasmus (Cape Town: Kwela Books, 2001), 114.

12   Alf Wannenburgh, 'Memories of Richard', *New Contrast* 71 18.3 (1990): 34.

13   Stephen Gray, personal interview, Johannesburg, October 1999; Es'kia Mphahlele and Rebecca Mphahlele, personal interview, Leboa, 11 August 1999.

14   William S. Mcfeely, 'Why Biography?' in *The Seductions of Biography*, ed. Mary Rhiel and David Suchoff (New York: Routledge, 1996), xi.

15   Stephen Gray, *Free-Lancers and Literary Biography in South Africa* (Amsterdam: Rodopi, 1999), xi.

16   Robert M Young, 'Biography: The Basic Discipline for Human Science', *Free Associations* 1.11 (1988): 108.

17   An example of my attempt to avoid mere sensationalising and trivialising of the sexual is how I had to decide on the extent to which I would share levels of detail about Rive's clandestine and very marginal sexual practices. With my larger research questions in mind, I have tried to make sense of the detail, revealing what is necessary for the argument and exploration, rather than merely describing all that I know unselectively.

18   Michael Holroyd, *Works on Paper* (London: Little, Brown and Company, 2002), 19.

19   Errol Morris, *Believing Is Seeing (Observations on the Mysteries of Photography)* (New York: Penguin Press, 2011), 118, 152, 164.

20   Virginia Woolf, *The Diary of Virginia Woolf*, ed. Anne Olivier Bell and A McNeillie (London: Hogarth Press, 1977–1984), Vol. 2, 263.

Part 1: 1930 – 1960

Chapter 1

1   Molly Billings, 'The Influenza Pandemic of 1918', http://virus.stanford.edu/uda/.

2   The term 'coloured' is an identity category that has been continually asserted and contested since its inception in South Africa in the late nineteenth century. Among those, like Rive, who have fiercely resisted the term, it was used in a qualified way, often placed in quotation marks in written texts or used with qualifiers such as 'so-called' or with fingers gesturing inverted commas in verbal discourse. In this book, it is the latter tradition that frames the use of the word, even though for stylistic reasons it is most often used without the qualifying markers. Historian Mohamed Adhikari, in *Against the Current: A Biography of Harold Cressy, 1889–1916* (Cape Town: Juta, 2012), 46, defines 'coloured person/people' as follows:

> Descended largely from Cape slaves, indigenous Khoisan communities and other black people who had been assimilated to Cape colonial culture by the late nineteenth century when colouredness emerged as a distinct social identity. Being also partly descended from European settlers, coloured people

have popularly been regarded as 'mixed race' and have held an intermediate status in the South African racial hierarchy, distinct from the historically dominant white minority and numerically preponderant African population.

3   Dougie Oakes, ed., *Illustrated History of South Africa: The Real Story* (Cape Town: Reader's Digest, 1995), 433; Vivian Bickford-Smith, Elizabeth van Heyningen and Nigel Worden, *Cape Town in the Twentieth Century* (Cape Town: David Philip, 1999), 135.

4   Oakes, *Illustrated History*, 263.

5   Details about the pandemic have also been sourced from JM Barry, *The Great Influenza: The Epic Story of the Deadliest Plague in History* (London: Penguin, 2005). Barry claims that in South African cities, 'those between the ages of twenty and forty accounted for 60 percent of the deaths' (239).

6   The year 1931 is the most common date of birth for Rive on websites discussing him and his work. The University of Cape Town Manuscripts and Archives collection, in a list of holdings for the 'Richard Rive Papers', compiled by Jill Gribble (1992), gives his date of birth as 1932 in its biographical description, while Stephen Gray cites 1931 (1999). Even at the time of Rive's death, the first article to appear about his murder in the *Cape Times*, by Malcolm Fried (1989), gives 1931 as his date of birth.

7   Richard Rive, *Writing Black* (Cape Town: David Philip, 1981), 3.

8   Ibid.

9   Richard Rive to Langston Hughes, 15 March 1962. Langston Hughes Papers, the James Weldon Johnson Collection in the Yale Collection of American Literature at the Beinecke Rare Book and Manuscript Library at Yale University, New Haven (hereafter Hughes Papers, Yale University). Copies are held at the National English Literary Museum (Nelm) in Grahamstown.

10   Rive, *Writing Black*, 1.

11   Ibid., 5.

12   Richard Rive, *Emergency* (New York: Collier Books, 1970), 37.

13   This and subsequent information attributed to Josias is derived from an interview with Freddie Josias, husband of Rive's now deceased sister Georgina, in Hanover Park, Cape Town, 29 June 2004.

14   Gilbert Reines and Ursula Reines, personal interview, London, 29 December 2005.

15   Rive, *Writing Black*, 6.

16   Ibid., 65–66.

17   Ibid., 6.

18   Rive to Hughes, 30 July 1954, Hughes Papers, Yale University.

19   Rive, *Writing Black*, 5.

20 Ibid., 6.
21 Ibid., 3.
22 Stephen Gray, *Free-Lancers and Literary Biography in South Africa* (Amsterdam: Rodopi, 1999), 159.
23 Rive, *Writing Black*, 3.
24 Rive, *Emergency*, 45.
25 Ibid., 51.
26 Reines, interview.
27 Harry Hendricks, 'A Tribute to Richard Rive', Athlone: Hewat Training College, 13 June 1989.
28 Rive, *Emergency*, 38.
29 Alf Wannenburgh, 'Death in Cape Town', *Mail & Guardian Review*, 7 February 1991.
30 Rive, *Emergency*, 21.
31 Reines, interview.
32 Rive, *Emergency*, 76, 21, 36.
33 Ariefi Manuel and Hazel Manuel, personal interview, Toronto, 7 March 2002.
34 Virginia Woolf, *Moments of Being* (London: Harcourt Brace & Company, 1985), 80.
35 Albert Adams, personal interview, London, 18 December 2005. Dennis Bullough, also known as Dennis Hatfield, was a well-known book critic for SABC radio and for local newspapers.
36 Es'kia Mphahlele and Rebecca Mphahlele, personal interview, Leboa, 11 August 1999.
37 Shaun Viljoen, 'Richard', in *Under Construction: 'Race' and Identity in South Africa Today*, ed. Natasha Distiller and Melissa Steyn (Johannesburg: Heinemann, 2004).
38 Judith Butler accounts for this phenomenon of the appearance of heterosexual norms within gay identities as follows:

    It is important to recognize the ways in which heterosexual norms reappear within gay identities, to affirm that gay and lesbian identities are not only structured in part by dominant heterosexual frames, but that they are *not* for that reason *determined* by them. They are running commentaries on those naturalised positions as well, parodic replays and resignifications of precisely those heterosexual structures that would consign gay life to discursive domains of unreality and unthinkability. ['Imitation and Gender Insubordination', in *Inside/Out: Lesbian Theories, Gay Theories*, ed. Diana Fuss (London: Routledge, 1991), 23.]

39 Ibid.
40 Rive, *Writing Black*, 6.

41   Rive, *Emergency*, 56.
42   This and subsequent information in this paragraph comes from a telephonic interview with Georgina Retief (née Rive), 29 June 2004.
43   Rive, *Writing Black*, 6.
44   Richard O Dudley, 'A Tribute to Richard Rive', Athlone, Hewat Training College, 13 June 1989.
45   Rive, *Writing Black*, 9.
46   Dudley, 'Tribute'.
47   Daryl R Lee, 'A Rival Protest: The Life and Work of Richard Rive, a South African Writer', PhD diss., Oxford University, 1998, 7. Lee's further claim that Rive 'was in step with Congress politics in his unswerving advocacy of the principle and practice of non-racialism' (9) is completely incorrect. Rive was very critical of political positions and practices of the ANC throughout his life. Also, Rive's non-racialism stemmed from his association with NEUM intellectuals and not from the ANC, whose policy was 'multiracialism' and, in effect, still is.
48   Rive to Hughes, 30 July 1954, Hughes Papers, Yale University.
49   Rive, *Writing Black*, 6.
50   Rive to Hughes, 10 February 1955, Hughes Papers, Yale University.
51   Reines, interview.
52   Peter Meyer, 'A Tribute to Richard Rive', Athlone, Hewat Training College, 13 June 1989.
53   Rive, *Writing Black*, 7.
54   Ibid., 9.

Chapter 2

55   Ibid., 10.
56   Richard Rive, 'On Being a Black Writer in South Africa: A Personal Essay', in *The Voice of the Black Writer in Africa: Senate Special Lectures*, ed. Tim Couzens and Es'kia Mphahlele (Johannesburg: Wits University Press, 1980), 21.
57   Es'kia Mphahlele, 'Landmarks of Literary History in South Africa: A Black Perspective – 1980', in *Es'kia* (Cape Town: Kwela Books, 2002), 307.
58   Richard Rive, 'The Black Writer and South African Literature', Hewat Occasional Papers Series 3, ed. Val Schnugh (Athlone: Hewat College of Education, 1990), 9, 6, 22.
59   Rive, *Writing Black*, 10.
60   Rive, *Emergency*, 68.
61   Rive, *Writing Black*, 10.
62   Harry Hendricks, 'A Tribute to Richard Rive', Athlone: Hewat Training College, 13 June 1989.

63 Ivan Abrahams, personal interview, Cape Town, April 1999.

64 In a letter to Hughes dated 30 July 1954, Rive also gives this date as 1951, contradicting the date (1952) he gives in *Writing Black* (111). The course at Hewat was a two-year offering, and the memories of Abrahams and Adams, and the Hewat magazine as well, place him there in 1950 and 1951.

65 Rive, *Writing Black*, 111.

66 Hendricks, 'Tribute'.

67 Meyer, 'Tribute'.

68 Alf Wannenburgh, 'Memories of Richard', *New Contrast* 71 18.3 (1990).

69 Rive to Hughes, 30 July 1954, Hughes Papers, Yale University.

70 Richard Rive [Mary X, pseud.], 'My Sister was a Playwhite', *Africa* (July 1955): 31.

71 Richard Rive, 'Mrs Janet September and the Siege of Sinton', *Contrast* 63 16.3 (1987): 9.

72 Peter Clarke to Langston Hughes, 16 November 1955, Hughes Papers, Yale University.

73 Rive, *Writing Black*, 11.

74 James Matthews, 'A Tribute to Richard Rive', Athlone: Hewat Training College, 13 June 1989.

75 Michael Chapman, ed., *The Drum Decade: Stories from the 1950s* (Pietermaritzburg: University of Natal Press, 1989), viii.

76 In the subsequent 1955 competition, which Hughes also judged, he deemed that only the submissions by Peter Clarke ('The Departure') and Rive ('Black and Brown Song') were excellent. Clarke again won first prize, as he had in the previous competition, a fact never mentioned by Rive, whose various accounts of the results of the competitions were deliberately ambiguous, possibly to give the impression that *he* had won first prize?

77 Hughes to Rive, 28 May 1954, Hughes Papers, Yale University.

78 Hughes to Clarke, 2 March 1955, Hughes Papers, Yale University.

79 The letter was posted from Rive's address at Flat 3, 17 Perth Street, Walmer Estate, and is undated, but was probably written in June 1954.

80 Richard Rive, *African Songs* (Berlin: Seven Seas, 1963), 104, 115.

81 Mphahlele, *Es'kia*, 307.

82 Rive, *African Songs*, 104.

83 Rive, *Writing Black*, 17.

84 Jayarani Raju and Catherine Dubbeld, *Richard Rive: A Select Bibliography* (Durban: University of Natal, 1990), 10.

85 Rive, *Writing Black*, 17; Raju and Dubbeld, *Richard Rive*, 10; Rive, *Writing Black*, 10.

86 Chapman, *Drum Decade*, 92.

87   Richard Rive, *Advance, Retreat: Selected Short Stories* (Cape Town: David Philip, 1983), 7.

88   Can Themba in Ursula A Barnett, *A Vision of Order: A Study of Black South African Literature in English (1914–1980)* (London: Sinclair Browne, 1983), 19.

89   Rive, *Writing Black*, 39.

90   Chapman, *Drum Decade*, 87.

91   In South Africa, the poem has appeared in poetry compilations edited by Gray, Pereira, Couzens and Patel and Malan (Raju and Dubbeld, *Richard Rive*, 18). In the United States, it first appeared in a collection called *Poems from Black Africa*, edited by Langston Hughes and published in 1963. In 2005, the poem was recommended reading in American schools during Black History Month.

92   Chapman, *Drum Decade*, viii.

93   Mphahlele, interview.

94   Ursula A Barnett, *A Vision of Order: A Study of Black South African Literature in English (1914–1980)* (London: Sinclair Browne, 1983), 19.

95   Es'kia Mphahlele, *Es'kia Continued* (Johannesburg: Stainbank & Associates, 2004). In a letter on a *Drum* letterhead to Langston Hughes, dated 30 January 1955, Mphahlele wrote: 'As you will see from the letterhead I am now working for DRUM as fiction editor – have been since last December.'

96   Rive, *Writing Black*, 22, 13.

97   Ibid., 17, 110, 13.

98   Ibid., 10, 17.

99   Ibid., 17.

100   Hendricks, 'Tribute'.

101   JC Kannemeyer, *Die Lewe en Werk van Uys Krige, die Goue Seun* (Cape Town: Tafelberg, 2002), 490.

102   Rive, *Writing Black*, 111.

103   Mphahlele, interview.

104   Carol Abrahamse, email to the author, 26 July 2005.

105   Manuel, interview.

106   Reines, interview.

107   Elza Miles, 'Triptych, for Peter Clarke', in *More than Brothers: Peter Clarke and James Matthews at 70*, ed. Hein Willemse (Cape Town: Kwela Books, 2000), 70.

108   Willemse, *More than Brothers*, 10.

109   Ibid., 14.

110   Arnold Rampersad, *The Life of Langston Hughes, Volume II (1941–1967): I Dream a World* (New York: Oxford University Press, 1988), 38.

109 Langston Hughes to Peter Abrahams, 28 February 1955, Hughes Papers, Yale University.
110 Es'kia Mphahlele to Langston Hughes, 27 July 1960, Hughes Papers, Yale University.
111 Gray, *Free-Lancers*, 159.
112 Ibid., 158.

Part 11: 1960 – 1970

Chapter 3

1   Richard Rive, *Writing Black* (Cape Town: David Philip, 1981), 18.
2   Ursula A Barnett, *A Vision of Order: A Study of Black South African Literature in English (1914–1980)* (London: Sinclair Browne, 1983), 129.
3   Rive, *Writing Black*, 19.
4   Daryl Lee provides a comprehensive review of the reception of the novel in 1964 and shortly thereafter. Lee quotes from positive reviews in the *London Times*, 15 October 1964, and in the *Irish Times*, 17 October 1964. See Daryl R Lee, 'A Rival Protest: The Life and Work of Richard Rive, a South African Writer', PhD diss., Oxford University, 1998, 122–137.
5   Es'kia Mphahlele, in Richard Rive, *Emergency* (New York: Collier Books, 1970), xvi.
6   Lewis Nkosi, '*African Songs* by Richard Rive', *Classic* 1.2 (1963): 41.
7   Ibid., 42. Pathetic fallacy ascribes human, emotional qualities to inanimate objects.
8   Richard Rive, Untitled response to Lewis Nkosi's review of *African Songs*, *Classic* 1.3 (1964): 75.
9   Rive, *Writing Black*, 143.
10 Lee, 'Rival Protest', 124.
11 Rive, *Writing Black*, 12–13.
12 In *Writing Black*, Rive lampoons ultra-left criticism of his work (18). In contrast, he does not talk about the kinds of criticism raised by academic critics such as Bernth Lindfors.
13 Bernth Lindfors, 'Form and Technique in the Novels of Richard Rive and Alex la Guma', *Journal of the New African Literature and the Arts* 2 (1966): 10.
14 Ibid., 11.
15 Ibid., 15.
16 Ibid., 12.
17 Barnett, *Vision of Order*, 130; Piniel Shava, *A People's Voice: Black South African Writing in the Twentieth Century* (London: Zed, 1989).
18 Barnett, *Vision of Order*, 131.

19   Rive, *Writing Black*, 19.
20   Lee, 'Rival Protest', 104.
21   Rive, *Emergency*, 163.
22   Ibid., 230.
23   Ibid., 85.
24   Ibid., 183.
25   Ibid., 138, 18.
26   Ibid., 208.
27   Richard Rive, 'Interview', by Chris van Wyk, *Wietie 2* (Johannesburg: Sable Books, 1980), 10.
28   Alf Wannenburgh, 'Memories of Richard', *New Contrast* 71 18.3 (1990), 33. The handwritten manuscript of *Emergency* is held at Nelm.
29   Ariefi Manuel and Hazel Manuel, personal interview, Toronto, 7 March 2002; Richard Rive to Langston Hughes, 30 July 1954, Langston Hughes Papers, the James Weldon Johnson Collection in the Yale Collection of American Literature at the Beinecke Rare Book and Manuscript Library at Yale University, New Haven (hereafter Hughes Papers, Yale University). Copies are held at the National English Literary Museum (Nelm) in Grahamstown.
30   Wannenburgh, 'Memories', 32.
31   Nadine Gordimer, 'Nadine Gordimer on the Murdered South African Writer Richard Rive', *Mail & Guardian: Review*, 7 February 1991, 25.
32   Rive, *Writing Black*, 18.
33   Peter D McDonald, *The Literature Police: Apartheid Censorship and its Cultural Consequences* (Oxford: Oxford University Press, 2009), 109.
34   Rive, *Writing Black*, 90.
35   Ibid.
36   McDonald, *Literature Police*, 109.
37   Jayarani Raju and Catherine Dubbeld, *Richard Rive: A Select Bibliography* (Durban: University of Natal, 1990), 10.
38   Rive, *Writing Black*, 18.
39   Wannenburgh, 'Memories', 29.
40   JM Coetzee, 'Writing Black', *English in Africa* 9.2 (1982): 72.
41   Tom Lodge, *Black Politics in South Africa since 1945* (London: Longman, 1983), 232.
42   Richard Rive, ed., *Quartet: New Voices from South Africa – Alex La Guma, James Matthews, Richard Rive, Alf Wannenburgh* (New York: Crown Publishers, 1963), 4–5.
43   Hewat Training College changed its name to Hewat College of Education, probably when the institution was transferred

from the Cape Education Department to the Coloured Affairs
Department in 1963.

44 Milton van Wyk, written response to personal interview, 24 June
1999.

45 Rive to Hughes, 30 July 1954, Hughes Papers, Yale University.
Rive is referring here to his graduation from Hewat College with
a teacher's diploma. He graduated with a BA from the University
of Cape Town (UCT) in 1962.

46 Lee, 'Rival Protest', 12.

47 Rive, *Writing Black*, 23.

48 Lee, 'Rival Protest', 11.

49 Desiree Lewis, 'Writing Hybrid Selves: Richard Rive and
Zoë Wicomb', in *Coloured by History, Shaped by Place: New
Perspectives on Coloured Identities in Cape Town*, ed. Zimitri
Erasmus (Cape Town: Kwela Books, 2001), 137. See also Grant
Farred, *Midfielder's Moment: Coloured Literature and Culture in
Contemporary South Africa* (Boulder, CO: Westview Press, 2000).

50 Lewis, 'Writing Hybrid Selves', 135. Even accepting the ines-
capable presence of colour-encoded racial markers in the context
of South Africa after the assumption of power by the National
Party in 1948, Rive seems to have internalised contradictory
notions of self that proclaim and deny particular identity
positions. Lewis concludes: 'Rive writes a hybridized identity that
not only responds to "racial hybridity", but also charts multiple
subject positions and unstable subjectivities' (146).

51 Mildred Poswa (Neville Alexander), 'Black Consciousness: A
Reactionary Tendency', *The Educational Journal*, March–May
(Cape Town: Teachers' League of South Africa, 1976).

52 Rive, quoted in Mark Bowman, 'Rive: Part 1 – 20 Years of Writing
about "Constitutionalised Racism" ', *South* (25 May 1989): n.p.

53 Rive, *Writing Black*, 19.

Chapter 4

54 Rive claims in *Writing Black* (19) that Mphahlele was refused a
passport and had to leave on an exit permit preventing him from
ever returning. David Attwell, however, says that Mphahlele left
on an ordinary passport, not an exit visa, after much internal
wrangling between the Native Commissioner, the departments of
Native Affairs and Internal Affairs, and the police in Pretoria. See
David Attwell, *Rewriting Modernity: Studies in Black South African
Literary History* (Pietermaritzburg: University of KwaZulu-Natal
Press, 2005), 114–115.

55 Rive, *Writing Black*, 71, 36.

56   Wannenburgh, 'Memories', 35.
57   Langston Hughes to Peter Abrahams, 30 May 1954, Hughes Papers, Yale University.
58   Rive to Hughes, 30 July 1954, Hughes Papers, Yale University.
59   Rive, *Writing Black*, 21.
60   Douglas Killam and Ruth Rowe, eds, *The Companion to African Literatures* (Oxford: James Currey, 2000), 148.
61   Barney Simon, 'My Years with *The Classic*: A Note', *English in Africa* 7.2 (September 1980): 75–80.
62   Rive, *Writing Black*, 38.
63   N Chabani Manganyi and David Attwell, eds, *Bury Me at the Marketplace: Es'kia Mphahlele and Company, Letters 1943–2006* (Johannesburg: Wits University Press, 2010), 104.
64   Rive, *Writing Black*, 36.
65   Ibid., 73.
66   Ibid., 82.
67   Stephen Gray, *Free-Lancers and Literary Biography in South Africa* (Amsterdam: Rodopi, 1999), 162.
68   Rive, *Writing Black*, 84.
69   Ibid., 83.
70   "Voorslag" (Afrikaans for "whiplash") was the name of an iconoclastic literary journal, first published in 1926, that was spearheaded by Roy Campbell and brought together three key early South African writers – Campbell, William Plomer and Laurens van der Post.
71   Ibid., 84.
72   Coetzee, 'Writing Black', 71.
73   Rive, *Writing Black*, 73.
74   Ibid., 35.
75   Ibid., 81.
76   Gilbert Reines and Ursula Reines, personal interview, London, 29 December 2005.
77   Rive, *Writing Black*, 102.
78   Ibid., 103.
79   This is from my own memory of Richard's behaviour at the time.
80   Rive, *Writing Black*, 109, 108.
81   Ibid., 107.
82   Ibid., 109.
83   Ibid., 112.
84   Recounted by Maeve Heneke in 2012.
85   Rive, *Writing Black*, 113.
86   Ibid., 114.
87   The transcript of the MA results for his ten modules, the subjects

of which ranged from American culture and education to American Negro literature and educational modules, were all passed in either grade A or B.

88 Rive, *Writing Black*, 114.

89 Richard Rive, 'Taos in Harlem: An Interview with Langston Hughes', in *Selected Writings* (Johannesburg: Ad Donker, 1977), 110–118.

90 Stonewall marked a turning point in the way the world related to homosexuality and the way homosexuals related to the world. The unexpected and protracted resistance to police harassment at the New York gay bar called the Stonewall Tavern in June 1969 marked the start of the worldwide gay liberation movement and annual gay marches.

91 Rive, 'Taos', 115. Countee Cullen (1903–1946) was a prominent poet and figure in the Harlem Renaissance. Unlike Hughes, Cullen questioned racial identification and chose to write in a more traditional poetic register rather than in contemporary idiom. He married but was rumoured to be homosexual – the 'tragedy' Rive refers to?

92 The other was to the unwelcome advances from a homosexual publisher in Greece, recorded in *Writing Black* (56), discussed a little later in this chapter.

93 Lee, 'Rival Protest', 18.

94 Manuel, interview.

95 Rive, *Writing Black*, 56.

96 Quoted in Arnold Rampersad, *The Life of Langston Hughes, Volume I (1902–1941): I, too, Sing America* (New York: Oxford University Press, 1986), 130.

97 Rive, 'Taos', 36.

98 Rive, *Writing Black*, vii.

99 Richard Rive, ed., *Modern African Prose* (London: Heinemann, 1964), 65.

100 David Levering Lewis, *The Portable Harlem Renaissance Reader* (New York: Penguin, 1994), 603.

101 Richard Rive, 'Storming Pretoria's Castle: To Write or Fight?' *New York Times Book Review*, 17 January 1988, 32. Scottsboro trial: 'During the 1930s, much of the world's attention was riveted on the "Scottsboro Boys", nine black youths falsely charged with raping two white women in Alabama. This case, more than any other event in the South during the 1930s, revealed the barbarous treatment of blacks' (http://www.pbs.org/wnet/jimcrow/stories_events_scotts.html). Camp Hill shootings: On 15 July 1931, a white mob raided a meeting of the Alabama Share Croppers Union being held in a church in Camp Hill. A shootout between

the mob and union members followed; one union member, Ralph Gray, was murdered, several men and women were injured, and at least 30 black men were later arrested (at least four others were lynched) (http://en.wikipedia.org/wiki/Camp_Hill,_Alabama).

102 Rive, *Writing Black*, 123.

103 Gray, *Free-Lancers*, 163.

104 Rive, *Writing Black*, 127.

105 Rive does not date these meetings in his memoir but mentions that Nortje was in his final year of study at the University of the Western Cape. Dirk Klopper gives the date as 1963 in the chronology of Nortje's life in *Anatomy of Dark: Collected Poems of Arthur Nortje* (Pretoria: Unisa Press, 2000).

106 Rive, *Writing Black*, 128.

107 Ibid.

108 Wannenburgh, 'Memories', 33.

109 Rive, *Writing Black*, 129.

110 Rive, 'Interview', 11.

111 George Hallett and Peter McKenzie, eds, *District Six Revisited* (Johannesburg: Wits University Press, 2007), 6.

112 Rive, *Writing Black*, 129.

113 Richard Rive, letter of application to University of Oxford, 26 July 1970, Magdalen College Archive, University of Oxford.

114 Richard Rive, completed application form for University of Oxford, 10 August 1970; Philip Segal, letter of reference for Richard Rive, n.d., Magdalen College Archive, University of Oxford.

115 Lindy Wilson, letter of reference for Richard Rive, 28 October 1970, Magdalen College Archive, University of Oxford.

Part 111: 1970 – 1980

Chapter 5

1   'Andrew' was published in HL Shore and M Shore-Bos, eds, *Come Back, Africa! Short Stories from South Africa by Phyllis Altman [and Others]* (New York: International Publishers, 1968), 143–150.

2   Personal correspondence from Michel Lobelle (July 2012), who worked for the service, reveals:

> Survey research in several countries at that time was used as a basis for an estimate that there were at that time around 28 million listeners in countries around the world who listened at least once a week to the BBC External Services in English. A very high proportion of that number, perhaps as much as 50 percent, was in Africa.

3   Quoted in Gwyneth Henderson, ed., *African Theatre: Eight Prize-Winning Plays for Radio* (London: Heinemann, 1973), 2.
4   Ibid.
5   Richard Rive to Langston Hughes, 5 January 1962, Nelm.
6   Richard Rive, 'The Visits', in *Selected Writings* (Johannesburg: Ad Donker, 1977), 58.
7   Allon White, *The Uses of Obscurity* (London: Routledge & Kegan Paul, 1981).
8   Rive, 'The Visits', 51.
9   Ibid.
10 Ibid.
11 Richard Rive, *Writing Black* (Cape Town: David Philip, 1981), 130.
12 Arthur Nortje is a well-known example of a South African who felt this sense of alienation. Rive mentions a character called Kobus (probably a pseudonym) from Stellenbosch who felt similarly estranged at Oxford. The South African writer David Medalie also says he had a horrid time at the institution and in the town.
13 Rive, *Writing Black*, 132.
14 Richard Rive, 'Four South Africans Abroad', *Contrast* 10.3 (1976): 56–57.
15 Albert Adams, personal interview, London, 18 December 2005.
16 Richard Rive, 'Interview', by Chris van Wyk, *Wietie 2* (Johannesburg: Sable Books, 1980), 13.
17 Stephen Gray, *Free-Lancers and Literary Biography in South Africa* (Amsterdam: Rodopi, 1999), 157.
18 Details about the academic and administrative aspects of the years at Oxford were taken from the administrative file on Rive held at Magdalen College Archive.
19 Ridley Beeton to Richard Rive, 19 January 1972, Magdalen College Archive.
20 Guy Butler to Richard Rive, n.d., Magdalen College Archive.
21 Clive Slingers, telephone interview, September 2004.
22 Magdalen College Archive.
23 Rive, *Writing Black*, 137.
24 Latief Parker, personal interview, Cape Town, 2006.
25 Bill Nasson, personal interview, Cape Town, 27 February 2013.
26 Rive, *Writing Black*, 144.
27 The Manuels claim that 'when he graduated he went to her [his sister Georgina] to say he was a doctor "of literature, not of medicine", something he often used to stress' (Ariefi Manuel and Hazel Manuel, personal interview, Toronto, 7 March 2002). The descrip-

tion of his proud and camp pose is my own reconstruction, not theirs.

28   Rive, *Writing Black*, 145.

Chapter 6

29   Rive, *Writing Black*, 148.
30   Alf Wannenburgh, 'Memories of Richard', *New Contrast* 71 18.3 (1990): 37.
31   This and the other quotes that follow are from a personal interview with Maeve Heneke, London, 30 December 2005.
32   Val Preteceille, personal interview, London, 28 December 2005.
33   Heneke, interview.
34   This interviewee asked to remain anonymous.
35   Adams, interview.
36   George Hallett, *Portraits of African Writers* (Johannesburg: Wits University Press, 2006).
37   Gray, *Free-Lancers*, 163.
38   Michael Chitter, 'Richard Rive: The Man', *Botsotso: Contemporary South African Culture* 13 (2004): 103.
39   Gray, *Free-Lancers*, 164.
40   Milton van Wyk, written response to personal interview, 24 June 1999.
41   Heneke, interview.
42   Rive, *Writing Black*, 149.
43   Ibid., 153.
44   Ibid., 154.
45   Richard Rive,ed. O*live Schreiner: Letters 1871–1899* (Cape Town: David Philip, 1987).
46   Gray, *Free-Lancers*, 165.
47   Jayarani Raju and Catherine Dubbeld, *Richard Rive: A Select Bibliography* (Durban: University of Natal, 1990).
48   Rive, *Selected Writings*, 70–71.
49   Ibid., 72.
50   David Attwell points to 'the growth of racial self-consciousness' that marked a shift in Mphahlele's thought away from non-racialism to pan-Africanism between the first edition of Mphahlele's *The African Image,* in 1962, and the revised one, which appeared in 1974. *Rewriting Modernity: Studies in Black South African Literary History* (Pietermaritzburg: University of KwaZulu-Natal Press, 2005), 130.
51   Rive, *Selected Writings*, 138.
52   'The same old parcels, just different labels' (Afrikaans mixed with English to convey a local variant of Afrikaans sometimes called *Kaaps*).

53 N Chabani Manganyi and David Attwell, eds, *Bury Me at the Marketplace: Es'kia Mphahlele and Company, Letters 1943–2006* (Johannesburg: Wits University Press, 2010), 374–375.
54 Manganyi and Attwell, *Bury Me*, 14.
55 Ibid., 375.
56 Rive, *Writing Black*, 159.
57 Ibid., 160–163.
58 Ibid., 161.
59 Ibid., 180.
60 Gray, *Free-Lancers*, 172.
61 Manuel, interview.
62 Rive, *Writing Black*, 195–196.
63 Information about Rutgers's association with Rive in this and subsequent sections was gleaned from various interviews and my own knowledge.
64 Rive, *Writing Black*, 213.
65 My suspicion that Rive would not 'play' at being gay, even in private, is confirmed by Judith Butler's contention that such play with identity 'is the way in which that "being" gets established, instituted, circulated, and confirmed' ('Imitation and Gender Insubordination', in *Inside/Out: Lesbian Theories, Gay Theories*, ed. Diana Fuss ([London: Routledge, 1991], 18). Rive resisted any such establishing and confirmation of his homosexuality.

Part 1V: 1980 – 1990

Chapter 7

1 Richard Rive, 'Interview', by Chris van Wyk, *Wietie 2* (Johannesburg: Sable Books, 1980), 10.
2 Michael Chitter, 'Richard Rive: The Man', *Botsotso: Contemporary South African Culture* 13 (2004): 104. The term 'Heathfield' applied to a wide suburban region denoting a number of smaller areas, which included working-class as well as middle-class residential zones. Windsor Park, however, a zone within Heathfield, was distinctly middle class.
3 Nadine Gordimer, 'Nadine Gordimer on the Murdered South African Writer Richard Rive', *Mail & Guardian Review*, 7 February 1991.
4 Stephen Gray, *Free-Lancers and Literary Biography in South Africa* (Amsterdam: Rodopi, 1999), 173.
5 Gilbert Reines and Ursula Reines, personal interview, London, 29 December 2005.
6 Gray, *Free-Lancers*, 169.
7 Albert Adams, personal interview, London, 18 December 2005.

8   Chitter, 'Richard Rive', 105–106.
9   Programme notes for 'A Tribute to Richard Rive', Athlone, Hewat Training College, 13 June 1989.
10   Gray, *Free-Lancers*, 173.
11   Rive, 'Interview', 10.
12   JM Coetzee, 'Writing Black', *English in Africa* 9.2 (1982): 73.
13   Alf Wannenburgh, 'Memories of Richard', *New Contrast* 71 18.3 (1990): 38.
14   Chitter, 'Richard Rive', 103. Chitter does not date this encounter but, after what seems like a good few months of contact between the two men, mentions the date 1984. So I assume this first meeting took place in late 1983 or in 1984.
15   Ibid., 104–105.
16   Rive, 'Interview', 13.
17   Richard Rive, ed., *Quartet: New Voices from South Africa – Alex La Guma, James Matthews, Richard Rive, Alf Wannenburgh* (New York: Crown Publishers, 1963), 142; Richard Rive, *Advance, Retreat: Selected Short Stories* (Cape Town: David Philip, 1983), 11.
18   Rive, *Quartet*, 143; *Advance, Retreat*, 12.
19   Margaret Daymond, 'Controlling Voices: A Review of *Advance, Retreat* by Richard Rive', *Reality: A Journal of Liberal and Radical Opinion* 16.4 (1984): 15.
20   Ibid., 16.
21   Rive, *Advance, Retreat*, 70.
22   Ibid., 69–70.
23   Ibid., 62, 64.
24   Ibid., 72.
25   Peter D McDonald, *The Literature Police: Apartheid Censorship and its Cultural Consequences* (Oxford: Oxford University Press, 2009), 203. Other details preceding the quote are also taken from McDonald.
26   Margaux Bergman, 'The Trojan Horse Massacre', http://www.athlone.co.za/heritage/history/0604200601_history.php.
27   Vincent Kolbe, 'Museum Beginnings', in *Recalling Community in Cape Town: Creating and Curating the District Six Museum*, ed. Ciraj Rassool and Sandra Prosalendis (Cape Town: District Six Museum, 2001), 15.
28   Anecdote told to me by Siraj Desai during an informal conversation, Salt River, 28 January 2006.
29   These last details about Small and Wissema and the Kramer/ Petersen musical are taken from Dawid de Villiers and Mathilda Slabbert, *David Kramer: A Biography* (Cape Town: Tafelberg, 2011), 214, 223.

30 Bill Nasson, personal interview, Cape Town, 27 February 2013.

31 Sir de Villiers Graaff was a lawyer and a member (and then leader) of the opposition United Party in South Africa's parliament from 1948 to 1977. He studied at UCT and also at Oxford. This icon of white Afrikanerdom had a noticeably brown complexion that could easily have made him 'coloured' in the racial classification system of apartheid South Africa.

32 Richard Rive, *'Buckingham Palace', District Six* (Cape Town: David Philip, 1986), 198.

33 Quoted in Peggy Delport, 'Signposts for Retrieval: A Visual Framework for Enabling Memory of Place and Time', in *Recalling Community in Cape Town: Creating and Curating the District Six Museum*, ed. Ciraj Rassool and Sandra Prosalendis (Cape Town: District Six Museum, 2001), 31.

34 De Villiers and Slabbert, *David Kramer*, 219.

35 Ibid., 234.

36 Richard Rive and Tim Couzens, *Seme: The Founder of the ANC*, UWC Mayibuye History Series (Johannesburg: Skotaville, 1991), 9.

37 Ibid., 23.

Chapter 8

38 Zoë Wicomb, 'Shame and Identity: The Case of the Coloured in South Africa', in *Writing South Africa: Literature, Apartheid and Democracy, 1970–1995*, ed. Derek Attridge and Rosemary Jolly (Cambridge: Cambridge University Press, 1998), 96.

39 Zakes Mda, 'Politics and the Theatre: Current Trends in South African Theatre', in *Theatre and Change in South Africa*, ed. Geoffrey V Davis and Anne Fuchs (Amsterdam: Harwood Academic, 1996), 193–218.

40 Mark Bowman, 'Rive: Part 1 – 20 Years of Writing about "Constitutionalised Racism" ', *South* (25 May 1989): n.p.

41 Rive, *'Buckingham Palace'*, 126.

42 Ibid., 76.

43 Robin Malan, 'Educational Notes', in Richard Rive, *'Buckingham Palace', District Six* (Cape Town: David Philip, 1996), 201.

44 The strong influence of Thomas on Rive's style in the novel was first pointed out to me by Colleen Radus, a colleague at Hewat College.

45 Wannenburgh, 'Memories', 31.

46 Rive, *'Buckingham Palace'*, 197.

47 Evelyn J Holtzhausen, 'An Interview with Richard Rive', *Upstream* 7.3 (1989): 4.

48 Rive, *'Buckingham Palace'*, 128.
49 Rive, *'Buckingham Palace'*, 188, 191.
50 Wannenburgh, 'Memories', 33.
51 Rive, *'Buckingham Palace'*, 85.
52 Wannenburgh, 'Memories', 31.
53 Even though Ian Rutgers lived at the house for the first two years, his presence must have been a frustrating one in that, like the student in 'The Visits', Rutgers was no doubt often absent, especially over weekends when he visited his girlfriend and family.
54 As Brenna Munro claims, 'Queer theory destabilises our ways of thinking about subjectivity and the social.' 'Queer Constitutions: Postcolonial Sexualities in Modern South African Writing', PhD diss. (Charlottesville: University of Virginia, 2005), 2.
55 Bowman, 'Rive: Part 1', n.p.
56 Basil Appollis, who played Rive in the 1989 Baxter production, shared this information with me in a talk I had with him in May 1998.
57 Grant Farred, personal interview, Cape Town, 7 May 2004. Farred says Rive expressed this wish in a conversation with him. I wondered whether Rive was saying this partly tongue in cheek, but Farred thought it was a serious comment.
58 Milton van Wyk, written response to personal interview, 24 June 1999.
59 Ibid.
60 Rive, *Writing Black*, 104.
61 Basil Appollis and Sylvia Vollenhoven, 'A Writer's Last Word', programme for the play (Cape Town: Baxter Theatre Centre, 1998).
62 Wannenburgh, 'Memories', 29.
63 Rive, *Writing Black*, 8.
64 Mda, 'Politics and the Theatre', 214.
65 The major productions I refer to are the Hewat College production under the direction of Colleen Radus with Shaun Viljoen and Marina Lotter acting as assistant directors, and scripted by Rive (1988); the Baxter production under the direction of Fred Abrahamse, with script by Rive (1989); the UCT Drama department production under the direction of Basil Appollis, with script adapted from Rive's original and the novel by Basil Appollis and Shaun Viljoen (2000); and the Artscape professional production under the direction of Basil Appollis, with script adapted from Rive's original and from the novel by Basil Appollis, Shaun Viljoen and the cast (2001). The two school productions I

refer to were by Garlandale High School, under the direction of and with original music composed by Basil Snayer and Edmund Bourne (2002), and an Artscape-funded school production called *Caledon Street, District Six,* under the direction of Fahruq Valley-Omar with choreography by Christopher Kindo (2004).

66 Gray, *Free-Lancers*, 158.
67 Holtzhausen, 'Interview', 5–6.
68 Ibid., 6.
69 Richard Rive, *Emergency Continued* (Cape Town: David Philip, 1990), 229.
70 Ibid., 45. The italics are used in the original; all letters to Abe are marked by italicisation.
71 Ibid., 183.
72 Ursula A Barnett, *A Vision of Order: A Study of Black South African Literature in English (1914–1980)* (London: Sinclair Browne, 1983), 130.
73 Rive, 'Buckingham Palace', 198.
74 Rive, *Emergency Continued*, 45.
75 Daryl R Lee, 'A Rival Protest: The Life and Work of Richard Rive, a South African Writer', PhD diss., Oxford University, 1998, 298.
76 Rive, *Emergency Continued*, 5.
77 Alf Wannenburgh, 'Rive's "Last Word" His Best'. Source unknown.
78 Richard Rive, 'Storming Pretoria's Castle: To Write or Fight?' *New York Times Book Review*, 17 January 1988, 1.
79 Rive, *Emergency Continued*, 139.
80 Ibid., 138, 143, 185.
81 Ibid., 184.
82 From Kathleen Hauke's electronic database, from a file called 'Richard Rive Draft', last reworked on 12 July 2004.
83 Hauke's claim that Heathfield is a section of Claremont, and that it was recently integrated, is wrong. And it was Elaine Cloete, not his housekeeper, who discovered Rive's body.
84 Alf Wannenburgh, 'Death in Cape Town', *Mail & Guardian Review*, 7 February 1991.
85 I have examined the police files on the case, including police photographs of the scene, held at the Police Museum in Pretoria. All information I have used in this research has already been made public through newspaper reports or by Wannenburgh, whom I guess must have been at the trial or used the fairly extensive newspaper reports on it.
86 I have a birthday on 2 June, the night before the murder, and had planned to invite Rive to join me and friends for a drink, but changed my mind about asking him. I of course wonder whether

the course of events would have been different, and the tragedy averted, if I had asked him.

87   Ivan Abrahams, personal interview, Cape Town, 18 March 2004.

88   Patrick Collings, 'Author Richard Rive Murdered', *Cape Times*, 5 June 1989.

89   Deela Khan, 'Man of Letters', epigraph to Jennifer M Johnstone, 'Authority and Displacement: A Reading of Richard Rive's Imaginative Writing', MA thesis, University of Natal, 1991.

90   Glen Retief, 'Keeping Sodom out of the Laager: State Repression of Homosexuality in Apartheid South Africa', in *Defiant Desire: Gay and Lesbian Lives in South Africa*, ed. Mark Gevisser and Edwin Cameron (Johannesburg: Ravan Press, 1994), 108.

91   This and other information in this paragraph is taken from the police file on the case kept in the Police Museum in Pretoria.

Epilogue

92   Rive, *Emergency Continued*, 185.

Select Bibliography

Abrahams, Peter. *Tell Freedom: Memories of Africa*. London: Faber and Faber, 1981 [1954].

Adhikari, Mohamed. *Against the Current: A Biography of Harold Cressy, 1889–1916*. Cape Town: Juta, 2012.

Alexander, Neville. *Thoughts on the New South Africa*. Johannesburg: Jacana Media, 2013.

Appollis, Basil and Sylvia Vollenhoven. 'A Writer's Last Word'. Programme for the play. Cape Town: Baxter Theatre Centre, 1998.

Attridge, Derek and Rosemary Jolly, eds. *Writing South Africa: Literature, Apartheid and Democracy, 1970–1995*. Cambridge: Cambridge University Press, 1998.

Attwell, David. *Rewriting Modernity: Studies in Black South African Literary History*. Pietermaritzburg: University of KwaZulu-Natal Press, 2005.

Baderoon, Gabeba. *The Dream in the Next Body*. Cape Town: Kwela Books and Snailpress, 2005.

Barnett, Ursula A. *A Vision of Order: A Study of Black South African Literature in English (1914–1980)*. London: Sinclair Browne, 1983.

Barry, John M. *The Great Influenza: The Epic Story of the Deadliest Plague in History*. London: Penguin, 2005.

Bickford-Smith, Vivian, Elizabeth van Heyningen and Nigel Worden. *Cape Town in the Twentieth Century*. Cape Town: David Philip, 1999.

Bond, Patrick. *Unsustainable South Africa: Environment, Development and Social Protest*. Pietermaritzburg: University of Natal Press, 2002.

Bowman, Mark. 'District Six: Part 2 – Warts and All'. *South* (1 June 1989): n.p.

———. 'Rive: Part 1 – 20 Years of Writing about "Constitutionalised Racism" '. *South* (25 May 1989): n.p.

Butler, Judith. 'Imitation and Gender Insubordination'. In *Inside/Out: Lesbian Theories, Gay Theories*, ed. Diana Fuss, 13–31. London: Routledge, 1991.

Chapman, Michael, ed. *The Drum Decade: Stories from the 1950s*. Pietermaritzburg: University of Natal Press, 1989.

Chitter, Michael. 'Richard Rive: The Man'. *Botsotso: Contemporary South African Culture* 13 (2004): 103–106.

Coetzee, JM. *White Writing*. New Haven: Yale University Press, 1988.

———. 'Writing Black'. *English in Africa* 9.2 (1982): 71–73.

Collings, Patrick. 'Author Richard Rive Murdered'. *Cape Times*, 5 June 1989.

Couzens, Tim and Es'kia Mphahlele, eds. *The Voice of the Black Writer in Africa: Senate Special Lectures.* Johannesburg: Wits University Press, 1980.

Daymond, Margaret. 'Controlling Voices: A Review of *Advance, Retreat* by Richard Rive'. *Reality: A Journal of Liberal and Radical Opinion* 16.4 (1984): 15–16.

Delport, Peggy. 'Signposts for Retrieval: A Visual Framework for Enabling Memory of Place and Time'. In *Recalling Community in Cape Town: Creating and Curating the District Six Museum,* ed. Ciraj Rassool and Sandra Prosalendis, 11–12. Cape Town: District Six Museum, 2001.

De Villiers, Dawid and Mathilda Slabbert. *David Kramer: A Biography.* Cape Town: Tafelberg, 2011.

Distiller, Natasha and Melissa Steyn, eds. *Under Construction: 'Race' and Identity in South Africa Today.* Johannesburg: Heinemann, 2004.

Drew, Alison. *Discordant Comrades: Identities and Loyalties on the South African Left.* Aldershot: Ashgate Publishing, 2000.

Dudley, Richard O. 'A Tribute to Richard Rive'. Athlone: Hewat Training College, 13 June 1989.

Ellmann, Richard. *Oscar Wilde.* New York: Knopf, 1988.

Erasmus, Zimitri, ed. *Coloured by History, Shaped by Place: New Perspectives on Coloured Identities in Cape Town.* Cape Town: Kwela Books, 2001.

Farred, Grant. *Midfielder's Moment: Coloured Literature and Culture in Contemporary South Africa.* Boulder, CO: Westview Press, 2000.

Fraser, Antonia, ed. *The Pleasure of Reading.* London: Bloomsbury, 1992.

Fried, Malcolm. 'Rive Was "Near Pinnacle"'. *Cape Times,* 5 June 1989.

Gevisser, Mark and Edwin Cameron, eds. *Defiant Desire: Gay and Lesbian Lives in South Africa.* Johannesburg: Ravan Press, 1994.

Gordimer, Nadine. 'Nadine Gordimer on the Murdered South African Writer Richard Rive'. *Mail & Guardian Review,* 7 February 1991.

Gray, Stephen. *Free-Lancers and Literary Biography in South Africa.* Amsterdam: Rodopi, 1999.

Gribble, Jill, ed. 'Richard Rive Papers Deposited with the University of Cape Town Libraries by Mr Leonard du Plooy'. Cape Town: University of Cape Town Libraries, 1992.

Hallett, George. *Portraits of African Writers.* Johannesburg: Wits University Press, 2006.

Hallett, George and Peter McKenzie, eds. *District Six Revisited.* Johannesburg: Wits University Press, 2007.

Hauke, Kathleen. 'Richard Rive Draft'. 12 July 2004.

Henderson, Gwyneth, ed. *African Theatre: Eight Prize-Winning Plays for Radio.* London: Heinemann, 1973.

Hendricks, Harry. 'A Tribute to Richard Rive'. Athlone: Hewat Training College, 13 June 1989.

Holroyd, Michael. *Works on Paper.* London: Little, Brown and Company, 2002.

Holtzhausen, Evelyn J. 'An Interview with Richard Rive'. *Upstream* 7.3 (1989): 4–6.

Hughes, Langston, ed. *An African Treasury: Articles, Essays, Stories, Poems by Black Africans.* New York: Crown Publishers, 1960.

———. *Poems from Black Africa.* Bloomington, IN: Indiana University Press, 1963.

Hughes, Langston, Papers, the James Weldon Johnson Collection in the Yale Collection of American Literature at the Beinecke Rare Book and Manuscript Library at Yale University, New Haven. Copies are held at the National English Literary Museum (Nelm) in Grahamstown.

Johnstone, Jennifer M. 'Authority and Displacement: A Reading of Richard Rive's Imaginative Writing'. MA thesis. Durban: University of Natal, 1991.

Kannemeyer, JC. *Die Lewe en Werk van Uys Krige, die Goue Seun.* Cape Town: Tafelberg, 2002.

Killam, Douglas and Ruth Rowe, eds. *The Companion to African Literatures.* Oxford: James Currey, 2000.

Klopper, Dirk, ed. *Anatomy of Dark: Collected Poems of Arthur Nortje.* Pretoria: Unisa Press, 2000.

Kolbe, Vincent. 'Museum Beginnings'. In *Recalling Community in Cape Town: Creating and Curating the District Six Museum,* ed. Ciraj Rassool and Sandra Prosalendis, 15–16. Cape Town: District Six Museum, 2001.

Lee, Daryl R. 'A Rival Protest: The Life and Work of Richard Rive, a South African Writer'. PhD diss. Oxford: Oxford University, 1998.

Lewis, David Levering. *The Portable Harlem Renaissance Reader.* New York: Penguin, 1994.

Lewis, Desiree. 'Writing Hybrid Selves: Richard Rive and Zoë Wicomb'. In *Coloured by History, Shaped by Place: New Perspectives on Coloured Identities in Cape Town,* ed. Zimitri Erasmus, 131–158. Cape Town: Kwela Books, 2001.

Lindfors, Bernth. 'Form and Technique in the Novels of Richard Rive and Alex la Guma'. *Journal of the New African Literature and the Arts* 2 (1966): 10–15.

Lodge, Tom. *Black Politics in South Africa since 1945.* London: Longman, 1983.

Magdalen College Archives, University of Oxford.

Malan, Robin. 'Educational Notes'. In *'Buckingham Palace', District Six*, Richard Rive, 199–212. Cape Town: David Philip, 1996.

Malan, Robin, ed. *Being Here: Modern Short Stories from Southern Africa*. Cape Town: David Philip, 1994.

Manganyi, N Chabani and David Attwell, eds. *Bury Me at the Marketplace: Es'kia Mphahlele and Company, Letters 1943–2006*. Johannesburg: Wits University Press, 2010.

Marais, Hein. *South Africa Pushed to the Limit: The Political Economy of Change*. Cape Town: University of Cape Town Press, 2011.

Matthews, James. 'A Tribute to Richard Rive'. Athone: Hewat Training College, 13 June 1989.

McDonald, Peter D. *The Literature Police: Apartheid Censorship and its Cultural Consequences*. Oxford: Oxford University Press, 2009.

McFeely, William S. 'Why Biography?' In *The Seductions of Biography*, ed. Mary Rhiel and David Suchoff, ix–xiii. New York: Routledge, 1996.

Mda, Zakes. 'Politics and the Theatre: Current Trends in South African Theatre'. In *Theatre and Change in South Africa*, ed. Geoffrey V Davis and Anne Fuchs, 193–218. Amsterdam: Harwood Academic, 1996.

Meyer, Peter. 'A Tribute to Richard Rive'. Athlone: Hewat Training College, 13 June 1989.

Miles, Elza. 'Triptych, for Peter Clarke'. In *More than Brothers: Peter Clarke and James Matthews at 70*, ed. Hein Willemse, 61–81. Cape Town: Kwela Books, 2000.

Mokone, Sarah. *Majority Rule: Some Notes*. Cape Town: Teachers' League of South Africa, 1982.

Moore, Gerald. *Seven African Writers*. London: Oxford University Press, 1962.

Morris, Errol. *Believing Is Seeing (Observations on the Mysteries of Photography)*. New York: Penguin Press, 2011.

Mphahlele, Es'kia. *Es'kia*. Cape Town: Kwela, 2002.

———. *Es'kia Continued*. Johannesburg: Stainbank & Associates, 2004.

———. 'Landmarks of Literary History in South Africa: A Black Perspective – 1980'. In *Es'kia*, 295–311. Cape Town: Kwela Books, 2002.

Munro, Brenna. 'Queer Constitutions: Postcolonial Sexualities in Modern South African Writing'. PhD diss. Charlottesville: University of Virginia, 2005.

———. *South Africa and the Dream of Love to Come*. Minneapolis: University of Minnesota Press, 2012.

Nkosi, Lewis. '*African Songs* by Richard Rive'. *Classic* 1.2 (1963): 41–42.

Oakes, Dougie, ed. *Illustrated History of South Africa: The Real Story*. Cape Town: Reader's Digest, 1995.

Poswa, Mildred (Neville Alexander). 'Black Consciousness: A Reactionary Tendency'. *The Educational Journal* 'March–May'. Cape Town: The Teachers' League of South Africa, 1976.

Pratt, Edward. 'A Tribute to Richard Rive'. Athlone: Hewat Training College, 13 June 1989.

Rabie, Jan, ed. *In Memoriam Ingrid Jonker*. Cape Town: Human & Rousseau, 1966.

Raju, Jayarani and Catherine Dubbeld. *Richard Rive: A Select Bibliography*. Durban: University of Natal, 1990.

Rampersad, Arnold. *The Life of Langston Hughes, Volume I (1902–1941): I, too, Sing America*. New York: Oxford University Press, 1986.

———. *The Life of Langston Hughes, Volume II (1941–1967): I Dream a World*. New York: Oxford University Press, 1988.

Retief, Glen. 'Keeping Sodom out of the Laager: State Repression of Homosexuality in Apartheid South Africa'. In *Defiant Desire: Gay and Lesbian Lives in South Africa*, ed. Mark Gevisser and Edwin Cameron, 99–111. Johannesburg: Ravan Press, 1994.

Rhiel, Mary and David Suchoff, eds. *The Seductions of Biography*. New York: Routledge, 1996.

Rive, Richard. *Advance, Retreat: Selected Short Stories*. Cape Town: David Philip, 1983.

———. *African Songs*. Berlin: Seven Seas, 1963.

———. 'Andrew'. In *Come Back, Africa! Short Stories from South Africa by Phyllis Altman [and Others]*, ed. HL Shore and M Shore-Bos, 143–150. New York: International Publishers, 1968.

———. 'Black Macbeth'. *Contrast* 49 13.1 (1980): 9–21.

———. 'The Black Writer and South African Literature'. Hewat Occasional Papers Series 3, ed. Val Schnugh. Athlone: Hewat College of Education, 1990.

———. *'Buckingham Palace', District Six*. Cape Town: David Philip, 1986.

———. *Emergency*. London: Faber and Faber, 1964.

———. *Emergency*. New York: Collier Books, 1970.

———. *Emergency Continued*. Cape Town: David Philip, 1990.

———. 'Four South Africans Abroad'. *Contrast* 39 10.3 (1976): 49–57.

———. 'Interview'. By Chris van Wyk. In *Wietie 2*, 10–13. Johannesburg: Sable Books, 1980.

———. *Make Like Slaves*. In *African Theatre: Eight Prize-Winning Plays for Radio*, ed. Gwyneth Henderson, 1–18. London: Heinemann, 1973.

———. 'Middle Passage'. *Contrast* 21 6.1 (1969): 37–44.

———. 'Mrs Janet September and the Siege of Sinton'. *Contrast* 63 16.3 (1987): 9–18.

———. [Mary X, pseud]. 'My Sister was a Playwhite'. *Africa* (July 1955): 27–31.

———. 'On Being a Black Writer in South Africa: A Personal Essay'. In *The Voice of the Black Writer in Africa: Senate Special Lectures*, ed. Tim Couzens and Es'kia Mphahlele, 21–24. Johannesburg: Wits University Press, 1980.

———. 'Riva'. *Staffrider* 2.1 (1979): 13–16.

———. *Selected Writings: Stories, Essays, Plays*. Johannesburg: Ad Donker, 1977.

———. 'Storming Pretoria's Castle: To Write or Fight?' *New York Times Book Review*, 17 January 1988.

———. 'Taos in Harlem: An Interview with Langston Hughes'. In *Selected Writings*, 110–118. Johannesburg: Ad Donker, 1977.

———. Untitled response to Lewis Nkosi's review of *African Songs*, *Classic* 1.3 (1964): 75.

———. 'The Visits'. In *Selected Writings*, 51–58. Johannesburg: Ad Donker, 1977.

———. *Writing Black*. Cape Town: David Philip, 1981.

Rive, Richard, ed. *Modern African Prose*. London: Heinemann, 1964.

———.*Olive Schreiner: Letters 1871–199*. Cape Town: David Philip, 1987.

———. *Quartet: New Voices from South Africa – Alex La Guma, James Matthews, Richard Rive, Alf Wannenburgh*. New York: Crown Publishers, 1963.

Rive, Richard and Tim Couzens. *Seme: The Founder of the ANC*. UWC Mayibuye History Series. Johannesburg: Skotaville, 1991.

Shava, Piniel. *A People's Voice: Black South African Writing in the Twentieth Century*. London: Zed Books, 1989.

Simon, Barney. 'My Years with *The Classic*: A Note'. *English in Africa* 7.2 (September 1980): 75–80.

Soudien, Crain. 'District Six and Its Uses in the Discussion About Non-Racialism'. In *Coloured by History, Shaped by Place: New Perspectives on Coloured Identities in Cape Town*, ed. Zimitri Erasmus, 114–130. Cape Town: Kwela Books, 2001.

Thomas, Dylan. *Under Milk Wood*. London: Dent, 1954.

Viljoen, Shaun C. 'Richard'. In *Under Construction: 'Race' and Identity in South Africa Today*, ed. Natasha Distiller and Melissa Steyn, 135–137. Johannesburg: Heinemann, 2004.

Wannenburgh, Alf. 'Death in Cape Town'. *Mail & Guardian Review*, 7 February 1991.

———. 'Memories of Richard'. *New Contrast* 71 18.3 (1990): 29–39.

———. 'Rive's "Last Word" His Best'. Source unknown.

West, Cornel. *Race Matters*. New York: Vintage Books, 2001.

White, Allon. *The Uses of Obscurity*. London: Routledge & Kegan Paul, 1981.

Wicomb, Zoë. 'Shame and Identity: The Case of the Coloured in South Africa'. In *Writing South Africa: Literature, Apartheid and Democracy, 1970-1995*, ed. Derek Attridge and Rosemary Jolly, 91–107. Cambridge: Cambridge University Press, 1998.

Willemse, Hein, ed. *More than Brothers: Peter Clarke and James Matthews at 70*. Cape Town: Kwela Books, 2000.

Willet, John and Ralph Manheim. *Bertolt Brecht Poems (1913-1956)*. London: Eyre Methuen, 1976.

Woolf, Virginia. *The Diary of Virginia Woolf*, ed. Anne Olivier Bell and A McNeillie. London: Hogarth Press, 1977–1984.

———. *Moments of Being*. London: Harcourt Brace, 1985.

Yeats, William B. *The Collected Poems of W.B. Yeats*. London: Macmillan, 1973.

Young, Robert M. 'Biography: The Basic Discipline for Human Science'. *Free Associations* 1.11 (1988): 108–130.

Index

Page numbers in bold indicate photographs.

Printed and bound by CPI Group (UK) Ltd, Croydon, CR0 4YY

09/06/2025

14685813-0001